THE
RADICAL FEW

THE
RADICAL FEW

Ordinary People Manifesting
the Extraordinary

Inspiring stories compiled by Sophie Sykes
Volume 2

Second Edition

Rosette Publishing, LLC

THE RADICAL FEW
Ordinary People Manifesting the Extraordinary
Inspiring stories compiled by Sophie Sykes. Volume 2

Second Edition

Book Cover Design by Melissa Peizer
Book Edited by Pat Richker

ISBN # 978-0-578-41132-3

Rosette Publishing, LLC
P.O. Box 1068, Rainier, WA 98576, USA

This book is dedicated to Ramtha the Enlightened One,
our Master Teacher,
who has taught us to live beyond ignorance.
He has given us the knowledge and the tools
to create a greater life.
One that is filled with joy,
unencumbered by our past —
something wonderful.

* * *

We also dedicate this book to JZ Knight,
who for over forty years has given us her brilliance and genius
through the living example of her life.
She is a woman who changes minds and awakens people,
takes chances, turns heads, listens.
She is unique, irreplaceable, intent upon making this
a brighter place for all.
She is a beacon of light — blazing a trail
that is burning bright with hope and love.

TABLE OF CONTENTS

ACKNOWLEDGMENTS xiii

FOREWORD 1

A MESSAGE FROM SOPHIE SYKES..............................1

    Analogical Archery® 5

    Blue Body® 5

    Consciousness and Energy® (C&E®) 6

    Candle Focus: 6

    Create Your Day® 6

    Fieldwork® 6

    Neighborhood Walk® 7

    The List 7

    The Tank® (The Labyrinth).. 7

    Twilight®, Visualization Process.............................. 7

INTRODUCTION: THE MISSION..................................9

    HUMAN HEALING AT A MOST PROFOUND LEVEL 11
        Miceal Ledwith

CHAPTER 1: HEALING ONESELF 15

    SOMETIMES IT TAKES AN ARMY 17
        Neil Kaber

    ATTITUDE IS EVERYTHING 23
        Joan Avnery

MAGICAL TWILIGHT® 27

Elizabeth Axe

YOU MUST LEARN TO THINK LIKE A GOD 31

Linda Barnes

A HEALER'S HEALING JOURNEY 35

Heidi Gould, with Jalene Smith

NO ONE HEALS THIS RAPIDLY — NO ONE! 43

Linda Liss

A HEALING IN THE MIRROR 47

Judy Audet Holsinger

HEALING MY BODY WITH LONG, QUIET FOCUS 49

Jaqueline Smith

MY CHOICE TO LIVE, GRANTED BY RAMTHA 55

David Tidwell

LIVING BEYOND MY FUTURE DEATH 59

Ektara Jarecki

TRANSCENDING PAIN: THE TRANSFORMATIONAL
POWER OF CHOICE 63

Calence Ethan Emerson

OVERCOMING EXTREME EMOTIONS 69

Lucy Jeanne

HEALING MY EYES 73

Debbie Christie, Master of Music

SEIZURES, A TUMOR, AND MAGIC 75

Brisa Chu 75

POWERFUL FOCUS — POWERFUL DETERMINATION 79

Iliana Valdes

BE CAREFUL WHAT YOU ASK FOR 83

Susan R. Louis 83

FROM THE MUNDANE TO THE REMARKABLE 89

Paul Daniel

DISCIPLINE, WILL, AND FOCUS CREATE MIRACLES 95

Marilyn Reardon

FOCUS SAVED MY LIFE 97

Donna Russo

A TALE OF TWO LIVES... 101

Suzann Hollar

HEALED IN A MOMENT 109

Bryan Liss

THE FAITH OF A MUSTARD SEED 113

Judy Andrew

INSIGHT 115

Jenny Gifford

CHAPTER 2: HEALING OTHERS 121

SAVING THE LIFE OF A COWORKER 123

Jacqueline Smith

CLIFFORD... 125

Terra Kram

BECOME LIKE A CHILD 127

Rosalie Saecker127

WHAT DO YOU HAVE TO LOSE BY SIMPLY TRYING?.. 131

Diane DuBuc

CHAPTER 3: HEALING OUR FAMILIES 137

THE PLAN 139

Sophie Sykes

ORCHIDS FOREVER — GOD IS A WHISPERER 145
  Karla Broschinski
MY SISTER UNDERSTANDS LIFE BEYOND DEATH 147
  Marian Clements

CHAPTER 4: HEALING OUR ANIMALS 151
  HORSES AND THE POWER OF C&E® 153
    Dr. Louie Enos, D.V.M., B.S.
  THE FROG, THE CAT, ... AND ME 159
    Jan Ferrari159
  DOGS, A CAT, AND MIRACLES 163
    Elizabeth Axe163

CHAPTER 5: HEALING OUR DNA 167
  CONFRONTING PREDETERMINED DNA 169
    Juliet Eichorn169

CHAPTER 6: HEALING OUR COMMUNITY 175
  ZEPHYR 177
    Michelle Horkings-Brigham177
  TZEDAKAH 191
    Steve Klein
  "WHERE TWO OR MORE ARE GATHERED..." 201
    Carolyn Chew
  LET NOTHING IN YOU HIDE YOUR LIGHT! 213
    Diane Dondero
  MY DEAL WITH RAMTHA 223
    James Brigham223

A TRIBUTE TO A WATER HERO 231
  *Sara Foster*231
DIVERSITY IN UNITY 233
  Jayne of The Triad Theater
THE REAL MESSAGE OF JESUS........................ 239
  Míceál Ledwith

CHAPTER 7: HEALING OUR WORLD 249
  "I REFUSE TO LET ANYTHING BLIND ME
  TO POSSIBILITY." 251
    *JZ Knight*251
  THE BLU ROOM — A PLACE OF MYSTERY 261
    Nancy Breidenthal
  THE BEAUTIFUL BLU ROOM EXPERIENCE 265
    Captain Cynthia Williams-Patnoe
  A WONDERFUL DREAM COMES TRUE............................ 269
    *Austin Hess*269
  RE-CREATING MY YEAR 273
    *Sharon Olson*273
  A MULTITUDE OF HEALINGS 281
    *Evonne LaForge*281
  THE MIRACLE 285
    *Nikki Bertone*285
  A DRAMATIC IMPROVEMENT IN DIABETES 287
    Jaime Leal-Anaya
  THE BLU ROOM AND BREAST CANCER 291
    Maggie Barragan
  RETURN OF OPTIMAL HEATH........................... 293
    Dr. Jo Linmans

A PORTAL TO ELSEWHERE 295
Rosa

A MAGNET FOR HAPPINESS! 296
Sandra

ALLOWING MYSELF TO BELIEVE..297
Inge

HOPE 298
Joan

FAMILY HEALING IN MISSOURI 299
Anna

SEBORRHEIC DERMATITIS..301
Diana301

HEALING STRABISMUS 302
Erika

CHARITY, COMPASSION, AND MERCY 303
Dr. Ana Maria Mihalcea, of the Mercy Blu Program

Donna's Heart Problems 303

Molly's Chronic Knee Pain...304

Bob's Psoriasis and Diabetes..305

Doris's Healing Pain from a Life-Altering Collision...................307

Pat's Chronic Open Wound Healed through Blu Room.................310

David's Healing Posttraumatic Stress Disorder 311

IN CLOSING: FINAL THOUGHTS...............................315

DESIGNING YOUR EXTRAORDINARY SELF 317

RAMTHA, JZ KNIGHT, AND RAMTHA'S SCHOOL OF
ENLIGHTENMENT...319

RAMTHA'S SELECTED GLOSSARY:

ADDITIONAL TERMS AND DISCIPLINES 321

ACKNOWLEDGMENTS

There is no question that the publication of *The Radical Few* could have ever happened without the enormous support of many people. I am tremendously grateful for all of those who contributed in a multitude of ways to bring this compilation into form.

First, I want to thank Ramtha and JZ Knight.[1] It was Ramtha who challenged me to finish the manuscript of these inspiring stories.[2] Because of this challenge and that inspiration, this book became my journey. It was a journey where I was tested to learn and apply the disciplines he has taught me — in short, to focus! His wisdom and guidance have helped this work to come forth into fruition.

This collection is both evidence and documentation from those students who had the courage and determination to heal themselves, others, animals, their families, and the very community in which they live. Their stories are like rare jewels, unique and shiny. To all of them I am deeply grateful for sharing their journey with the world. May these stories be shared and passed on to inspire others in all walks of life.

I am also deeply grateful to Rebecca Hardwick and Marilyn Reardon for their unwavering dedication and immense patience. Becca's support in creating an enormous database and orchestrating the administrative duties was invaluable to me. Marilyn has given not only hundreds of hours to editing the first round of over sixty-five stories but has stood by me and given me support and advice with persistent encouragement. Many times, when the chaos and the magnitude of this production were at its peak, it was Marilyn who stepped in with a quiet and gentle word of encouragement.

---

[1] See "About Ramtha, JZ Knight, and Ramtha's School of Enlightenment" at the end of this book. See also *Ramtha, A Beginner's Guide to Creating Reality*, Third Edition (JZK Publishing, 2004) for Ramtha's introduction to his teachings, his exercises of the mind and techniques of focus, and his School of Enlightenment.

[2] See *In the Age of the Miraculous. Miracles, Extraordinary Experiences, and Discoveries. Stories Compiled by Sophie Sykes. Vol 1* (Rainier: Rosette Publishing, LLC, 2015).

I would also like to thank my family, my sons John and Jim, and all my friends who have given me so much loving support over the past years: Marilyn Reardon, Paulina Amador, Rebecca Hardwick, Carolyn Chew, Nancy Driscoll, Nancy Breidenthal, Lucy Jeanne, Pamela Roberts-Aue, Neil Kaber, Miceal Ledwith, Jenny Gifford, Diane D'Acuti, Aly Marvin, Lyn Quale, Din Wilkie, Luby Missov, Ruth Bennett, Steven Carrell, Helene Goslin, and Kate Morgan.

A special thanks goes to Pamela Roberts-Aue and Ruth Sparrow for their generous contributions. Without them this book could not have existed.

Above all, I want to thank Mike Wright, Pat Richker, Jaime Leal-Anaya, Melissa Peizer, and Michelle Horkings-Brigham who brought their wisdom and experience together to prepare this extraordinary volume for professional printing. Mike's guidance, precision, and intelligence have been like navigational markers, providing guidance and direction for Chapter 7 of this manuscript. Melissa Peizer's artistic and brilliant design of the cover is compelling and joyful. Jaime's excellent editorial work for this volume 2 is greatly appreciated. Michelle's book design in preparation for printing this second edition has been done with extraordinary skill and a meticulous attention to detail.

Finally, I am profoundly grateful to Pat Richker, who has invested in this book beyond measure. Pat's extraordinary editing skills and expertise, her absolute commitment to excellence, has made this book shine with clarity and professionalism. Her generosity, her patience, and her unwavering love is palpable in this book.

"What I have never experienced is what I want to have.
I long to sit in the company of great beings.
I long to dine with them.
I long to spend long moments in some tranquil place.
And if they like to drink ale, I will drink ale.
If they are drinking wine, we will have wine,
whatever their pleasure.

"But I long to have a camaraderie with beings that
have made it and that have seen such sights that
I couldn't even dream of seeing, that I could engage
in such knowledge and such language,
and that they would know my very thought and know my
hunger for knowledge and my desire to expand,
and by their pleasure they would accompany me.
And they would know by my heart and by my Spirit that
I am not entangled of anything, and that if they asked of my
company to go to some far and remarkable place,
I surely have nothing in this world that would own me
enough to keep me from such a destiny.

"I want to see. I want to see the kingdoms of the fifth level.
I want to dance with Shiva.
I want to go to the center of the sun.
I want to know things that I couldn't even form the questions
to know in my former self. And I want, with all of my might,
that one day I should be so lofty myself that
such as I would seek to be in my audience,
and that I would entertain them and bestow upon them
and give to them the gift of life.
Those are the ones I want to take home.

— Ramtha the Enlightened One
Boktau II, July 1, 1997

Foreword:

A Message From Sophie Sykes

Let's imagine that it is 100 years in the future. You are walking through the living room of your home and your eyes fall upon a book resting on top of your dining room table. You slowly pick up the book and read the title, *The Radical Few*. You open the book and wonder, "Who are the people in this compilation? Where did they come from? How did this book endure the passage of time and appear here 100 years after it was published?" You open the book and now you float back in time. You find yourself sitting in a room with a group of ordinary people — people of all ages, gender, color, size, ethnic origins, and languages — who have focused their attention on healing themselves, their families, their animals, their community, their attitudes, and their very well-being into a state of joy. They are alive, present. In their pursuit of joy, they have discovered a way to activate the extraordinary. They have insisted upon overcoming their limitations, their humanity, to intentionally create a wonderful, healthy life that is filled with the love of God. Through all of these people there runs a common thread. That thread for each here is to meet, engage, and become God. This is the message of our Master Teacher, Ramtha the Enlightened One, "Behold God." These ordinary people show us their journey is one filled with a powerful passion to live a dynamic life, free of disease, overwhelming attitudes, and emotions. Their journey illustrates their bravery and what they had to do to overcome their past and become anew. They are the Radical Few.

Imagine you are sitting among them and the questions beg to be asked: How did they do it? What activates extraordinary healing? What is the key that unlocks the door that shapes our experiences and determines the well-being and health of our life? How could it be possible that the key to a joyful, healthy life is within us, yet perhaps never recognized? How could something so simple be seemingly not within our grasp? These people assure us that is possible, and yet what is required is a passionate desire to learn and the will to apply the knowledge and test it with a fiery and unwavering dedication. This is the journey one takes to become a living experience of the extraordinary.

As our Master Teacher says, the journey of the radical few is about ". . . honorable, meaningful, enriched people of superb mental excellence. And all of those attributes do not belong to the world; they belong to God and are reflected in the human being."[3] Ramtha continues, "That is why the miracles happen, because the truth is vitally alive in your midst."

The stories in the book you hold in your hands illustrate the journey of what each person engaged and underwent to evoke change. Is this not what Jesus meant when he said, "He who believes in me will also do the works that I do; and greater works than these will he do." The people in this book are not saints, mystics, or gurus. They are ordinary people, just like you and me. The only difference is they have the knowledge and courage to do something new.

Chapter 1 is entitled: *Healing Oneself.* This section describes those who have utilized the teachings, as taught to us by our Master Teacher, and applied their focus to designing a new reality. Here we are shown that it is becoming commonplace to design and create a reality with no sickness, no unhappiness, and no suffering. According to Ramtha's teachings we have the ability to draw upon the disciplines applying Blue Body®, Fieldwork®, Neighborhood Walk®, and The Tank® — the labyrinth — to grow and develop extraordinary health through focus. Through the application of these disciplines we

---

[3] *Ramtha, The Mind Gladiators of the Future* (Hun Nal Ye Publishing, 2016).

are taught that we access vast potentials through our thoughts once focused upon. These stories include miraculous healings: those who have healed breast cancer, tumors, shattered bones, cystic masses, Parkinson's disease, punctured lungs, heart attacks, and more.

The second chapter is entitled: *Healing Others*. In this chapter we see the power of the divine residing in each person as they apply their knowledge in a magnificent way to heal others. In one case, a student delivered a coworker from death.

In Chapter 3, *Healing Our Families*, we find individuals who through their unflappable love of family have found healing and restoration for themselves, their parents, and siblings. Through their efforts we can gain a greater understanding of the true message of Christ: "It is not I who perform these great works but the Father who lives within me."

Healing Our Animals is the subject of Chapter 4. Here you can read the most tender and exquisite stories of those individuals who have healed cats, horses, dogs, and their owners. Again, these stories stand as a testament and evidence of the power working through these individuals which they have used to heal our beloved animals.

Chapter 5 addresses the profound challenges with *Healing Our DNA*. In this chapter Juliet Eichorn reveals her journey with her genetics and DNA, and the territory she traversed in making known the unknown. Hers is a genuine story of bravery and love told for the first time to enlighten many who have suffered from mental illness.

Those individuals who have opened the door to truth and applied their wisdom and focus have been the sentinels of our community. Chapter 6 is entitled: *Healing Our Community*. This chapter represents a group of radical individuals who through their tenacity and steadfast determination have brought change and healing. The first story in this chapter is about a man who, although he does not stand alone in his efforts for spiritual evolution, has been the person in our community that has taught us the meaning of the Greek word "agape," unconditional love, and what it means to be "empowered." His name is Mícéál Ledwith. He is one of the Radical Few. Like others in this chapter, his efforts have brought healing, restoration, knowledge, and empowerment to a great group of community members, young and old, who are seeking answers to improve their lives by practicing unconditional love. Through his bravery and brilliance, along with the other individuals in this chapter, we have been given some heretical truth — not always easy to swallow but always new and empowering. There is hope. They show us ways we can change our deeply embedded subconscious programs and live, knowing that, as Jesus said, the kingdom of heaven is not here or there but within you.

In Chapter 7 we meet a rare individual who knows how to put these concepts into practice and utilize them to create something wonderful in our daily lives. This individual is JZ Knight, who is literally *Healing Our World* with The Blu Room that she created. The Blu Room is bringing forth the evidence of healing. As she says, "Our Future Medicine is Frequency Medicine." In this section JZ Knight explains to us about the Blu Room and the effects it has on its participants. In this chapter you will find clear and undeniable examples of people using the Blu Room to change the state of their health. JZ Knight explains that in the Blu Room, "There is a sense of improved health and well-being. Focus deepens. There is increased creativity and greater self-awareness. And just one session will last a person two to three days. All of this is as a result of three main factors in the creation of this phenomenal room: its geometry, its stasis of mind, and its delivery of Vitamin D."[4]

Beyond this current breakthrough in science lies an even greater understanding of the profound impact of ultraviolet-blue light and the effect it offers us for healing. With all of the current advancements in science and frequency medicine, where the scientist, the physician, and the students of the Pacific Northwest meet on common ground, we can truly see the potentials for

---

[4] Taken from the *Rob Simone Talk Show* interview from March 21, 2017.

healing and for a miraculous future. Just as you are holding this book in the palm of your hand, you are holding a talisman of your future. You have now become part of the question: What more lies latent waiting to be discovered?

Recent discoveries in genetics, cellular biology, neurophysiology and quantum physics are some of the important components of the model taught at RSE.

Ramtha's School of enlightenment (RSE), created by Ramtha the Enlightened One, is an academy of the mind. Ramtha's teachings emphasize that each individual is responsible for their own reality: Your thoughts and attitudes affect and create your life, and you can intentionally change your life by artfully changing your thoughts. This model includes distinctive techniques that are intended to demonstrate the power of consciousness in a person's life. These techniques teach students how to access the extraordinary abilities of the brain in order to bring forth an extraordinary life. Ramtha's techniques include:

Analogical Archery®: Discipline created by Ramtha to provide students immediate feedback of their ability to manifest reality. Students are taught to broaden and refine the focused power of the mind while blindfolded.

Blue Body®: The body that belongs to the fourth plane of existence, the bridge consciousness, and the ultraviolet frequency band. The Blue Body® is the lord over the lightbody and the physical plane. It is also a discipline taught by Ramtha in which the students lift their conscious awareness to the consciousness of the fourth plane. This discipline allows the Blue Body® to be accessed and the fourth seal to be opened for the purpose of healing or changing the physical body. This technique is taught exclusively at Ramtha's School of Enlightenment.

Consciousness and Energy® (C&E®): "The breath of power." Abbreviation of Consciousness & Energy®. This is the service mark of the fundamental discipline of manifestation and the raising of consciousness taught in Ramtha's School of Enlightenment. Through this discipline the students learn to create an analogical state of mind, open up their higher seals, and create reality from the Void. A Beginning C&E® Workshop is the name of the introductory workshop for beginning students in which they learn the fundamental concepts and disciplines of Ramtha's teachings. The teachings of the Beginning C&E® Workshop can be found in *Ramtha, A Beginner's Guide to Creating Reality,* Third Ed. (Yelm: JZK Publishing, a division of JZK, Inc., 2004.) This technique is taught exclusively at Ramtha's School of Enlightenment.

Candle Focus: Discipline taught by Ramtha to still the sensory and analytical mind and reach the state of analogical mind.

Create Your Day®: Discipline created by Ramtha for raising consciousness and energy and intentionally creating a plan of events and experiences for the day very early in the morning before the activities of the day begin. This technique is taught exclusively at Ramtha's School of Enlightenment.

Fieldwork®: This is one of the fundamental disciplines of Ramtha's School of Enlightenment. The students are taught to create a symbol of something they want to know and experience and draw it on a paper card. These cards are placed with the blank side facing out on the fence rails of a large field. The students blindfold themselves and focus on their symbol, allowing their body to walk freely to find their card through the application of the law of consciousness and energy and analogical mind. This technique is taught exclusively at Ramtha's School of Enlightenment.

Neighborhood Walk®: Discipline created by JZ Knight for raising consciousness and energy to intentionally modify our brain's neuronet and preestablished patterns of thinking that we no longer desire and to replace them with new ones of our own choice. This technique is taught exclusively at Ramtha's School of Enlightenment.

The List: The List is the discipline taught by Ramtha where the student gets to write a list of items they desire to know and experience and then learn to focus on it in an analogical state of consciousness. The List is the map used to design, change, and reprogram the neuronet of the person. It is the tool that helps to bring meaningful and lasting changes in the person and their reality. This technique is taught exclusively at Ramtha's School of Enlightenment.

The Tank® (The Labyrinth): It is the name given to the labyrinth used as part of the disciplines of Ramtha's School of Enlightenment. The students are taught to find the entry to this labyrinth blindfolded and move through it focusing on the Void without touching the walls or using the eyes or the senses. The objective of this discipline is to find, blindfolded, the center of the labyrinth or a room designated and representative of the Void.

Twilight®, Visualization Process: It is the process used to practice the discipline of the List or other visualization formats. The student learns to access the alpha state in the brain with focused intent in a state similar to deep sleep, yet retaining their conscious awareness.

Utilizing these disciplines, the students of RSE confront personal adversity and have taken on the challenge of conquering themselves in order to know themselves greater. The byproducts of this school are the marvelous achievements accomplished by these determined individuals to change their lives in pursuit of truth.

* * *

I invite you now to enter into the room and share the experiences of these ordinary people who have used their knowledge to create a healthy and wholesome life. These stories are more than mere miracles. They are an invitation for you to become and discover your magnificent life. I wish you the most extraordinary journey!

INTRODUCTION: THE MISSION

"You can do anything.
The key is focus."
"One day I will have turned out Christs
from this school
and the world will rejoice,
for this is the mission."

– Ramtha

HUMAN HEALING AT A MOST PROFOUND LEVEL

Miceal Ledwith

Almost a decade ago some friends suggested they would like to have me come to their homes and elaborate on some of the ideas concerning our subconscious programs and the ways they disempower us. The aim was to undermine and weaken the subconscious programs that have crippled the effect of the message of Jesus in all our lives. In short, the project was about spiritual healing at the most profound level. The word spread, and several groups formed. My friends named it "The Conversations," and thanks to the superb pioneering abilities of the seven "Hosts" of the Conversations, and the extraordinary dedication and commitment of the participants, the sessions continued on a monthly basis for almost seven years, during which time we covered close to seventy themes. I am not aware of any similar phenomenon ever having occurred anywhere else. The sessions resulted in my recent book, *Saving Jesus*.

It was a serious commitment, but it is only with that amount of dedicated focus over time that many matters can be brought into clear perspective and a major amount of healing at the deepest level of the human psyche can take place.

It is clear that the powerful tradition that saw Jesus as Suffering Savior had its roots in an utter inability to profoundly accept the significance of his central teaching: "You are all Gods." That same inability spawned a host of other equally unfounded beliefs that unfortunately constitute the majority of the religious belief systems with which we are familiar today in the West.

An individual who on a daily basis could heal the sick, walk on water, raise the dead, and feed a multitude of five thousand people with a few fish and a couple of loaves of bread, Jesus was obviously going to gain attention and spark a lot of questions.

11

Most of those who observed him were utterly unable to envisage that a human being could ever perform such extraordinary phenomena. It was way beyond their mind-set. They had forgotten that message of the ancient Sages concerning the enormous power within the human person and how it could be used by any human being who was willing to make the effort to bring it under conscious direction. No, an entity who did these extraordinary phenomena had to have come down directly from God.

Jesus often referred to "the Father." It is worth noting that the word "Ramtha" means "Father" in the ancient Lemurian language. Relatively early on in Christian history it began to be postulated that since Jesus referred to "the Father," there must be another, more "senior," divine person behind the scenes. So it was concluded that Jesus was God's son, in fact God's only son, and that he was let down from heaven to teach people to live in a God-fearing way so that they could go to heaven when they died. The enormous release of power that happened on the first Pentecost Sunday was understood as the visitation of another Being in the Godhead to which Jesus was thought to have made reference: the Spirit. Then the puzzle began as to how this third individual would fit in, and so emerged the belief in the Holy Trinity: the conception of a father, a son, and a Holy Spirit, a group of three who are yet only one. And then followed the method of authentically following Jesus, with which we were all familiar: sins and virtues. Jesus is supposed to have taught a certain way of living which, if we practiced it, would bring us a reward after we die, and so we would go to heaven rather than purgatory or hell.

All in all, it was a view of reality that saw God as some form of human being enlarged. It was a partner belief to that incredible degree of narcissism needed to convince oneself that the Earth was the only place in the vastness of the galaxies where intelligent life could be found. It was assumed without question that such intelligent life would be in humanoid form. But surely it is axiomatic that the Spirit emanating from the Source, which we all possess in equal degree, can take on material form in a multitude of ways, not just in humanoid form. Perhaps the reality is that few, if any, of those ways of incarnating Spirit into material form may afford us the comfort of them being even remotely similar to the human form, which we have so long taken blindly as the standard.

It would be hard to image a belief system that could do more damage to the heart of what Jesus taught than ours has done.

That is the belief system that has been served up to us for so long in Christianity. In fact, it is also substantially true of all the belief systems of the three major religions of the West. Nobody is necessarily imputing massive ill will here or wishing in the slightest degree to ignore the massive amount of good that Christianity, for example, has done in the world, especially over the last few centuries. That holds true even when we recognize what happened with the Inquisition and the Crusades. We should feel glad that such good was done, but we also need to recognize that this system was not what Jesus came to establish, and the sooner we recognize that, then the sooner we will begin the great journey of following what he really taught and becoming the powerful beings that he desired we should be.

In many ways the religious belief systems today are steering eerily close to the mind-set of that notorious statement made in 1899 by Charles H. Duell, the U.S. Patent Commissioner: "Everything that can be invented has been invented." A closed mind is a wonderful thing to lose in any field of inquiry, but especially in traversing the labyrinths of transcendent issues of ultimate concern.

Some no doubt will find such advice disturbing, especially if they have little or no knowledge of the facts on which their faith is based. The normal reaction of such people is to reject out of hand all such considerations as I have recounted briefly here. Such individuals or groups cannot face the potential level of personal insecurity that would result if they made such a rejection. The most satisfying and instinctive reaction of all such people is, as usual, to try to kill or defame the messenger, rather than try to heal the roots of their own deep insecurity.

But if we do set out on the marvelous journey towards accomplishing what Jesus intended for us, even on a modest scale, it will soon herald the end of the bizarre scenarios of sickness, misery, lack, powerlessness, and victimization that have continued — despite all Jesus accomplished — to characterize the history of our race for the last two thousand years. Jesus is an Ascended Master. But even an Ascended Master must occasionally wonder what went astray? To have one's message hijacked is bad enough, but to see it turned so completely on its head? The version of his message that has been retailed for so long not only does not empower us but is being used as an instrument to create all over again that very state of disempowerment from which he came to deliver us in the first place. That must surely give great pause. Ascended Masters are not noted for fading into retirement after they have achieved their goal, for once that stage is reached, the options open to them increase exponentially. That indicates that the Ascended Master Jesus is extremely unlikely to be sitting in comfort in retirement in heaven — as we so often fondly imagine, if we bother to imagine at all — but rather has already embarked on making known the unknown at even greater levels now. As the two-thousandth anniversary of his mission dawns, and if we ourselves decide to embark seriously on our own adventures of powerfully creating in the quantum field, it is not unrealistic to hope that, without dying, we can at some stage tell Jesus in person that we have finally got what he meant and that we are acting on it now. To him, I am sure, that would be the most congruous and appreciated two-thousandth anniversary gift.

CHAPTER 1: HEALING ONESELF

*"There have been a small host of masters
appear here on your plane for eons in your time
to teach you this same teaching,
that God is one and the same as you
and that the kingdom of heaven
is within your kingdom."*

— Ramtha

SOMETIMES IT TAKES AN ARMY

Neil Kaber

It was summertime and I had family visiting. My son, his wife, and my two-year-old grandson, who I had never met in person, flew in from the East Coast. One of the things we did for fun was taking several walks. Although as a diabetic I knew there were risks for me doing so much walking, I decided to do them. There were two parts to my deciding to go. First, it was because I was really excited to be with my family again and, second, because of my deep-down feelings that they expected me to be with them as much as possible. I didn't think about whether that was true or not; I just automatically assumed it was. It did turn out from the walks that all the action in my feet caused a large blister on my left foot near my big toe.

When my family left, I went to my podiatrist to check my toe. I waited as he assessed me. He found that this blister had opened up into a large wound that developed into a diabetic ulcer. After the assessment, my doctor calmly began to draw with his finger on my foot where he thought the surgeon would amputate. He looked knowingly at me and said, "I believe the infection has gone into the bone. Osteomyelitis is not curable and the infected bone needs to be cut away." While he was calmly telling me this news, sweat was pouring out of me! I just wanted to escape from this scene from hell as fast as I could. He looked at me and said, "Go to the hospital and have it evaluated. They will run some tests and we will know how to proceed."

I waited a few days but then I started getting chills at night. My doctor had warned me about this and said that the chills were a sign that an infection was present. So in the morning I drove myself to the hospital to be evaluated to see if I had the dreaded bone infection. When I left home for the hospital, I figured I would be there for a few hours. As it turned out, the tests showed

I did have a bone infection and they kept me for six days, during which I had an intravenous (IV) antibiotic dripped into me continuously, day and night.

A bone infection is very dangerous to the body but it was also a big concern to me because I knew it was going to force me to stop my main exercise, bicycling. I love bicycling. I bike for the floating, dreamy pleasure it brings me. Also, the diabetic oral medication I take doesn't lower my blood sugar enough and biking lowers my glucose levels. Add to this that pedaling puts less exercise stress on my feet than walking, it's clear how important bicycling is to me. Another aspect of my biking is that as I ride, I sometimes do my Neighborhood Walk®, one of the disciplines I learned as a student at Ramtha's School of Enlightenment (RSE). Instead of walking, which puts stress on my feet, I do my "walk" on my bike. If done consistently, this discipline creates new neurological connections in the brain which can change reality, including creating healing in the body. All of these wonderful benefits are the reasons I had been bicycling two times a day, seven days a week, for a long time. I didn't want to have to stop!

Nine years prior, I had worked as a Hyperbaric Oxygen Technician. I had done this work for three years, and because of my experience I absolutely knew a better way to deal with the infection than amputating my foot. Hyperbaric, which involves a person entering a chamber to receive oxygen at higher than atmospheric pressure, is a radical alternative therapy for most traditional doctors. It just doesn't fit into the box of an allopathic doctor's training. I looked at the doctors and said, "I want several weeks of simultaneous antibiotic IV and hyperbaric oxygen treatments." All of them shook their heads and said, "No, you need the amputation. Then the hyperbaric will help heal the surgery." I told them emphatically, "You have it all backwards. The hyperbaric will prevent the surgery and I will still have my whole foot." I knew what I was talking about. They were not in agreement and continued to assume I would need amputation.

Previous to my going into the hospital, I had barely slept in two weeks. I discovered this insomnia was also due to the infection. The insomnia continued in the hospital. I was worn out. This was only made worse by the temporary end of my bicycling.

I thought about my training at RSE with Ramtha. I was in my late thirties when I took my beginning class and have attended for over thirty years. Learning at RSE has been, and is, the most exciting journey I have ever been on. Without this cutting-edge school of the mind, my life would be creating me instead of me creating my life. I learned how my MIND is MATTER. I learned how to develop focused intent and the science of how focus works in the human brain. And the disciplines Ramtha taught where I had to apply what I learned brought everything to life. All the disciplines helped me to create a new and improved life. With an open mind, strong will, and sharply focused intent, I had learned that I can create anything. I CAN have it my way. I would not know how it will happen, but it will. Now I had an opportunity to use my mind as matter and my strong will to have it my way!

I drew a card that said, "NEIL HYPERBARIC YES." Despite my exhaustion, I focused on this card many times a day, every day. There was also a whiteboard in my hospital room where daily therapies are written down. I erased a large space and wrote NEIL HYPERBARIC YES. On top of this, several times a day I walked the halls, dragging my IV stand, creating a new reality with the Neighborhood Walk® saying, "NEIL HYPERBARIC YES."

I had to be a salesman for hyperbaric therapy to every doctor who saw me. And my doctors changed so often that I had to start my campaign from the beginning with every one of them.

Eventually, my podiatrist came into my room. He started drawing on my foot again. With all my remaining strength I yelled, "NO!" The amount of sheer power of that "NO" stunned everyone present, including me. It was a "NO" without arguments, options, or negotiations. After my declaration, my doctor decided to go along with my plan. My remaining days in the hospital were devoted to convincing the other doctors until, eventually, they agreed with my idea despite the fact they thought it would be ineffective. But *I knew* it would be effective. And in my mind I celebrated — MY FOCUS WORKED!!

Before I could be released from the hospital to pursue hyperbaric treatment, I had to be trained by a nurse to perform home IV infusions of the antibiotic. I had a tube inserted into my arm going through a vein to just above my heart to facilitate this home process. It's called a PIC line. Then I was released from the hospital. Driving home after three weeks of practically no sleep, and using my energy to constantly fight doctors about my treatment, was an amazing testament to my will. Will is a gravity that can hold me together even in the most difficult situations. And my will was turned up to ten!

When I arrived home, it was dark and I was worn out beyond words. If I had had enough energy left, I would have cried. But I could not go to bed yet because I had to start my first home antibiotic IV infusion. As I tried to start, I could not recall enough of my training. My kind and patient son lives with me and he read through the instructions one by one. Somehow we got the dining room table cleaned off and sterilized and together we made it through the infusion. Now the challenge had begun. Every eight hours — at 8 a.m., 4 p.m., and 12 a.m. — I had to do my own IV infusions in sterile conditions. It required following the protocol with precision. I could not make mistakes on any of the many steps involved. If anything went amiss, foreign matter could get into my heart and cause devastating problems. Still running on will, I proceeded.

Simultaneous with my infusions, I drove thirty miles each way every day for my hyperbaric treatments. This made additional demands on me but my strong will kept me going.

During the half hour it took to infuse the antibiotic at home, I would focus. I had just finished reading *Joan of Arc* by Mark Twain. This is the most vivid and accurate description ever written of her life and the army she assembled and led. The characters and battles were still fresh in my mind. During each infusion I put on blinders and visualized Joan's army going down the tube — from the syringe all the way into my bloodstream and down into the infected bone. I made the infection as green, round blobs with faces on them. Here came the army, on horseback, led by Joan. The Paladin, her standard bearer, and the Dwarf, who was tall and formidable, were there, the Paladin leading the charge and the Dwarf following with his axe. I watched as the army came closer and closer. Then the battle began. With swords, battle-axes, and arrows flying, they moved forward into every hiding place and crevasse in the bone. They hacked the staphylococcus bacteria to pieces. None could run fast enough to escape the wrath of this most noble and formidable fighting force. There were splattered blobs everywhere. A few last arrows and my thirty-minute battle was over until the next infusion, eight hours later.

I asked myself, "What is happening here? In my PRESENT state I bring alive an army from the PAST to create a FUTURE healing. I know that the present, past, and future can happen all at once!" Quantum physics says that all time exists simultaneously in the quantum state, and I knew that that was exactly what I was doing. I also had learned from Ramtha that disease is caused by habitual, repetitive attitudes. Hence I committed to uncovering the attitude from the past and bringing it into my present and conquering it with my will so I could have a new future.

The days and weeks went by and I contemplated continuously on what attitude was behind this disease. Many experiences came up which were like a review of my life. After days of review, it became crystal clear to me how I created this whole incident. The driving attitude that I discovered that created the diabetic ulcer on my foot and the other illnesses that I had suffered from for most of my life were:

I sacrifice myself for other's needs.

Being a martyr, I feel obligated to do what other important people want.

I do not want to disappoint other people.

This last attitude was so deeply ingrained in me that I was totally unaware of it. I cannot emphasize enough how big of a realization this was. It changed my whole way of being.

As I looked back, I realized that when my family arrived that summer, my foot was already tender. I could have thought more lovingly about myself and the condition of my body and decided to stay home instead of doing all the walking. Deep down, I knew better. But because of the hidden attitude that drove me, I chose self-sacrifice. I followed what I thought other people wanted instead of following my own knowingness. And the attitude went further than that. I had a made-up loyalty to my family. I told myself to just "suck it up and do it for the family."

After uncovering these attitudes, now when I find myself being a martyr, I catch it and make a different decision that includes loving myself. This was my realization and my wisdom gained from this whole experience. Wisdom often comes after great suffering, and it was so for me.

My hyperbaric treatments were five days a week and the infusions were seven days a week, every eight hours. But I never gave up. There were a lot of Joan of Arc battles, but I was driven to be healed completely of this foreign invader. For me, there were no other options!

Many weeks later when I visited my podiatrist, the large, gaping wound was healed and the infection was gone. An x-ray confirmed it. He was extremely surprised but remained cautious. He saw me once a week for about three weeks until he gave me the okay to start biking again. I was overjoyed like a child on Christmas morning when I heard his words. I started biking just a half mile a day. Then it became one mile a day. Finally I built up to riding forty to fifty miles a week, which is what I do now. I am feeling strong and well again and, most importantly of all, I am really vigilant about identifying and eliminating old attitudes, as I know they were the ultimate source of my disease.

ATTITUDE IS EVERYTHING

Joan Avnery

"You have a tumor on your uterus." My doctor continued speaking slowly and clearly, "It is the size of a tennis ball and it is too big to remove by operation. If it were smaller we could cut it out. But in your case we need to remove your uterus." I stared into my doctor's eyes and said, "Can you explain to me how big it is and where it is located?" On the back of a small napkin he drew a diagram of my uterus and showed the tumor. He spent a long time explaining everything to me. I was grateful that he didn't rush to say that surgery was needed immediately. I picked up the diagram and went straight to the hospital where another x-ray was performed and my surgery was scheduled.

On the way to the hospital, I began to worry. Although I was forty-eight years old at the time, I still wanted children. My Aunt Alice had had a baby boy at age fifty-two, so I didn't think it would be unusual for me to do the same. Also, my husband really wanted a baby! But now, with the thought of losing my entire uterus, I became upset and sad. I was also in pain from my monthly cycles and had lost quite a bit of blood. As a result, my blood level plunged seriously low and my pulse, which had always been low, went even lower. It was not good news.

The nurse scheduled me for my hysterectomy on the following Wednesday. Before she had finished entering me into the calendar, I stopped and firmly said, "Give me three weeks. I will return for another examination at the end of the month, and if the tumor is still there I will schedule surgery."

I went straight home and drew a healing card to focus on, based on the doctor's explanation and diagram.

At home I began to contemplate how could I have manifested a tumor? What came to me was a memory from long ago. I remembered starting my period when I was ten and on holiday with my aunt who lives in England. I was a skinny little girl who had not yet been told about developing and having a menstrual cycle. When I saw the blood on my underwear, I locked myself in the bathroom and began to cry. "I am probably going die!" I sobbed. I knew two of my grandparents had died of cancer and now I was sure it was happening to me.

Hearing my distress, my aunt came to the door and asked, "Joany, what are you doing?" When I opened the door she immediately knew but would not tell me about menstrual cycles. "We'll wait until your mother comes to visit and she will tell you what is happening to you. Until then you must go to bed with a hot water bottle." At that moment I knew that I must be dying of cancer. So intense fear set in at the age of ten when my period began. I also realized now at age forty-eight that although I really wanted children, I had something more in me that was blocking me from getting pregnant.

Further contemplation brought me back to the time when I was three months' pregnant and had a miscarriage. Before the baby miscarried, I had a dream where I saw the baby going into a big white room and I woke up screaming, "Don't take my baby!" Yet my first baby was taken by a miscarriage, and I was filled with unworthiness and even more fear. Now facing a hysterectomy, I realized how much I really wanted a baby and how much fear, loss, and unworthiness were getting in the way of my having a healthy uterus. That was what I wanted to conquer — feelings of fear, loss, and unworthiness.

I first learned how to draw a focus card in February of 1989 when I went to a Ramtha's School of Enlightenment (RSE) retreat at Estes Park in Colorado. This was the second RSE event that I attended. What brought me to Ramtha's school was an accident that occurred in which I had a near-death experience. Since then I had never stopped wondering about what happened that day.

At that time of the accident I was twenty-one and studying French in Paris at the Alliance Française. I had been out with a friend in the countryside. At the end of our afternoon together, my friend offered to give me a lift into the city. I accepted. On the way, the car went out of control on the slippery road and rolled onto a field. As the car rolled, I was thrown against the door. The door handle punched deeply into my back and then my friend landed on top of me. At that moment I left my body and started floating. There was a beautiful, yellow field. I saw a tunnel and started going up. A voice said, "Oh, no, it is too early. Go back." When I came back into my body there were policemen and an ambulance. I had cut my foot, and blood was coming from every direction. They very carefully removed me from the car into the ambulance. I then realized that they thought I had broken my back.

After this out-of-body experience, I realized that I wanted to learn more about what had happened to me and I wondered whether I could do it again without having a car accident. Also, I realized that I was no longer afraid of death. Suddenly I began to ponder the supernatural and I sought out RSE as a way of getting answers to my questions.

Soon after, I became interested in healing modalities and was invited to go to a "Healers for Peace" conference outside Copenhagen, Denmark. A group of us met there to see the healers from the Philippines and the United States. While we were walking down the hallway, we passed a room where the healers were getting ready to lecture. I noticed a small television that was playing the video of Ramtha from Hawaii. When I passed the television, I heard a voice in my head answer the question I had been pondering over and over since the car accident: What happens when we die? I stopped and said to my friends, "I want to look at this." I looked at the video and took down the address for RSE. The school quickly sent me the information I requested. Amazingly, exactly two weeks later there was a Beginning Event in November in London.

At that time I didn't have much money, but when I returned home outside of Copenhagen there was a check in my mailbox for the exact amount that was required for the event.

That was the beginning of my journey.

Now, ten years later, I was faced with having a hysterectomy and accepting that I would never have children. I said to myself, "No, I will focus and change this situation." Every morning and every night I would focus on seeing my uterus being healed and perfect and would send it love. My drawing of my uterus was shaped as a heart.

After nearly a month I went back to the hospital to have my examination. To the surprise of the doctors, it showed that the tumor was completely gone. My doctor was stunned. "It is gone," he said.

I asked him, adamantly, "Are you sure?"

"Yes," he said. "That happens sometimes." I looked at him and smiled and thought, "Yes, and when you have learned how to focus, it happens all the time."

Since then I have tried to obtain my x-rays and medical records. This miraculous healing occurred when I was in Denmark. Since then, the hospital where I was treated has been converted into apartments and the hospital merged with another hospital in northern Copenhagen. When I called that hospital, they had no records older than five years ago.

For all these years I have kept the card I drew to remind myself how important my thoughts are. This miracle taught me that anything is possible and never to let anyone tell me otherwise. I knew that I had healed my uterus but, more importantly, I healed my attitudes of fear and loss.

MAGICAL TWILIGHT®

Elizabeth Axe

I received a phone call on the morning of June 30, 2010, and immediately my life changed. Ten days earlier I had what seemed like a gallstone. I was nauseous and uncomfortable. Even after doing a liver cleanse I felt weak and unwell, so I decided to visit my doctor.

I had been experiencing pain in my breast, so while the doctor was examining me I had her check my breast. She found a lump. Breast cancer is not normally painful but in my case the pain was caused by a pulled back muscle. From the moment the doctor found the lump, I felt like I had boarded a train that was careening out of control — certainly out of my control.

She scheduled an appointment for me later that day for a mammogram and explained that they would send the results to her and she would let me know.

I left the doctor's office shaking. My mind was numb. How could this be happening to me? I was fifty-one years old and otherwise healthy, if a little overweight. Compared to most Americans, I ate well — mostly organic, homegrown vegetables from the garden. I did not smoke, took over-the-counter medicine only on rare occasions, and drank moderate amounts of red wine. I was a happily married mother of three grown children. How could this be happening to me?

I kept telling myself, "Most detected masses were benign. Don't panic!" It didn't help. I focused on it being benign but my God had other plans.

Within twenty minutes of that fateful phone call, I pulled myself together. I had the tools to heal myself. I had healed our animals on many occasions. I could do this. I knew the first thing I had to overcome was fear. Knowledge conquers fear, so I got on the Internet and started an intriguing journey to learn as much as I could about what was happening in my body and what alternatives I had to chemotherapy and radiation. I already decided that I was not going down that path.

As a student at Ramtha's School of Enlightenment (RSE), I had heard Ramtha say that while ultraviolet-blue frequency can cure anything, we human personalities sometimes need to have the support of physical aids, be that conventional medication, diet, or alternatives. They help us to know we are doing something while the mind and body get on with healing. So along with the disciplines I learned at RSE, I changed my diet and did all that I could to support my immune system.

I contemplated surgery and eventually decided that I was interested in hearing what the surgeon had to say. However, when he said with a big smile on his face — as if he were giving me the best news ever — that with my kind of cancer and the early stage I had caught it, my life expectancy was ten years. I looked at him and thought two very Anglo-Saxon words! I was fifty-one and had not had grandchildren yet!! There was absolutely NO way I was dying at sixty!

I very quickly realized that although I had been a student of RSE since 1988 and had used the disciplines to manifest many things, I really had never truly known what focus was. There is nothing like a bout of mortality to bring things into sharp focus.

My research quickly told me that tumors create their own connections to a blood supply. So I realized that if I could cut the blood supply to the tumor, it was not going to go anywhere else in my body and was not going to get bigger. My discipline of choice for this was Twilight® Visualization. I had learned that Twilight® is a discipline wherein I lie perfectly still in focus until the subconscious mind is free to work.

Once I was deep in Twilight®, I began to visualize the tumor, snipping each of the connections until it was isolated. My doctor scheduled me for a thermogram six weeks later and according to the results, I had achieved isolating the tumor from the blood supply. "Great! I will be rid of this in no time," I thought.

One important thought that came to me while snipping connections to the tumor was that I had created this group of cells. They were made of me, therefore fighting them would be fighting myself. Instead I saw that I had to love them into becoming normal cells once again, just like a mother loves an errant child back into the fold.

I am glad it took quite a bit longer. I learned so much about myself, I let go of so many things, I forgave myself for so much. I spent many hours in disciplines. But although the tumor did not grow and it only shrank a little, I knew that I had not gotten to the root cause.

I kept calling the root cause forth and eventually, when I was so bored of focusing on healing that I forgot for long periods of time I even had cancer, the runners — experiences that make us aware of what we need to know — came forth. Through these runners I understood what had started the tumor growth. What to do about it? Twilight®, of course.

I went down the stairs deep into Twilight® and asked the "entity at the door" to help me. Immediately a video started playing that showed me the situation that brought about the huge emotional shock that had caused the tumor to start to grow. I watched it in complete detachment as if I were watching something that absolutely had nothing to do with me. In true observation is forgiveness. When the scenes were completed, I went through all the participants and forgave them, finishing with myself.

The next day I went to see my traditional Chinese medicine doctor for my regular weekly treatment. She was intimately aware of my tumor. Halfway through the session when she came to my breast, she exclaimed, "It is no longer there. It's gone!" The tumor had been dissolved and I know it happened the moment I had resolved the past into wisdom.

YOU MUST LEARN TO THINK LIKE A GOD

Linda Barnes

On June 11, 2017, I became semiconscious and unable to function. A friend came to check on me and called an ambulance after repeatedly asking for, and finally getting, my permission. I had no idea the condition I was in or why I was in such a state. I could hardly breathe and went in and out of consciousness.

An ambulance quickly arrived and transported me to St. Peter Hospital in Olympia, Washington. Fluid was filling up my chest cavity and my gut. It was later explained to me that I was drowning in my own body fluid because of anaphylactic shock swelling, which was combined with a severe bacterial infection present in my abdomen. The anaphylactic swelling occurred inside my body rather than in my face and throat, so it could not be seen. Consequently, the bacteria rapidly multiplied the fluid to fill my entire body cavity. I remember suddenly sitting upright on the stretcher and projectile vomiting a large stream of water beyond the stretcher and then gasping to get air. I then passed out again.

There was no room available in the hospital, so I spent a day in an emergency room bed waiting for a room. I then was moved upstairs to a room on the thirty-third floor only to be moved the next day to another room, and then moved a third time to yet another room. I finally stayed in this small room facing east for the next two and a half months while a countless number of doctors, nurses, and specialists tried to figure out, first, what was wrong, then where the infection had come from, and how to make me well.

After a couple of days in my room I fell asleep and woke up elsewhere. There were no people, places, or things. There were no black Voids or bright lights. All that existed was just me staring into an open space. I looked into it and said, "I don't know what to do." All of a sudden a picture flashed into view. A voice, sounding like a young child, squealed "*I know*." As a student of RSE I did know what to do. I had to go into my Blue Body® and talk to my God within.

Suddenly I was in a new place where I began the process of building my Blue Body®. I knew I fell asleep a number of times as I was creating my Blue Body®, but each time I awoke and continued the process and finally it was complete. I turned my head to the left to look at my God and have a chat. And there it was — my God. It was not any thing. There was no light, no whirling ball of energy, no voice, nor any "thing." There was no time. It was just knowingness in a timeless place.

I had a wordless conversation with my God, and at some point the conversation was done. Suddenly pictures began to appear. I would enter and become part of a picture/experience and each time I knew exactly what I wanted to do.

I was then sitting in complete darkness. There was a small hole, and I crawled into it and just sat there. I looked all around and there was nothing but me sitting in this darkness. I thought, "I don't want to be here," and instantly I was not there anymore.

The last picture that I saw was a small child about two and a half years old sitting on the floor in the corner of an empty room. The child was waiting for something. I walked into the room and squatted down next to the child and said, "Today is going to be different. We are going to do what you want to do." I stood and offered my hand. I continued talking as we left the room. "Tell me what you want. What do you like? This is your time. You decide." We left the room to do what the child wanted to do. I fell asleep.

When I woke up I was first surprised and then a little disappointed. I was in my hospital room. During the period that I created and lived in my Blue Body®, I had no memory of being in my hospital room. The only memories I had were of the other realm — the pictures that would flash before me and the experiences that I had in the pictures. After waking up in my hospital room, I realized that I had been in the other realm for about nine days. During those nine days my body had been in the hospital bed taking the pills and answering the nurses' questions, but I had no awareness of that. To this day I have no memory of it.

After waking up, I had plenty of time during my hospital stay to ponder what I had seen and done and what it all meant. I realized that I now knew what unconditional love felt like. I had more of an understanding of Oneness with other living creatures. I knew that I would be well but the body would need time to get there. I learned that I have to define who and what I am. I heard a voice in my head say, "You must learn to think like a God." I thought about the fact that I have lived countless lives and have done it all. I knew that life is about balance and moderation and that Oneness is not herd mentality. Oneness is recognizing and honoring the value of each individual to be unique. It is the divinity in us that makes us One. My job is to define and evolve me. That is a full-time job.

A HEALER'S HEALING JOURNEY

Heidi Gould, with Jalene Smith

Today is March 5, 2018. I feel such joy and peace. I have been given an opportunity to live life anew. From this opportunity, I have had a profound experience in learning to truly love myself. Because of the challenge I faced, I was forced to go deeper into the recesses of my brain to tap into the calm place in the center where I am at one with the God within me. What an experience to surrender to that God and allow my body to be taken care of and healed! I am so very grateful to be on the other side of this challenge. As a result of it, I know the power of my mind and have gained an enormous amount of knowledge and experience. I have used the knowledge I have been taught these past twenty-three years as a student of my Master Teacher, Ramtha, and his daughter, JZ Knight, to heal my body. After doing healing work on others for thirty years, I can now say without a doubt that the power of my mind has healed me. When faced with this "dis-ease," I knew that it was my personality that had created it and knew it would take something greater than my personality to heal me.

To begin at the beginning: On February 16, 2018, my doctor presented to my partner Jalene and me the results of a CT scan taken the previous day. She was quite surprised and emotional to tell us there was a cystic mass attached to my right ovary, fallopian tube, appendix, rectum, and omentum (a portion of the stomach) about the size of an avocado. She also made note that there was abnormal cellular activity throughout my abdomen and possibly in the colon. She believed it indicated ovarian cancer and prepared me for an urgent surgery and chemotherapy. She referred me to a gynecologic oncologist surgeon in Bellevue, Washington, and also wanted me to get a specific blood test — a CA-125. This test came back at a score of 816;

the healthy range is from 0 to 35. My doctor said this was not unexpected. Both tumor size and the CA-125 blood test are considered markers for ovarian cancer. We were in shock. We were numb, and very sad. It felt like it was a bad dream, but it was real.

Even with an urgent request from my doctor, I would not be able to see the surgeon for ten days. I knew I wanted surgery immediately and this was a blow.

But when Jalene and I got home, I realized this was an opportunity to use these ten days to get emotionally, mentally, physically, and spiritually prepared for the surgery for its greatest future outcome. We took this time to embrace all the wonderful teachings and disciplines we had learned at Ramtha's School of Enlightenment (RSE) and to call on the assistance of friends and family to focus with us on healing. We realized that sharing this journey with our friends, family, and RSE community would be part of the healing, even though my first response was to keep this to ourselves. It turned out that learning to be truthful without shame and to accept the love given to me by others were all part of my healing.

I also realized that this disease was an "initiation" and many of the great masters have gone through major health crises. I knew that I was the creator of the cystic mass and had been well-prepared in this lifetime for this kind of challenge. How many lifetimes have I gotten to this place of challenge and died, only to come back again and again and again? Too many.

I have had a few brushes with death in this life. The most significant was a near-death experience when I was sixteen and almost drowned. This experience taught me that there is more to me than my body. Something outside of me had saved me from death, and from this experience I knew deep inside myself that I was not destined to live an ordinary life. I recalled that while drowning, I went from panic and fear to surrender. I know now that it was my surrender to that something inside me that saved my life then and that this deep surrender would save me now.

During the ten days that I was waiting to see the surgeon, I felt very vulnerable. I became very present with all that was happening around me, including those little thoughts that popped into my head. For example, when I ran into an old acquaintance at the grocery store who is more overweight than I am, I felt judgment come up in me. As I peeked into his grocery cart and saw his choice of food, I asked myself, "Why is he not taking care of himself?" Then I questioned myself, "Why am I judging him?" "Why am I judging me?" "STOP AND SELF-CORRECT."

So as I waited, I did a lot of self-correcting and have continued to do so. The judgments I held about everything I ate, drank, and thought were transformed into pure observation where every moment became a healing experience.

I passionately engaged my RSE disciplines, during which I found myself moving to a place in my brain that was centering, calming, and strength-enhancing. I listened to Wholetones music, which carries specific frequencies that lightened my mood and elevated my Spirit. I used other advanced technologies available to me as well. While using a Keshe electromagnetic-gravitational device designed by Dr. Rodrigo Vildosola, I felt a weight lifting off me in the area of my right pelvis. It was quite profound and very much a physical sensation. It was only much later when I was able to make the connection between this experience and the card I had drawn at the RSE Create Your Year event held in January. I had made a card of a blue-and-yellow Orb with a black, rotating atom coming out of it. At the time I didn't really know what it was or what it meant. I thought of it as activating myself through the frequencies of the electromagnetic spectrum to Point Zero. It was only upon later reflection that I realized that it was healing the tumor/mass and making it disappear into the Void.

In addition to these modalities, JZ Knight, the creator of the Blu Room technology, graciously allowed me to use her original Blu Room. Upon entering the room, the sheet lifted up like a soft wind had breezed through. I happily lay down and immediately relaxed into a deep, timeless state, feeling a pink glow around me. I also asked naturopathic physician, Dr. Andrew Iverson, to put together a nutritional regimen of the highest quality herbs and foods to prepare my body for surgery and my recovery. I followed through on all his recommendations.

Jalene and I had been doing the discipline of Consciousness & Energy® daily for the past year and continued to do so. We also engaged the Neighborhood Walk®, candle focus, and making cards. When I walked my property, I said to the trees, "I will be here with you in twenty-five years and we will spend many moments together." I hugged a tree that I have hugged in the past. A friend reminded me to see myself come in my front door after the surgery with my health restored, so during this time of waiting I continued to see myself returning home healthy.

I realized that people in our RSE community often keep our illnesses and difficult times to ourselves. I did not want to do that. I knew that an important part of my healing was to be truthful and accept the love others wanted to give me. Knowing the power of the minds and the strength of focus of our student community, Jalene and I decided to send out an email to school friends in both the United States, Hong Kong, Korea, Australia, and Canada. We wanted to prevent rumors and allow us to directly communicate with them.

I had to cancel clients that had scheduled with me for the next three months, which caused me to feel even more vulnerable. I had to admit to them that I had health issues that needed to be addressed. This was very humbling since I do healing work as a profession. But I knew that sharing this truthfully would be part of my healing.

Finally the day arrived to meet with the surgeon and schedule surgery. We met Michelle Benoit, M.D. Her specialty is gynecologic oncology surgery. She took my history, did an exam, and reviewed the CT scan and blood work.

I was given my options. I told her I wanted to have the surgery to remove the mass as soon as possible. I asked her if I could get in right away, thinking she would admit me for surgery that week. She saw new patients on Monday and did surgery Tuesday through Friday. I had been focused on surgery for Tuesday or Wednesday. She said she could possibly schedule it for the end of the week, but we should go out and check her schedule with the front desk. I later found out her schedule usually had a six-to-eight-week wait for surgery. But we gladly accepted an opening the next day, Tuesday morning. It was a "great sign." Jalene and I had been focusing on "Next-Day Surgery" during the week before and we had successfully manifested it!

Dr. Benoit prepared us for the worst, telling us she would remove the tumor, ovaries, tubes, appendix, and any lymph nodes that were suspect. She expected to remove some of the large intestine as well, and I would need to use a colostomy bag until healing occurred. I would then undergo another surgery to reconnect the colon. She said I would need chemotherapy for six months and she would put in two ports: one in my abdomen and another in the shoulder area for the chemotherapy which would follow. Given the CT scan and the CA-125 blood work, there was no indication given by Dr. Benoit that it may not be cancerous.

Jalene and I called friends to take care of our home and animals and let our friends know the day and time of the surgery so they could focus with us. Our friends were there for us and encouraged us with their knowingness that everything would be all right. We found a hotel near the hospital and checked in for the amount of time I would be in the hospital so Jalene could be close by.

In preparation for surgery, I drank the preparation liquids and cleaned my body with special presurgery wipes. Every day I focused on my healing images and did my Neighborhood Walk® at the hotel. During my disciplines I had to work a lot to conquer the emotions stirring in my mind and body about what I was about to face.

The morning of the surgery I did my Neighborhood Walk® in the hotel parking lot. There was a sense of relief that the surgery would finally be happening. I was not as nervous as I thought I would be, given the grim future that my surgeon told me awaited. Somehow I had knowingness that I would be all right.

I met the surgical team and my surgeon. They were all very kind and I felt a sense of trust that I was in "good/God's" hands. When they rolled me down the hall, I closed my eyes so I would not see all the people and surroundings in the hospital on the way to the surgery suite. Upon arrival in surgery, I marveled to myself that this was such a large room. I commented to the team that this was my "blue room" and they were my "blue team." They must have wondered what I was talking about!

I quickly went under with the anesthesia and don't remember anything until I awoke in recovery. The surgeon was quite surprised at what she found during surgery. She came into the waiting area to tell Jalene that the initial pathology report was that the tumor was benign and there was no evidence of cancer. However, she did make the decision to remove my appendix and greater omentum because of statistical "at-risk" factors. But finding no signs of cancer, and being an oncology surgeon, she said her work was complete at this time and she was going to close me up. She said she may have to operate again if the more detailed pathology reports that were still pending came back positive for cancer and hoped we would not mind. I can only imagine the joy and relief Jalene must have felt.

I was moved to a hospital room and Jalene was waiting. WOW! She told me what the surgeon had told her — benign results! Although I was attached to an IV and a catheter and could not eat, I was overjoyed!

I progressed rapidly. My vital signs were really good and I was encouraged to get out of the hospital bed and walk the next day, Wednesday. Although there was a lot of abdominal and back pain, I walked so much the nurses were surprised. They said they have to usually push most people to walk. In my room

I sat in the chair with a heating pad on my back and focused with music. The television was rarely on.

Upon my discharge on Friday morning, the surgeon told me that the final pathology report was also negative. Jalene and I drove home that Friday amazed at how changed we were by this incredible experience. Then we realized that the RSE Dimensional Mind event was starting that night. I could participate in the event! This would be the icing on the cake — I could keep my mind in the frequency of the blue realm while my body continued its healing.

I cherish this great opportunity I have gone through. I now know without doubt that surrendering to the God within me and allowing love of self truly awakens the healer within.

NO ONE HEALS THIS RAPIDLY — NO ONE!

Linda Liss

The car wreck occurred in early 1998. My youngest daughter Sarah, who was four years old at the time, was in her car seat on the passenger side in back. I was driving to pick up my oldest daughter when the wreck occurred. A young couple on their way from a friend's house were rummaging through their CDs when the young man unknowingly veered into my lane. I was driving a small car and, to his horror, his pickup truck actually went over the top of my vehicle totally destroying my car roof. Thank God Sarah was basically uninjured! She had been safe in the back seat. I was not so fortunate.

Every rib on my left side had been broken; some, multiple times. My left collarbone had been broken and the left scapula shattered. My left lung had been punctured. I was apparently unconscious after the wreck, although I have since been told by paramedics that the drugs given in such circumstances often wipe one's memory. I do, however, have one memory of all of this. I remember lying on a gurney outside of the ambulance looking at the night sky and distinctly remember knowing that I had been severely injured and that the only important thing was to find my kids. Where were they? I have since been told that Sarah was put into the ambulance in the front seat and that the paramedics actually looked for Kate along the side of the road because I kept insisting they find her and had been unable to tell them where she actually was.

Rumors were that my heart had stopped on the way to the hospital. That I cannot verify. Ramtha later told me that I had died and that my God had told me, "You shall not pass." I have been told by many that I was a terrible sight to behold when I was brought into the emergency room on the gurney. Many students from Ramtha's School of Enlightenment (RSE) came to the emergency room to focus on me. I was truly blessed and I am eternally grateful to these wonderful, fellow students.

That night my parents and brother were told that it was highly unlikely that I would survive the night. Interestingly, my father later told me that when he went to bed that first night he saw me surrounded by a blue light. My father knew nothing about Blue Body® healing at that time.

I have no recollection of the first few days in ICU. I do remember what seemed to be hours of endless "space" that I went in and out of. I distinctly remember being grateful for the many hours of Fieldwork® I had done at Ramtha's school because I knew from those experiences that I could focus my way through this. I also remember a moment where food sounded terrible to me and another memory where I realized that I could not hold my loved ones due to my injuries. Upon this realization, I suddenly imagined a huge buffet of food and was not interested. At this moment I wondered, "What else is there when you can't eat and you can't hold those you love?" At that moment I asked my God to show me what more there is to life. Immediately my answer came. I realized in that moment that my life had truly been all about my body.

I am convinced that what actually saved me through all of this were Ramtha's teachings and disciplines, and my wonderful boyfriend Bryan. Once Bryan was able to get into the Intensive Care Unit to see me — a whole story in itself! — he was the greatest gift I could ever have. Although we have since married, Bryan and I were a couple at the time of the car wreck and both of us had been in Ramtha's school for numerous years.

I am no longer sure of the actual order of events during my stay at the hospital. During the first days in the hospital I was given six pints of blood. I also needed to have a hole drilled into the lung that had been punctured in the car wreck. I think the lung had been filling with fluid and now needed to be drained. This was a painful process that required bandaging. But this bandage was subsequently forgotten by the nurses, which caused further problems.

Bryan and I began writing to one another in the hospital because at first I could not speak. I did not like the morphine I was being given due to the fact that I felt it kept me from thinking clearly. Together with the medical staff, Bryan and I made a decision to have me self-administer the morphine. This resulted in my ability to be completely off the drug unusually quickly. Once off of the morphine, I tried using other types of pain medication but they all caused my heart to become erratic. In their place I used ibuprofen, which did offer some relief.

At some point during all of this, the doctors had become concerned that my spinal cord had been damaged. I remember the very profound moment communicating with Bryan when I refused to accept that I could have any spinal challenges. I insisted that this would not be a problem. The doctors ordered an MRI to verify the state of my spine. I was put into this very tight capsule and told not to move and to hold my breath until they told me that I could breathe again. They warned me if I moved, I might have to do the whole procedure over again. You can imagine how difficult this experience was after having had a collapsed lung and further lung complications.

While in the MRI machine I remembered my many experiences in The Tank® overcoming fears of tight spaces. And, believe me, I was truly grateful for those experiences! To my great relief I only had to do this procedure once, and to everyone's relief it showed my spine was fine.

One day one of the doctors came into my room. She realized that the nurses had not changed the bandage on my chest where a hole had been made for drainage. The wound had become infected because of the soiled bandages and lack of care. She was very concerned about this infection. She was also upset that I was eating so much. I had started becoming ravenous! She was worried that due to my multiple injuries, my intestines would not yet be functioning properly. I told her that wasn't a concern because they were working properly. She looked somewhat surprised that my body was returning to normal so rapidly but didn't say anything.

Within the next few days the same doctor returned. Her eyes almost popped out of her head when she saw how rapidly the wound on my chest had healed! Again, she made no comment other than to say that things were coming along fine.

My recovery seemed slow to me at first, but actually it was quite rapid. I was healing! When possible, Bryan would shut the door and engage the Consciousness & Energy® (C&E®) discipline to help me alleviate the pain. It worked! From the very beginning Bryan and I put the teachings foremost in our minds. Ramtha's teachings filled our every thought. I had a magnificent Blue Body® card on my table and pictures of blue webs on the walls. Every night in my hospital room we played the "cricket" CD, with the subliminal messages, that was prepared for students in Ramtha's school. We didn't care what the medical personnel thought about any of this. In addition, during these years Steve Klein held a weekly healing group where Ramtha students gathered at his home and participated in the teachings of Blue Body® healing. I was one of the people being focused on. For this I am truly grateful for all their wonderful love.

The day we left the hospital I thanked every doctor. They seemed quiet, yet happy that I was well. I wondered why none of them commented on what we thought was a rather speedy recovery, but Bryan and I left the hospital happy. We knew that I still had a long road ahead but that we had gotten through all of the serious issues quite well.

Three months later I was scheduled for a checkup with the doctor who had discovered the problem with my chest bandage. As I was leaving, she finally said it. "No one comes through these hospital doors in the condition you were in and heals that rapidly — no one!" I told her, as I had through the entire experience, that it was because of Ramtha's school.

I am now well and fully functional in my life. The fact that I am is a testament not only to the care I received in the hospital but also to the magnificent Blue Body® training that we students all receive at Ramtha's school.

A HEALING IN THE MIRROR

Judy Audet Holsinger

When I was in the seventh grade, I began wearing glasses because I was myopic. Myopia is the inability to see clearly at a distance. Some refer to it as shortsightedness or nearsightedness. I didn't think much about it because my father wore glasses and so did my favorite aunt. It seemed natural to me.

In my late twenties I began to question *why* I was shortsighted. As I observed myself over the years, I realized that I held a lot of tension in my head, face, and eyes but I wasn't sure what created the tension or how to let it go.

In 1980 I met Ramtha the Enlightened One and resonated with his teachings. In 1988 he created Ramtha's School of Enlightenment (RSE) and I have continued to attend his school to the present time. In RSE I was taught to observe myself in all areas of my life. I still wasn't figuring out why I had myopic vision but I did begin to wonder in what areas of my life I was "shortsighted." What was I unwilling to see or what was I afraid to see?

Two years ago I had cataract surgery. When I took the patch off my eye for the first time, I was astounded by my perfect vision. I was thrilled that everything I saw was totally clear. However, after a year I was back to being mildly myopic again. My question again was, "Why?"

One of the disciplines I was taught at RSE was mirror work, and I continued doing the mirror discipline at home in a very consistent manner. After engaging mirror work for a number of years, one day driving down the road I realized my vision was crystal clear. "WOW! How did that happen?" I asked myself. As I drove on, I pondered this. Then suddenly I realized that when I was doing my mirror work, I had to relax my eyes in order to do it correctly. There was an actual physical sensation of relaxation behind my eyes. So as I was observing myself while driving, I noticed that I was experiencing the same feeling behind my eyes that I experienced during mirror work. Again, WOW! Is this the answer I have been looking for? All I have to do is consciously relax the muscles behind my eyes to have perfect vision?

The answer is yes. However, I found it is not quite that easy because my pattern is always to tense my eye muscles. I know it takes constant vigilance, at least until it becomes a habit, so I still constantly remind myself to be aware of that pattern.

Mirror work is a discipline that takes diligent focus in a relatively relaxed manner. Because I became consciously aware that my eye muscles were very relaxed both when doing the discipline and when I was seeing clearly as I drove, I felt that making the connection between the two was truly a miracle. Even if I intellectually knew I was holding tension, where else could I have learned how to relax my eyes so wonderfully? And the greatest part is that I taught it to myself. I was not attempting to heal my eyes when I started doing mirror work, but as a result of that discipline I now have the knowledge of how the healing came about. It just happened to be a wonderful, unexpected result of the Great Work, for which I will be forever grateful.

HEALING MY BODY WITH LONG, QUIET FOCUS

Jaqueline Smith

I was living in Illinois and had completed my college degree at Eastern Illinois University. After graduation I went to work as a draftsperson, but my dream was to become an actress in Hollywood. So as soon as I saved enough money, I bought an airline ticket and off I went to Los Angeles.

Fortunately, I had college friends who were living there and was able to stay with them until I could "break into the industry." I worked for a year and a half at various jobs until one day a coworker at Price Waterhouse handed me a newspaper clipping of a job ad for temporary workers at one of the major studios. Although I did not have one bit of background for any of the jobs, I was determined to get my foot in the door of a studio. So I went the very next day to try to get a job.

There were three jobs available: a set painter, a grip — whatever that was — and a greenery person. I had no idea of what the grip or greenery job was and I had done almost no painting in my life. But painting was the only job I knew anything about. I knew it had to involve paint and brushes. So that is what I ended up being hired to do. I began rolling paint onto backgrounds for movie sets at Burbank Studios. Because I was a temporary worker, I was making $2.50 an hour — this was 1976. When I was eventually offered a regular, full-time job as a set painter, I took it gladly, as it paid union-level wages of $8.10 an hour. Wow!

I was at Burbank Studios for a year when I was offered a job at 20th Century Fox. I began as a set painter, but one day the grip gang needed an extra person. Grip gangs take down and store lighting, scaffolding, and movie and television sets. I was sent over to help and ended up being a grip for many years at Fox.

It was while working as a grip at 20th Century Fox that I had an on-the-job accident.

It was Christmastime 1990 and Fox had built a Christmas display up on Dolly Street. Dolly Street was named after the movie, *Hello Dolly,* and it was one of the primary streets used in filming the movie. Along with several other grips, I was assigned to take down and remove this display.

We were in the process of taking down a parallel stand — a large, heavy support for the display lighting. This was done by taking the stand apart, piece by piece, and lowering it down using a rope rigging. The grip who was in charge of letting the stand down did not have it secured properly. The parallel side swung out toward me. I jumped backwards to avoid being struck. But as I jumped, I fell back over a twelve-by-two-foot wooden box in which we stored a projection screen. It caught me at the back of my knees and I fell backwards onto the base of my spine. I did not think I was hurt, but the lot steward for our union insisted I go to our lot's on-site clinic and report the accident.

The next day I awoke with a pinched nerve running around my midsection and in severe pain from my coccyx to the middle of my back. I called an acupuncturist and was able to get in and see her that day. Fortunately, she was able to get rid of my pinched nerve, but the intense pain in the rest of my back remained.

I made an appointment with my doctor and found out, over a course of diagnostics, that I had twenty-three percent soft tissue damage around my spine. This damage meant I could not sit without support. I could not ride my bike or get down on my knees to cut fabric, which I did when working in the canvas sewing room. I had become physically very limited and was unable to continue to work at my job. As a result, 20th Century Fox awarded me a settlement and a long-term medical reimbursement for the injury.

My reaction to all this was, "There's no way I am going to be physically limited!" And that's where my journey to heal myself began.

At this time I had no knowledge of how to heal myself, so I was looking for anything or anyone who could heal my back. I had heard of psychic healers and decided to visit one. After my visit I had no results whatsoever. Then I heard that gurus were able to heal you with their holy ash, vibhuti, so I went off to see an Indian guru that was visiting in Los Angeles. I was given the holy ash and told to drink it in a glass of water every day. I must tell you it does not taste that good! I took it and, again, there were no results.

After having no results with these supposed healers, I turned to deep tissue work with a Heller practitioner which, over the course of three years, did help somewhat. At this time I also decided to take yoga classes. I did yoga for a year and a half and found that it helped me greatly. However, I still could not sit for long periods of time without my back hurting.

One day I got a call from a friend of mine. She was coming down to visit me from this strange place called Yelm, Washington. She told me about the school she was attending. It was called Ramtha's School of Enlightenment (RSE). After telling me all the things that students were taught in the school, it sounded right up my alley. I took my first Beginner's course in April 1991. At that time we were required to take three classes to be able to continue our study and attend the advanced classes. During my first three events I had a very hard time sitting on my pillow on the floor of the arena, where classes are held. My back hurt continually.

It was during my fourth event, the Primary Retreat, that I had my healing experience.

During this event, Ramtha sent the students out to what he named "Paradise Beach" for three days and three nights. We were to sit up, deeply focused, the entire time. I understood that if we were truly focused for that length of time, we would experience a deep peace and bliss — a paradise. But as I sat out there, I really did not find anything "paradise" about it. After having lived in Los Angeles for so long, my mind would not shut up. Sitting and attempting to focus for three days and nights was torture. Thankfully, I did have moments when my mind became quiet and I was able to focus, but due to my injured back, I was not able to sit up for the full time. I sat for as long as I could and then I would lie down, usually during the nights.

After the three days were up, Ramtha had us go to the name-field to do Fieldwork®. Fieldwork® is one of the disciplines Ramtha taught us. It involves being blindfolded and moving in deep focus across a large field to come to a card we had drawn earlier with a symbol of something we desired to have manifested in our life. After many hours of participating in this discipline, Ramtha called the field and had us gather around him. I remember an elderly gentleman telling Ramtha about his healing experience on Paradise Beach. I heard Ramtha tell him that he had healed himself by being impeccable and sitting up all three days and nights in a very focused state.

The next day we had Fieldwork® again. After many hours, I came to the fence and I knew the card next to the one I had come to was mine. The end of the card was curled up and I could see the letter E and I recognized that's what my name ended in. I took my card off the fence and went up to the Red Guards — the people appointed to facilitate Fieldwork® — and told them what had happened. I thought they would tape my card on my chest, as is done when a student finds their card. Instead, they said they were going to put it back up on the fence. They said I should be able to find it again, because the card was already in my bands — the electrical field around my body. They told me that Ramtha loves us being impeccable. So off I went, focusing on my card for the rest of the day but did not find it again.

The next day I came into the arena and put my pillow down to do disciplines. When I sat down I noticed I had no pain in my back at all. It had been years since I had felt no pain in my lower back. I was amazed!

Later that day we were back on the field doing Fieldwork®
and I found one of my cards. I went up to Ramtha and started
telling him about my miraculous healing experience. I asked him
if it had anything to do with my impeccable experience with my
card the day before. I told Ramtha that I remembered how he
had told the elderly gentleman how he had healed himself by his
impeccable focus. He looked at me and asked if I needed an
excuse to heal myself. I said, "No." Ramtha told me that anytime
you sit in long, quiet focus, your body heals.

I walked away with the wisdom from the Master Teacher
and knew that I had healed my back with my own focus. I
learned that day that what Ramtha said is true — that all the
power lies within ourselves and we really can do the miraculous.

MY CHOICE TO LIVE, GRANTED BY RAMTHA

David Tidwell

I have been a student of Ramtha's School of Enlightenment (RSE) for twenty-five years. During my time as a student I knew of numerous miraculous healings of fellow students. Most of these "miracles" occurred as a result of the student's focused healing efforts. However, I attribute my returning to life to the intervention of my Master Teacher, Ramtha. This is my story.

On April 22, 2014, my wife Rosalind was away working in Tumwater for four days. It was 1:20 a.m. on that day when I awoke with a severe burning pain in my chest. I had experienced acid reflux for many years, so at first I dismissed it. But this time my chest felt like it was exploding with fire. I decided to drive to the Veterans Administration Hospital in Lakewood, Washington, about forty minutes from my house.

By the time I got halfway down our gravel driveway, the pain became so severe that I decided to go to my next-door neighbor for help. I was very grateful that my neighbor was home and that she arrived at the door quickly, despite the fact that I had awakened her. I asked that she take me to the Veterans Administration Hospital. As a fellow student at RSE, she did not oppose me. But Ramtha students are taught how to access a view of the future. She immediately went into an analogical state and saw that I would not survive the trip. So she sat me down and called 9-1-1, the number for medical emergencies.

The ambulance and medics came very quickly. By the time they arrived, I was convinced that I was having a heart attack. Again I asked to be taken to the Veteran's Hospital because, as a Vietnam veteran, that is where I had been instructed to receive care. The medics took my vital signs and told me I was having a heart attack. They made a call to St. Peter Hospital in Olympia — the nearest hospital — and gave me medication. As I was getting on the stretcher, I started feeling very dizzy. They strapped me in and we were gone.

During the drive to St. Peter Hospital the pain was terrible. After what seemed an interminably long time, the medic beside me called to the driver, "Pull over. I'm losing him!" I looked up at him and told him, "I'm okay," but he was busily preparing the heart resuscitator. I then lost consciousness. Later I heard the medic say to the driver, "Put the pedal to the metal." I lost consciousness again.

In the hospital I awoke briefly to see two doctors pushing me at a run on a wheeled gurney. Again I lost consciousness.

When I became aware again, it was dark. I felt I was in the Void — the place where I heard Ramtha say that all potentials exist. As I looked around I saw a pair of dark eyes that were shining with beautiful light. A voice asked me, "What do you want?"

Somehow I knew it was my Teacher, Ramtha. I said, "Hi, Ram." As a student of RSE I had heard Ramtha tell us that when our Spirit self leaves the body at physical death, he will meet us. And there were his eyes, looking at me and shining with an indescribable spiritual light, and Ramtha asking me what I wanted.

I thought about Ramtha's question for a few moments and then said, "If I have to go, it is okay. But I would rather be healed, with no sickness or dying." Ram just said, "Okay."

Again I floated away in a sea of darkness.

The doctors at St. Peter performed emergency surgery on my heart and put in two stents to keep the blood flow going. After the surgery the doctors told my wife that I needed to be transported via helicopter to Seattle to be admitted to the University of Washington Medical Center. However, there was too much equipment needed to sustain my life and the medivac helicopter did not have space for it all. Instead, I had to be transported via ambulance. At this point my wife Rosalind was told that I had only a forty percent chance in surviving the ambulance transport.

Although I don't remember being transported, I remember waking up sometime later. I was in a hospital bed looking at a big box about three feet square that was suspended from the ceiling. It was lowered down on my chest. I found out later that it was taking further tests on my heart. I also heard the doctors around me talking. One doctor said, "He sure knew what he was doing." It seems the doctor at St. Peter Hospital had done all the right things that would save me.

The days in the hospital passed and eventually I was able to sit up. One by one the multitude of tubes, including the feeding tube, was removed and I was able to eat. I was weak, but I knew I was getting better every day.

My recovery from dying twice during this ordeal was exceptionally swift. My wife told me that the doctors expressed surprise at how quickly I was able to recover. And because of the speed of recovery, I was released to go directly home after ten days spent in the University of Washington hospital.

Although I am still on medication for my heart, I know without a doubt that Ramtha met me and asked me what I wanted. When I made my decision to live and asked Ram to heal me and give my life back to me, I know my desire was granted by this grand Teacher.

LIVING BEYOND MY FUTURE DEATH

Ektara Jarecki

During the early 1980s, I went looking for spiritual truth as I traveled around Europe. I found bits and pieces but no one had answered my deepest queries. I had almost given up when I found Ramtha, the Master Teacher, at Ramtha's School of Enlightenment (RSE). It happened in 1986.

That year my husband David and I watched Ramtha's teaching, *Change: The Days to Come,* which talked about large changes the Earth would experience in the future. From that point on, the criteria for our lives changed. We moved away from the San Francisco area to central California where we thought we had found our dreamland.

A short time after moving into our new home, I started to have a recurring dream. In the dream, David was working on an incline running an orange tractor. As I walked up to say something to him, the tractor rolled over on me, killing me. Night after night I had the same dream. We had five acres with seventy-four fruit and nut trees, gardens, berries, and a greenhouse. A tractor would have been a great help, but David was aware of my dream and knew how upset it had made me. So he chose not to buy one.

After we had been on the property for about one year, my daughter came to live with us. One morning she came into the kitchen very upset. That night she had had a dream that a tractor rolled over and killed me. I then told her about the recurring dream I was having — the same one she had had. It was my second warning.

About two years after my recurring dreams began, David and I decided to attend an RSE event in Yelm. At this event I heard Ramtha tell us that we were going to go through a process where we would live beyond our future death. I heard him ask us to spend some time contemplating our death on our timeline and to see it as clearly as we could. I also heard Ramtha tell us to choose a talisman, which is an unusual object that would appear in the scene and capture our attention. The appearance of the talisman in the future would confirm that my destiny had been changed and my death avoided. Of course I knew immediately that it would be my dream of the tractor.

We prepared for the process and Ramtha gave us instructions how to proceed. As I proceeded through the process, I chose to change the color of the tractor to green and to put David and me on flat ground. After that, I visualized having a conversation with him and then walking away as he continued working. I chose my talisman to be a bright red tulip. Because I had already experienced so many miracles in this amazing school, I absolutely trusted that this would work.

Many years went by. By this time we had moved to Yelm and I had stopped thinking about those dreams — they no longer occurred — until one day when I was in the kitchen making lunch. David had borrowed his friend's John Deere tractor and was tilling our garden. He was working about two hundred feet from the house. When I finished making lunch, I walked out to tell him that lunch was ready. About halfway there, a scene unfolded in front of my eyes. It was very fast, like a projector on fast forward. I watched as the blur of this new reality I created in Ramtha's process so many years ago passed through my awareness. It was colorful and stunning and then at the end, there was the bright red flash, and I saw my red tulip talisman! I knew immediately without a doubt that it was my recurring dream with the new ending that I created! I saw the red tulip confirm that this day I *had* changed a former timeline and had survived beyond a timeline that would have resulted in my death. This was to be the first of four times that I had changed timelines and avoided potential death.

The implications of this humbled me to the core of my being. My beloved God gave me the dream, and my Teacher,

Ramtha, gave me the means to shift my timeline to live beyond my death. I am blessed and grateful beyond measure.

By sharing this experience, it is my hope that you who are reading this will reach beyond your limitations and, through the Lord God of your being, bring the miraculous into your reality and know that anything is possible, even living beyond timelines of future deaths.

TRANSCENDING PAIN: THE TRANSFORMATIONAL POWER OF CHOICE

Calence Ethan Emerson

I have spent a good portion of my life studying alternative medicine, including bioenergetics. As strange as it sounds, I was somewhat disappointed that I never had a reason to experience the modalities I had learned so much about. Despite a few serious injuries from being an adventurous kid, I have always been physically healthy and resilient with one exception — an inflexible right hip.

I am sure you remember stretching your quads in gym class, grabbing your foot from behind and pulling it close to your rear end. My gym teacher called it the "quad stretch" but it should have been called the "let's-see-how-many-times-Ethan-falls-over" stretch. I was convinced my teacher created that exercise to torture me.

No apparent reason existed for the discrepancy in flexibility between my left and right hips. While I could almost put my left leg behind my head when sitting, I could not pull my right leg into a simple cross-legged position without experiencing pain.

As I learned later in my adult life, my physical pain was the result of emotional trauma. I unraveled it all when I chose to take on my life with Ramtha's disciplines beginning in 2012.

Through dedicated application of Ramtha's teachings and engaging some outrageous runners — experiences that teach us something about ourselves — I unraveled and transformed a series of deeply buried beliefs, which had been controlling my entire paradigm of existence and causing my physical pain.

Before moving to Yelm, I lived in the beachfront city of Santa Cruz, California. I shared a cozy townhome with my best friend and her husband on West Cliff Drive overlooking the resplendent Pacific Ocean. I often spent the night patrolling the cliff under twinkling stars, observing waves race toward the shore like eager electric currents, crashing, pausing, and returning to begin anew.

I was working for a bioenergetic healthcare company that used pulsed LED lights to encode healing frequencies into water. I loved my job. I spent day and night organizing massive amounts of scientific data, writing content for an energy-medicine, authority website, reading scientific papers, and explaining our modality in detail to laymen, traditional physicians, chiropractors, and alternative practitioners.

This was all part of a beautiful dream I had consciously created, so when I was fired from my job in March of 2016, I had a difficult time letting go.

Within a week of being fired, I was assailed by severe sciatica, lower back pain, knee pain, and hip joint pain. Some days I could not get out of bed. I carried a cushion to sit on everywhere I went. If I had to stand for more than five minutes, my hips would creak like the Tin Man from Oz. I was well aware that my pain was rooted in fear and lack as a result of losing my job. *I was worrying about money and my future.*

I wasn't interested in finding another corporate job just to make the rent. Where I lived, unless you wanted five roommates and a house full of marijuana, you had to make a minimum of $50,000 a year just to survive. And I wasn't willing to play the corporate game anymore. I was D – O – N – E, like a Thanksgiving turkey.

I wanted to live life on *my terms.* And in the space of my new freedom, I saw my opportunity. For years it had been my dream to attend an event in person at Ramtha's School of Enlightenment (RSE), and I wasn't going to put it off any longer. I got rid of nearly everything I owned, manifested a cargo van, and moved to Yelm.

I arrived in Yelm in June of 2016 — just in time to attend July's 101 Beginner's Retreat. JZ Knight had generously gifted this event to all students, so it was packed. This was my first event at RSE, and I was ecstatic.

A couple of days into the event, as I made my way to my pallet in the Great Hall, I gazed intently at the brilliant blue star on the wall above the large double doors. We students had just come back from a meal break and were getting ready to engage the Blue Body® Dance. Although I had been learning from Ramtha for four years, this was my first time learning the dance.

We were to begin with the discipline of Consciousness & Energy® (C&E®). As I settled down on top of my cushion waiting for the session to start, I crossed my legs, folded a small pillow in half, and placed it under my right leg to support my inflexible hip — something I had been doing for four years during the discipline of C&E®. My leg could not rest on the cushion, and without the support of an extra pillow it would bounce uncontrollably in the air, painfully pulling on my tendons.

Although my right hip flexor had been tight since childhood, no amount of stretching or yoga made a difference. The sciatica and hip joint pain made my pain worse. And sitting in the half lotus position like the yoga pros? I could barely sit in a chair at that time.

After C&E® we prepared ourselves for the Blue Body® Dance. I chose two specific areas to focus on: an eighteen-year-old broken toe that healed incorrectly and my right hip. As I danced, I felt a freedom that can only be described as a lightening of my whole self. I was consumed by blue and surrendered completely.

After the dance, lying on the floor as we were instructed to do, I felt a tingling sensation followed by the feeling of fine threads bursting out of my big toe. Moments later, I felt the same fine threads bursting forth from my right hip. Inner warmth became my body's only sensation, and I was in bliss.

When instructed to sit up, I folded my legs underneath me and immediately noticed my right leg went all the way down to the floor without resistance or pain. To further test my discovery, I pulled my right foot on top of my left thigh into the half lotus position and smiled with eyes wide open and glistening. *My hip flexor had been healed during the dance!*

Perhaps part of the reason I experienced this healing is because simply participating in the Blue Body® Dance was a breakthrough for me. When I was younger, I grew up dancing. But something happened in my life, and I equated dancing with personal failure. I had refused to dance ever since. However, not only did I surrender to the Blue Body® Dance with no expectations, but in doing so I gave up being my past.

Through the consistent application of Ramtha's teachings and disciplines, my world has undergone a deep and profound transformation. It feels like my life has been turned inside out. The healing I have experienced is not limited to the Blue Body® Dance. Perhaps my deepest healing has taken place through the discipline of Consciousness & Energy®. In my experience, in addition to manifesting desires, this discipline continues to bring the shards of unresolved emotions to the surface for me to acknowledge and dissolve. Through C&E® I have drilled my way through a labyrinth of programming and beliefs that have been running my life since childhood. Through a series of impossible-to-ignore runners and a few close calls, I came face to face with how I was showing up in the world and where I was playing small. After certain sessions of C&E®, I was gifted the opportunity to see where I had been unsuccessfully attempting to re-create my past for the sake of redemption. I was presented with unmistakable mirrors in people, places, things, times, and events to help me see what I had refused to see.

Being willing to take on everything in my path, I experienced a profound inner healing that has provided me with the freedom to be, do, and have a life filled with love, joy, and bliss. But most of all, I have learned more about who I am. I no longer need to make lemonade out of lemons. I can appreciate a lemon for being a lemon and tap into its wisdom through shareable waves of compassion. No sugar needed.

In my experience, the biggest benefit of engaging in this level of self-transformation to heal old traumas, both physical and psychological, is this: the details of my life read like a movie script. Synchronicity lives in my pocket and it is only a matter of time before something new and "wonder-full" unfolds.

OVERCOMING EXTREME EMOTIONS

Lucy Jeanne

Most of my life I have been known as the one who talks and laughs too loud. From my teen years and beyond, I was also the one who suffered bouts of severe depression and crying. I didn't know psychological terminology then — just that once I started crying I could not stop, and my face got red and splotchy. Years later I realized my trigger-happy nervous system magnified reactions to upsetting news beyond all reason. By the time my brain's neurotransmitters had spun the story, it felt like nothing would ever be right again. My sobbing felt uncontrollable.

I was born into a family with generations of creativity, special gifts, and genius. I have since learned that this kind of genetic wiring in the brain rides on a current of emotion. The packages of traits and sensitivities are different for each person, resulting in unique patterns of behavior. But without understanding my own brain chemistry, I was vulnerable to extreme reactions. Empathic to a degree, I could sense something was wrong and would often feel depressed for no apparent reason. Fears and emotions seemed like rogue lifeforms beyond my input or control.

I wasn't just afraid of the dark, as most young children are — my fear was mortal terror. Every night I would lock my bedroom door before getting into bed, then cover up completely with blankets, leaving only a small breathing hole. Often, to my horror, I would forget whether I had locked my bedroom door. I would lie under the covers trembling in fear, trying to decide if it would be worse to make a quick leap to check the lock or stay safe under the covers and wonder. Any noise I heard in the dark house would send jolts of fear through my body. Eventually I would fall asleep from exhaustion. This lasted throughout childhood and well into my young adult years whenever I was alone at night. At twenty, the night terrors continued when my first husband, a Navy Corpsman, had overnight hospital duty and I was home alone with our infant son.

Traumatized by loud noises — balloons breaking, cars backfiring, fireworks — and sudden lights like old-fashioned flash cameras, I was the little one hiding in closets to avoid family photos, or covering my eyes just as the camera flashed, or crawling under blankets and crying at Fourth of July picnics.

Beginning after the flow of youthful hormones began and extending into adulthood, my rush of wild emotions escalated. In the most extreme situations, like during a perceived failure or a relationship breakup, I was a sobbing mass of protoplasm. The anguish was unbearable. All thoughts focused on finding relief from pain. In that context, killing myself seemed like a viable, practical answer — the permanent solution. I had actually written suicide notes and carried them in my purse, just in case.

In my early forties I had a life-changing moment during one such episode. As I was contemplating the unthinkable, a very direct, clear thought came into my head: "No. This time you have to live." This time? — *THIS TIME*? Suddenly the suicide solution didn't sound permanent after all. I had done this before in previous lives? You mean I need to keep coming back to this agony until I conquer it?

After that experience, my inner dialogue became "I don't care what it takes — I *WILL* live."

I was first introduced to Ramtha's teachings in 1989. It was a long and circuitous journey in this life to arrive at my school, but the first time I saw Ram, I knew he was my Master Teacher. Since then I have conquered various internal demons using his teachings and applying the disciplines.

The perfect storm year was 1999. My fourth marriage, the one I was certain would last forever, was crumbling. Another of my cobbled-together families was being torn apart. Our life had seemed rich with potential and we had come so far together in our personal evolution. Now he was sitting at the kitchen table with divorce papers for us to fill out. My nervous system went into meltdown mode. I was never going to stop crying. As I sobbed convulsively, I had a distinct memory of Ramtha saying, "An emotional storm can't exist in the fourth seal or above where there is no polarity." Could it be true? If I used my C&E® (Consciousness & Energy®) breath to move energy into my fourth seal, would I be at peace? What did I have to lose?

Still crying, I grabbed my fleece cape, my blinders, my focus cushion, and a handful of Kleenex (in case it didn't work). I walked down to the creek bed near our home and picked a nice spot. Once seated and prepared to begin, I had one of those rare, unforgettable, extended moments of no-time. I observed myself in a series of slow-motion scenes, flashbacks from my past like a mini-life review. It was excruciatingly humbling. I finally saw what I had never understood before — that every cell of my being did not want to stop crying. I watched. I could not muster any will to move energy. My body wanted to keep the drama going — scenes from my life played out. I heard people saying, "You just want to cry!" I sat there and kept observing myself.

Finally I did a few embarrassing attempts at my power breath ... pathetic. I was spitting all over. I continued, observing my body as an unwilling participant. Eventually I began to feel some momentum building in my breathing. Still observing myself, I kept on until my breath actually began to look and sound like real C&E®. After a time of serious breathing, I stopped to check my state and immediately felt pain flooding back into my chest. I then became a power-breathing machine. I blew myself into a fog of oblivion. I didn't know how long I had been gone or where I had been. I touched my chest area all over. The pain was gone.

I dried my eyes, picked up my things, and went back into the house. My husband was in the living room. I said, "If we're going to do this divorce, let's work it out together. We don't need lawyers. Let's remain friends and help each other get a start in our new lives." He looked at me as if his emotional-freak wife had been kidnapped by aliens. But we went on to do all of that, got a friendly divorce, and are still friends to this day.

I thought I had just discovered the best method for neutralizing an emotional storm — a great trick to use for the rest of my life. But there have been no more incidents. Nearly twenty years later my transformation holds strong. Unfinished emotional issues from past lives seemed to have fallen backward like a stack of cards. That lesson was finally complete. I still have laughter — it is my trademark — joy, and feel passion deeply, but without addictive, run-amok reactions.

The body itself can be expressing rage, fear, or anguish, but if we are observing our own reactions, we are not "being" them. With powerful will, the conscious choice to observe ourselves means we are in a level of awareness beyond emotion.

I had never spoken about this incident with Ramtha. Yet during an elegant Feast in 2010, he walked over and pointed his finger at me and saying tonight you celebrate what you have overcome. When we overcome, then we are happy!

HEALING MY EYES

Debbie Christie, Master of Music

When I was around nine years old, I wanted to wear glasses. Other kids in my class were wearing them and I thought they were cool. I found an eye doctor and convinced Mom that I needed them. She made an appointment and I got glasses. But the glasses were bifocals for reading — not what I had in mind. Now understanding that there were nearsightedness and farsightedness, I decided I didn't need glasses to read but to see far away. My eyes went from farsighted to nearsighted, and I got the cool glasses without lines in them.

In high school, wearing glasses was not cool anymore, so I got contacts. What was once cool had become a royal inconvenience.

My eyes were now -3.00 diopters, and that's where they were when I moved to Yelm in 1985 to be close to Ramtha. I went back to glasses.

When I started playing music for Ramtha, my focus was continually on him to know what to play and read any cues he may give me. When meeting Ramtha before sessions, I didn't like looking into his eyes through windows and often took them off. A strengthened desire to not need corrective lenses derived from this.

When Ramtha introduced webbing and the Blue Body® Dance, I would web my eyes and focus on them through every dance. I always webbed them, even though for the most part I was playing music for the dance.

There was an event where I created a Fieldwork® card of a ram's head to represent Ramtha and becoming as he was.

Shortly after that, I wasn't seeing as well and thought my eyes were getting worse. When I had them checked, they had actually improved from -3.00 diopters to -1.5 diopters.

I told Ramtha about the card I had focused on and the improvement in my eyesight. He shared with me that a ram's eyesight is very keen and that my continual focus on him was healing my eyes.

I included my eyesight on my list — which I eventually replaced with other things — continued with the webs during the Blue Body® Dance, and of course kept my focus on Ramtha. I didn't really think about my eyes. Healing my eyes became more of a detached observation of common thought rather than a daily focus.

As the years passed, my eyesight slowly got better and the strength of my contacts/glasses lessened, fluctuating between -1.00 right, -1.00 left, and -.75 right, -.50 left.

At the end of 2015, I again thought my eyes had gotten worse when in fact they had improved again: -.50 right, -.25 left. By the fall of 2016, I noticed I no longer needed right-eye correction and the lens for my left was too strong. I wore the -.25 in my left, or not. As of the fall of 2017, I no longer needed corrective lenses.

Ramtha always said that you can uncreate what you have created. For me this is the most prominent example of uncreating a creation, because I knew when I consciously created bad eyesight and why.

Detached observation through common thought — I discovered a learning in this and it has provided for me much contemplation about creating personal reality.

SEIZURES, A TUMOR, AND MAGIC

Brisa Chu

In October 2004, I was living in southern Taiwan. At that time I was involved in a bad relationship. I knew my partner was cheating on me and that he had continuously lied to me, yet I did not confront him.

The day finally came that he moved out of my apartment and I knew I was going to be alone. That same day I had an epileptic seizure for the first time in my life. The seizures continued every day for six months. It was like living in a war every day. My body shook, and my emotions were wild and crazy. It felt like my brain was going through a thunderstorm. After the attacks, I always had to think really hard to remember who I was and how people, places, things, and events in my life were related to me.

The seizures eventually became so severe that I was hospitalized for over a month, during which time the medical staff had to hold me down so that they could inject a tranquilizer into my body. When I left the hospital, I was given a prescription for a drug I was to take. But after taking the pills, I knew that the prescription was damaging to my body because I was weak and felt constantly dizzy. Despite this, I kept taking the pills because at the time I did not see an alternative.

After I left the hospital, the symptoms were reduced but didn't go away. For over a decade I fought with this psychosomatic situation. I continued to be filled with intense emotions which created stresses that my body had to deal with. Under this emotional pressure, my body was always fatigued and I had difficulty concentrating. Eventually, I made a decision not to be traumatized by my body anymore. I insisted on building my will to fight for my health. From this decision I tried a number of different healing modalities. Although not curing me, they were part of my journey to heal myself.

Over the course of my life I had often asked for spiritual help. I studied Buddhism for a long time, but I was still confused. How was my physical and mental situation going to end? In Eastern culture all the spiritual answers led to karma, demons, and hellfire. As I pondered these answers, I came to the decision that they were nothing more than a group of philosophies. I wanted real answers, a real way out.

Then in 2015 I started my study at Ramtha's School of Enlightenment (RSE). I learned an amazing amount of knowledge as well as the disciplines of Conscious & Energy® (C&E®) and the Neighborhood Walk®. I came home from my studies and used the disciplines every day to change my health. Although some seizures still occur, the frequency and the degree of impact have been reduced a great deal. My body no longer collapses with a seizure, and I have become much healthier not only physically but also emotionally. To my great relief, I also stopped having nightmares.

In the beginning of 2016, a tumor started to appear on the palm of my right hand. It was accompanied by mild pain. I went to an orthopedic physician and had an x-ray. The physician told me that an operation would be needed to remove it, and a further test was ordered — an ultrasound.

Before I could schedule the ultrasound, I attended the RSE Advanced Retreat in Taiwan. I did C&E®, the Neighborhood Walk®, and candle focus, always focusing on my health. After a few days at the event I found that the tumor had disappeared. That was like finding my card in the field. Magic happened!

This has been my journey. I believe everyone has their own to take. I now know I can create everything I want and desire. I can be abundant and fulfilled, just like the boy in *The Alchemist*, by Paulo Coelho: "When I have been truly searching for my treasure, every day has been luminous, because I've known that every hour was part of the dream that I would find it. When I have been truly searching for my treasure, I've discovered things along the way that I never would have seen had I not had the courage to try things that seemed impossible for a shepherd to achieve."

This wonderful School of Ancient Wisdom provided me with abundant knowledge and specific disciplines so I could become, through my own efforts, my own truth. I am very grateful.

POWERFUL FOCUS — POWERFUL DETERMINATION

Iliana Valdes

I am an orthopedic surgeon from Cali, Colombia. I attended my first event at Ramtha's School of Enlightenment (RSE) in April 2006 in Cuenca, Ecuador. I immediately fell in love with Ramtha and his philosophy and have been a student ever since.

None of my extensive schooling to become a doctor had ever explained the brain and its function as clearly as Ramtha's teachings had done. And there was no medical training at all about the brain's relationship to quantum physics. All of this new knowledge was very exciting to me. But most exciting of all was learning about Blue Body® healing. I was eager to see how I could apply it to myself and my patients.

At the Cuenca event, the teachers spoke of the upcoming Assay to be held in Yelm, Washington. An Assay is an event where your spiritual development is tested by participating in the disciplines taught at RSE. I immediately decided to go. I am passionate about learning, and I knew it was going to be a great adventure. Little did I know what an adventure it would be! The first day of Assay, Ramtha came to teach us. I was utterly riveted by both his presence and what he was teaching. It was everything and more I hoped to experience at this event. When Ramtha concluded his teaching, we students were released to eat and relax.

Later that first night, I started to play with some of the children who were attending Assay with their parents. We were running up and down, playing around, and having a lot of fun. One of the girls did a cartwheel and she asked me if I could do one. I knew I had done them in my youth and thought, "Why not?" and went ahead and did it. I landed at a wrong angle on my right foot. All I heard was a crack and then I fell down. The girls asked if I was okay, and I said, "Yes," but I had to stop playing. They went away giggling. The pain in my foot was intense, throbbing. I slowly moved my ankle and knew the problem was not there. I removed my shoe and immediately my foot became so swollen I could not move my toes. A Red Guard — a person appointed to assist at events — came to me and asked if I needed anything. I asked for some pain relievers and ice. I hoped it would be better in the morning. Despite the pain relievers, I didn't sleep at all that night. I wept, thinking of all the money I spent to come to Assay and now I would miss the event because of my foolishness. How did I ever think I could do cartwheels?

The next morning I could not walk. The Red Guard provided me with crutches so I could move around. Two seats to my right a boy had sprained his ankle the day before too and also was on crutches. That night Ramtha came to teach again and said that some people are faking diseases just to skip his disciplines. I was so angry I cried that whole night, knowing I was certainly not faking.

The morning of the next day the little boy came to me and said, "Hey, I don't need my crutches anymore!" That struck me, and so I started focusing on leaving the crutches behind and that I was fully healed and well.

By that afternoon I left one crutch behind. The Tank® discipline was scheduled for the next morning and I really wanted to participate. I kept my focus and by the next morning I had discarded the second crutch. As an orthopedic surgeon, I knew the expected outcome of walking on a fractured foot before it was healed. But I was determined to live The Tank® experience fully.

The Tank® discipline takes place in a very large labyrinth on the RSE campus. Students are blindfolded and must find their way through it solely using a focused mind. So from the very beginning of The Tank® discipline I focused on my Blue Body®. I found an entrance to the labyrinth and took it. As soon as I entered, a fellow student stepped on my foot. I screamed. I was in excruciating pain. I stopped, took a big breath, and said,

"Okay, this is it." I only had one question: "Iliana, are you going to focus on your pain or on the Void?" It took just seconds for me to decide it was going to be on the Void. With this decision, time stopped. The pain immediately went away and I continued on my journey through the labyrinth.

During the entire six-hour journey in The Tank® discipline, I totally forgot about my foot. When The Tank® test ended and we were heading back toward the arena where we meet for teachings, a throbbing pain in my foot returned. I started limping. I fell on my knees and laughed. "Focus does work!" I thought. Great!

When the Assay event was over, I returned to Colombia. I went to an orthopedic surgeon for an evaluation of my foot. X-rays showed that there was a fracture of my fourth metatarsal bone and two dislocations. As a result of these injuries, it was necessary for me to have surgery. The surgeon did an open reduction of the dislocations and of the fracture and installed screws and pins. The surgeon told me I could not step on my foot for at least two months and warned that I could have residual pain after surgery.

Because I wanted to return to RSE for an upcoming event, I decided after the surgery to apply intense focus during my Neighborhood Walk® discipline. I did this daily at my home. Every day, walking with my crutches in a slight trancelike state, I declared that my foot was well and strong.

When I went back to my surgeon six weeks after the surgery, the fracture had totally healed. This was a remarkably fast healing. A fracture usually takes eight to twelve weeks to heal. To this day my foot is well. There is no residual pain whatsoever. Through this experience I demonstrated to myself that there is nothing more powerful than focused thought and great determination, and nothing more valuable than the knowledge gained at Ramtha's school.

BE CAREFUL WHAT YOU ASK FOR

Susan R. Louis

It was September 1994.

I was cracking, slowly, under the immense emotional and mental pain of leaving the man I adored. We truly loved one another deeply and had a fabulous relationship in every way, except that he could not accept my attending Ramtha's School of Enlightenment (RSE).

I had just started a new job at the local newspaper and threw myself into it with every fiber of my being, trying to keep myself too busy to feel the pain of the separation. I tutored after work and worked extra duties editing. I was exhausted.

On my way to work one morning, while driving down Highway 507 towards Yelm, I said out loud to my God, "I need some time. I have no time to think or contemplate." In my head I heard, "Is it okay if you have an accident?" Huh? Uh, yeah. "Okay," I agreed, thinking it might end with a sprained ankle or broken leg.

Months later, I went to see my mother and brother in Illinois for the Christmas holidays. I returned home, and as I was leaving SeaTac Airport I unconsciously mentally said, "Oh, it didn't happen." I had thought if I were going to have an accident, it would be around my family and the people I went to school with in high school. That mental statement must have been the "okay" button. Less than three days later, I was attempting to cross Highway 507 in my little red Toyota Tercel in downtown Rainier when it happened.

I was at the stop sign, where I always put on my seat belt. There was a long, white semitruck delivering beer to the local tavern to my left, blocking my view of oncoming traffic. I proceeded, looking left and only seeing the long, white expanse of the truck. In the middle of the intersection, my driver's window and head were met by a white Ford F-150 coming along at thirty miles per hour.

Be careful what you ask for! I asked for time to rest and contemplate. I have always been extremely flexible, so my neck and hips just popped back into their proper place. But my skull was another story.

I was fortunate. Two off-duty EMTs were having breakfast at the tavern. They rushed out after they heard the crash, took the shattered glass out of my eyes, and got me as ready as possible for the ambulance ride to the hospital.

A bonus was that I had recently interviewed Rita Hutcheson, the Rainier Fire Chief, and Kathleen Devin, the local Fire Commissioner. Both were former Army nurses and happened to be on call that morning. The two quickly appeared on the scene. Before the ambulance arrived, my body was flailing all over the place. Rita told me later that when the brain is injured, the body doesn't have direction. But in my unconscious state, I responded to her voice and calmed down, so she rode with me all the way to the hospital.

Back in Rainier, synchronicities were again helping me out. I had been going to see Rainier's police department every week for the newspaper. Chief Randy Schleis knew who I was, so he called my employer and told them what had happened to me. My coworkers called my roommate, who found a way to have my mother called in Chicago. Amazingly, my mother got to the hospital as I got out of brain surgery seven hours later.

I was in a coma, head shaved and bandaged, with an IV, and a feeding tube coming out of me. My mother Ruth always said she was an agnostic. But when she walked through my hospital room doorway and saw me, she looked up to the ceiling and commanded of God, "Not my kid!" She insisted I recover and be well.

At Ramtha's School of Enlightenment (RSE), we had recently learned about Eldon Taylor's genius work with subliminal recordings. My friends wasted no time in getting a tape player and instructing the hospital staff that no television was to be on during my coma. Instead, the subliminal tape — with the healing message — was to be played continually.

I found out later that for the first three days in the hospital, my cranial pressure was so high that I wasn't expected to live. RSE's New Year's Eve event was being held during this time, and one of Ramtha's appointed teachers at the time, Greg Simmons, announced my dire predicament to everyone in attendance in the arena. My friend said she went out to do Fieldwork® and she found many cards with my name on them. The focus worked! After that night my cranial pressure normalized and I was out of the danger zone. I am eternally grateful to all who focused on my healing.

I stayed safely in my coma for another week. It was such a healing time for my body and mind. All I remember is the blackness, a feeling of complete love and acceptance, and my Teacher's eyes.

On a Sunday morning, despite the morphine, feeding tube, and IV, I woke up from the coma. The nursing staff found me wandering down the hallways of the hospital. After more days went by, I normalized and was sent to a neighboring hospital for a week of rehabilitation. From there I was released to go home. The focus, prayers, sweat lodge ceremony, and subliminal recordings had all done their work.

Most of my body was fine; it was my brain that was still injured. The Broca's area, the verbal area of the brain, was damaged — not good for a reporter! I could speak, but only very, very slowly. The part of my brain that found words was also not working up to speed. And worse, the brain part that told my mouth muscles how to form sounds was damaged too. Once a perfect speller, I was disheartened when I could not even spell "daughter" when I returned to work part time.

The most devastating injury to my brain, however, was my memory. I could say a question, but it felt like it took me forever to find the words and speak them. Then the painful part: the person would answer and I would only remember the first three words they had said. It was so frustrating. I knew the person had replied, but for the life of me the rest of the answer was gone like a puff of smoke. My speech therapist tested me and discovered that my short-term memory was only at five percent capacity.

In June of that summer, there was an Assay being held at my school and a healing retreat held in August. It was the first time in the six years I had been in school that we were instructed to speak aloud in disciplines. It was hell for me. In the June Assay, we were to say a long prayer aloud to our Holy Spirit during our healing discipline. In August, we did Fieldwork® blindfolded saying, "I now release the attitude that created this condition," over and over. It took me a "L – O – N – G" time to get that sentence out of my mouth.

At that retreat, Ram taught a new healing technique. I lay down amid seven beautiful students for the healing. Later, when Ram had us write down a lengthy passage, amazingly I remembered every word! Students around me were asking *me* the words he had said. My memory, in one healing, went from five percent to one hundred percent!

It was on the third day of the healing retreat when Greg Simmons sat down at my head as I lay on my mat in the arena. Six other students gathered around my body and began to prepare for the healing. I remember looking at Greg before I put my blinders down and said "Okay" to myself. I had been in "speech hell" for seven months. I was consciously agreeing to have the big enchilada of healing that day.

Earlier in the retreat, I was mentally squirming about my loss of speech. Wasn't I supposed to know why I created it? What was the attitude that created this condition anyway? That moment when I said "Okay" was the moment of acceptance. I finally didn't care why I created the injury — I just wanted my ability to speak to return.

At the end of the healing inside the arena, Ram instructed us to go to the name-field without talking and continue our work. I got to the name-field, put my blinders down, and started the discipline. "I now release the attitude that created this condition." It came out of my mouth effortlessly. WHAT?!?!

I repeated, "I now release the attitude that created this condition." "Oh, my God! I can talk, I can talk!!!" I yelled in my head. Everyone was diligently doing their Fieldwork®, so I could not share my exciting news. I stood there, sobbing in joy. At least that is what I thought I was doing.

"Wham!" I hit the fence where we had all put up our healing cards. I hit it somewhat hard, with my nose. I had been crying behind my blinders in such joy that I hadn't even known I was moving. I lifted my blinders and then turned the card over. "My brain is healed. Susan Louis."

FROM THE MUNDANE TO THE REMARKABLE

Paul Daniel

By the time I was forty years old, a very strong suspicion arose inside of me that all is not quite what it seems to be — what society, social structures, and institutions made me believe what the purpose and meaning of life is. By that age I had done and experienced an amazing amount of things.

I was raised in a middle-class, Afrikaans family, completed my schooling, and went on to study social sciences, psychology, and sociology. I achieved both my degrees cum laude and then lectured at UNISA (University of South Africa, City of Pretoria) and RAU (Rand Afrikaans University, City of Johannesburg). Eventually I became bored with lecturing and so opted to begin my two-year, compulsory military training, which I completed. After that, I wanted some out-of-the-box adventures and decided to backpack around Europe for a year with 1,000 rand in my pocket. I soon ran out of money and quickly needed a lot more to continue my travels.

I chose to work in the sex industry as a gay male prostitute. What an experience that was for this Afrikaans boy! On my return to South Africa, I continued to lecture at RAU but soon became bored again. I then began a career in sales selling timeshares, which led me to selling real estate in Hyde Park and Sandhurst for a period of ten years.

I was very successful, earned copious amounts of money, and was regarded by colleagues as an ideal — someone who had everything. The accolades, applause, and rewards just kept piling up. I was in the top-performing five percent of *the leading* property group in South Africa. I had everything I wanted, including a beautiful Bushveld farm an hour out of Sandton, exotic holidays, and money, money, money! I was at the top of my game.

My assumption, of course, was that I have now reached fulfillment and so true joy and happiness would follow. That was, after all, the promise from social culture and institutions. I discovered that was absolutely not so. My despair, disappointment, and confusion were huge. How can this be? Why am I still not happy and filled with joy?

I then added more adventures to my life in order to fill this obvious gap that I felt. They now came in the form of drugs, crack, and cocaine. It started off being fun and seemed to do the trick, but only for a short while. Soon I became a full-fledged addict, spending close to 50,000 rand per month on my addiction. Surprisingly, I was still a very successful property broker with the same company in the same suburbs. I was also still the same unhappy and unfulfilled person. The meaning and purpose of life still escaped me.

This all reached a point when I confronted myself with an ultimatum: I either find true meaning for being alive — because I could not imagine living another forty years like this — or I would continue using drugs at the same pace, knowing that it would soon end in death. The signs were already there. In other words, if success, money, and having everything that everybody apparently dreamed about was not going to result in joy, I would rather go out with a bang.

With the limited understanding I had at that time, I spent weeks and months searching for answers to all those fundamental, yet elusive, questions: Who and what am I? What is the purpose of my life? Where do I come from? Where am I going? Despite my attempts, I did not find any truth or resolution to my quandary. I kept coming up empty-handed.

I was once told if in need, ask for help and you will receive it. One day, arriving back at my farm, I stood at my gate and screamed into the heavens, "I really need some answers!!" With rivers of tears pouring from my eyes, I got into my car, turned around and drove back to Sandton. I decided to go to all the holistic shops I knew of to see if I could find anything that could help me. I knew it had to be self-help. By the end of that day and at the last shop, still no answers. But I wasn't going home empty-handed. My head in my hands, leaning on that counter, I spotted a single copy of the *Namaste* spiritual magazine. I bought it, drove toward home, and smoked yet another crack pipe.

Arriving back at my farm gate, I turned the car off and fluttered through the magazine landing on a two-page article with the heading, "A Spiritual View on Drug Addiction." Amazed, I quickly read the article. The essence of the message was that the Spirit world — God — does not judge drug addicts but that I was encouraged to conquer and master it. By doing this, wisdom can be gained for all humanity. I remember feeling slightly elevated.

I fluttered the pages again and it opened to another two-page article. A beautiful lady called Kim had the courage to write her life story — truthfully. She wrote how she found, after her life was in a mess, a School of Ancient Wisdom called Ramtha's School of Enlightenment (RSE). The extraordinary teachings of this school contained knowledge and wisdom that could be found nowhere else on Earth. They turned her life around from a spiral of devastation to the truly remarkable. I was not only hugely inspired, but a surge of energy flooded my body leaving me feeling a profound excitement and joy. It hit me that I had just found my answer. Adjacent to the article was an ad for the school, a Beginner's course, which was a nine-day retreat near Magaliesberg. Two weeks later I drove into the resort, astounded as I watched myself throw my crack pipe away just before entering.

The content of the teachings, its obvious truths and wisdoms, left me spellbound for nine beautiful days, so much so that I had no thought or desire for drugs, nor did feelings of despair and meaninglessness cross my mind or enter my body. I was given answers to all of my questions and, to my amazement, this was not another religion but a School of Ancient Wisdom. The greater purpose and meaning of life flooded my consciousness. My search was finally over. I was completely empowered by Ramtha's teachings. I learned that the knowledge that is taught is coupled with the opportunity to actually experience it during the event. That way, I would leave with my own wisdom of what was taught. The school was precisely what I needed to do my quantum leap into becoming a remarkable, meaningful life.

Today I am fifty-three years young, have been addiction-free for ten years, live in a state of joy, peace, and happiness, and found my absolute purpose and meaning in life. I am on a journey of the extraordinary. Men and women are truly the creators of their own reality and destiny. The power to manifest has always resided inside us, and our brain is more powerful than any quantum computer ever designed.

I learned with ease and confidence to truly become remarkable. This school welcomes and embraces everyone, whatever their creed, culture, race, or sexual orientation. All are equal and treated as divine. I, the hopeless one, have become absolutely in love with my life. I am in a constant state of joy. I have learned to master my limitations, to reverse my aging, to create radiant health and fabulous wealth without enslavement, and to unlock my potential to create anything I desire, no matter how outrageous. My mind has opened to accept my own inner power. We are truly the most remarkable biological, neurological, and spiritual beings that have ever existed on this Earth. We are such powerful beings creating not only our own personal reality but also creating a new and astounding world around us.

The entire reason for this exposé of my life journey will be lost if I don't summarize the quintessential truth that lies hidden within the message. I have all of my life looked for joy outside of myself. In other words, I tried to find it in a good education, the adventures and excitement of sex and drugs, my successful career, tons of cash, the things I have accumulated, and the relationships I have had. But none of those worked. It was only when I learned that the source of joy and happiness is not in the people, places, things, times, and events that I brought into my life but has everything to do with the hidden truth that I am not only my body. The fabric and essence of what I am is of a divine, spiritual nature — the God within — the power of the infinite intelligence of my subconscious mind. The unlocking of that knowingness brought about my joy and happiness. Now my life has become an open canvas for creation, to always make known the unknown through adventure. The future is bright and is awaiting me!

As Ramtha says, the power is within each of us.

DISCIPLINE, WILL, AND FOCUS CREATE MIRACLES

Marilyn Reardon

Anyone who has ever had a urinary tract infection (UTI), whether a man or a woman, will know it is not life-threatening — it just feels that way!

I had been on a camping trip and, as can happen when there is not the usual amount of attention to sanitation, I contracted a UTI. I had been a student at Ramtha's School of Enlightenment (RSE) for a number of years and had been taught a discipline by Ramtha called Blue Body® healing. So once I was home from the trip, I engaged the Blue Body® discipline. But to my dismay and increasing pain, the infection was getting worse.

I decided it was time to visit my doctor and be prescribed some antibiotics to deal with the infection. At the time I was living in Mossyrock, Washington. Mossyrock is located in rural Lewis County and it was a forty-five-minute drive from my house to my doctor's office in Centralia. I got in my car, desperately hoping I could make the journey without needing to stop, and drove onto Highway 12 toward town. Not more than ten minutes down the road, I had to stop behind a line of traffic. We were being held back for road construction and, unusually, there was a sign that informed us that it might be as long as a twenty-minute wait.

My first reaction was to be a victim. How could this be happening today? Why did I come at exactly the time the construction crews would close the road? I sat there for a few minutes, victimized, then the memory of Ramtha's voice resounded in my head. JUST DO IT!

I readjusted my attitude and began to apply Blue Body® healing focus. Because the pain was so intense, my will and my focus had to be even more intense. I sat there in the strongest focus I had ever achieved until the line of traffic was allowed to proceed.

I arrived at the doctor's office and was escorted to an exam room. The nurse instructed me how to give a urine sample and said he would be back to get it from me. He said it would be analyzed immediately and the doctor would be in to see me as soon as the results were available. When I handed the nurse my sample, he commented on the unusual amount of blood in the sample, indicating a severe infection. I waited.

Sometime later the doctor walked into the room, shaking his head. The first words out of his mouth were, "I have never seen anything like this. All the indications of a severe infection are there, but there is also an enormous number of white blood cells, far in excess of what I would normally see. Your body is taking care of this infection on its own. I can prescribe you an antibiotic if you like, but you don't need it." I said to him, "I cured it with my mind." He looked at me in surprise but only said the usual, "If your symptoms get worse, make an appointment to come in."

I walked out of the exam room grinning from ear to ear. What wonderful knowledge Ramtha has imparted. It works! And the lesson I learned from this experience is what it takes to reach the threshold of will and focus to bring about a healing. Being held back on the highway forced me, out of desperation, to *really focus,* to really bring up my will. I realized there is a reason Ramtha calls the many practices he teaches "disciplines." Affecting reality, whether it is the reality inside my body or the reality I experience as outside myself, takes discipline. It takes, as we students have been taught, "fighting for control of the frontal lobe" of our brain. My desperation led me to be more disciplined, more willful, and more focused than ever before. And the prize was there, awaiting me at the end — a miracle of healing.

FOCUS SAVED MY LIFE

Donna Russo

In November of 2009, I arrived from Australia for my third adventure to Yelm — and what an adventure it was!

Charlie Roy picked me up at SeaTac Airport and we chatted away while heading to Yelm. As we passed the magnificent sight of Mount Rainier, I said out loud, "Wow! I would like to go there!" Every time I flew over Mount Rainier I was consumed with an insatiable appetite to visit this beckoning mountain. There was, and still is, an attraction to this mountain that I cannot put into words. It's a calling, a knowing, and a familiarity with this majestic being.

The following day, Charlie offered to have someone drive me up the mountain, but a voice in my head said, "Go alone." So I did. I borrowed Charlie's car and arrived without incident enjoying peaceful walks around the mountain during this early winter. I relished being with myself.

After the winter snows fell upon the spectacular mountain, rivers were flowing and life was vibrant. I sat alone on one of the riverbanks enjoying the sunny day and the sounds of running water and birds.

I drove a little further up the mountain to the hotel parking lot. Unable to travel further due to road closures caused by heavy snow, I decided to venture by foot into the mountain. My peaceful state was interrupted by sudden thoughts of possible dangerous, wild animals and a fear of meeting one while alone and defenseless. I thought, "They have bears and cougars here. What would I do if I came across one? Am I taking a risk walking in the mountains alone?"

The day before my hike, I purchased a hunting knife to use for cutting food during the event at Ramtha's School of Enlightenment in the coming days. Just then I remembered the knife in my backpack and took it out. "At least if I encounter an animal, I have some form of defense. Now it is not a risk," I thought to myself. I began to thread the knife and its leather holster through my belt. Just as I was doing this, I slipped on ice, falling down with my legs across the trail close to the edge. Terrifyingly, the edge of the trail had a steep drop. Unable to get up without slipping and moving closer to the edge, I removed my knife and dug it into the ice, leveraging myself away.

The ice was thin, and as I pulled on the knife with all my might, it released and stabbed me on the right side of my torso. Immediately a voice said, "Get up," and without conscious awareness I found myself standing and bleeding heavily from my side. Miraculously, I collected my backpack and knife and went into trance, covering my bleeding side with snow as I headed to my car. I had no tears and made no noise. Focus was my only awareness.

I continually changed the snow as it became saturated in blood. No thought or fear came to mind, despite the fact I knew my life was hanging in the balance. Two people passed me on the trail and I said, "Hi. Be careful — there's ice on the path," and continued to my car.

I arrived at the hotel car park and decided to seek help. The hotel was locked, but I could hear voices inside. I knocked on the door to no avail. As I searched for another entrance and help, I fell twice on ice, which impacted the wound and caused more bleeding. Unable to find anyone and knowing I needed help, I went toward my car.

I noticed a group of four people outside their car lightheartedly chatting. There was a tug of war in my mind. Should I ask for help or just drive to a medical facility? With great effort and pain, I physically got in my car. Then a voice in my head said, "Go over and ask for help."

I went over to the group in a state of surreal composure and asked if they had a bandage. They asked, "What did you do?" I showed them my wound. I hadn't looked at my injury, not wanting to shock myself. Given the look on their faces, I knew it was serious. They did have a bandage, which they applied, and offered to drive me to a hospital. But I insisted I would be okay and that I would drive myself. They said they would follow me down the mountain.

As I drove down the mountain with the other people following, a beautiful eagle appeared, flying directly in front of my windshield. At that moment I had a sense of being led and looked after. Not far down the mountain we had to stop for roadwork. One of the girls from the car behind ran to see if I was okay, and I said, "Yes, I am focused," and kept going.

The disciplines that I learned at RSE taught me that all things are possible in a focused state, even when the outcome is unknown. I willfully held a vision of arriving safely, not allowing failure or fear as an option. All the way to Yelm I repeated, "Stay focused, stay awake, stay to the right." We drive on the left in Australia. Because the situation was so serious, my focus was deeper and more intense than I had ever experienced before.

I finally arrived at the Yelm Family Medicine clinic and proceeded to the counter saying, "I have hurt myself and need help." The person said, "Take a seat," and I did. The waiting room was busy, full of people waiting for assistance. After a short while, I went back to the counter and said, "I am bleeding and need help."

The receptionist called a nurse, who took me around the back to inspect my wound. Seeing it, she immediately summoned the doctor.

There was much interest in how the injury occurred, so I told my story. As the doctor was inspecting my wound, he said, "You are very lucky, as you just missed your stomach." The knife blade was four inches long and had protruded two and one-half inches into my body. Before the doctor could begin placing stitches, it was necessary to clean the wound. Because I had placed snow on top of my merino wool shirt, it left fibers in the cut. The doctor placed a cloth with disinfectant on the cut. This was extremely painful and liken to having lemon juice on an open wound. I cried out for the first time.

After that I don't remember much detail, other than being stitched up and feeling very heavy in the body. Through will, I managed to drive to my hotel and get ready for bed.

Before arriving in Yelm, I had read about students seeing numbers, suits, and symbols on the back of playing cards. They saw the card before turning it over. I was excited by this and packed my cards to practice staring at them on the plane. Disappointingly, I did not see any resemblance of number, suit or symbol.

Once settled into my hotel bed, I decided to look at my cards again. Strange symbols, numbers, and suits began to appear on the back of cards. I stayed staring at my cards for hours. It was wonderfully calming to be in this gentle state of tranced focus. Finally I fell asleep and woke the next day with the thought, "Was that all a dream?" Again, I picked up my cards and was astonished that I could still see symbols, numbers, and suits. I could not get enough of looking at the "magical" cards.

Since then, I have contemplated much about my experience on the mountain. I came to realize that the length and intensity of my focus while driving and saying, "Stay focused, stay awake, stay right" had an effect of bringing my mind to an entirely new state. This was so exciting! I am grateful this new state of mind has created many wondrous experiences in my life, which continue to this day.

A TALE OF TWO LIVES

Suzann Hollar

What happened to me in 1995 changed my life irrevocably. It had been a long day and I arrived home about 9:30 p.m. Samantha, my two-year-old, was in her baby seat in the front seat of the van and was happy to be home. I walked around my van and opened the passenger door to take Samantha out. When I began to take her from her baby seat, I blacked out and went unconscious. The next thing I remember was that I was lying flat on my back on the ground with Samantha on my chest. "What happened?" I wondered. I slowly got up and nothing hurt, so I picked up Samantha and went into the house. For days I thought about what happened. What was going on? Why didn't I remember anything? What should I do? I found excuse after excuse to ignore my episode. Finally after several months a small voice inside me screamed, "NOW!" I booked an appointment with my primary doctor. The diagnosis was that I had a benign brain tumor the size of a golf ball. My surgeon said, "Go home and put your affairs in order."

I panicked! What am I going to do? I am a single mom, barely able to pay my bills, and now I have a brain tumor! I turned to the only thing I knew how to do — apply what I had learned at Ramtha's School of Enlightenment (RSE).

Back in 1986 I traveled from Southern California to Yucca Valley, California, to attend my first RSE event. This event became the first and greatest learning of my life and shaped literally every part of my life in a miraculous way in the years ahead. When I stepped into the dining hall where the event was being held, I noticed there were people smiling, hugging, and chatting away with an animation and vitality that I had never experienced before. It was at this first event that I would begin to learn the knowledge taught at RSE and to have my first experiences applying the knowledge. And at this event I would have the honor of meeting our Master Teacher. Just before he arrived, the music came on and was playing loudly. Everyone was dancing and filled with excitement.

Once Ramtha began to teach, I listened closely to what he had to say and found myself beginning to cry. Something he said had deeply touched my soul and I continued to cry for four more days at the event. Finally, I could not stand it! I decided to relax and let go of whatever it was that was bothering me. I went to the showers that were provided for us at the event venue. The water streamed down my face and the soap smelled heavenly. Suddenly I heard a boisterous laugh coming from inside my head. I knew that I was hearing information from my future. The information was telling me, "STOP JUDGING." I saw that I had long been judging everything — people, places, events, and things. This voice reminded me to look for the God in everything. As I thought more about this I realized that, via my judgments, I had given my power away to things outside myself and had never looked at *who I was*. This information in my head challenged me to find the specific lesson each person in my life was offering to me. I began to understand that doing this would enable me to change my life and become the *real* Suzann. It was what I needed to learn for what was to come. I dried off, dressed, and went back into the hall. During the whole event I made certain that I listened, contemplated, engaged with the people around me, and observed all the judgments that I had held about them.

After returning home, I continued to contemplate the knowledge I was learning at RSE and decided to attend the next event in Estes Park, Colorado. This was 1989. During that event, our Teacher, Ramtha, said that there were three people in the audience that had timelines that needed to be changed. He then led us through a process on how to do that. I proceeded to do everything he instructed us to do with great intent. As it turned out, I was one of the three people. Little did I know at the time that my work during this discipline would save my life.

For a number of weeks before Estes Park, I had dreamed nightly about a catastrophic car accident. I was not used to frightening, repetitive dreams, so this was very strange. Yet during the event I didn't connect these dreams to the need to change a timeline.

Not long after I returned home from the event, the car accident actually happened. I was driving down a steep road covered in black ice. My car went out of my control. I knew that I would not be able to stop. I froze when I saw the road curving toward the edge of a cliff. Just then I saw a two-foot-high tree stump that could stop me from falling into the steep ravine. Seconds before I was going to make impact, I slammed on the breaks with both feet. The car lifted straight up, turned ninety degrees, and landed on top of the tree stump. My life flashed before my eyes. I was frozen. I was in shock. I sat there, unable to think or move, when a car came around the curve and stopped. A man came to the passenger's side door. I climbed over the gearshift and he carefully helped me out. The driver's side door could not be opened because it was hanging over the cliff! He called for help, I was taken home, and my car was hauled away. Later, the insurance adjuster said that there was not a single mark on the upper body of the car — no damage at all — but the underbelly was mangled.

The next day a friend took me back to the site of the accident to get over my fear of driving. As we pulled up to the place where the accident occurred, we both screamed, "The tree stump is gone!" There were no signs of a tree — no roots, nothing. The road had no marks. There was no sign at all that something had happened there. No one I knew could understand how I could have survived. My friends were baffled. I was baffled. It was a miracle! From this terrifying and miraculous experience, I learned how wise it is to always listen carefully to Ramtha and to do the disciplines as instructed. I had actually changed a disastrous timeline during that event in Estes Park because I listened and did the disciplines the way Ramtha had taught us.

Nine years after that first RSE event and facing brain tumor surgery, I realized that with the help of Ramtha's disciplines and my love of my God within, I was ready. The surgery lasted nine hours and the outcome did not look good. The doctors described the surgery as a "traumatic brain injury." I was in a coma for three days and to this day I have no memory of time, people, or any events. The residual effects of this surgery have become my greatest challenge for the last twenty years.

When I came home from the hospital I was deaf in one ear and had virtually no balance. I had to relearn basic skills. Imagine that your life is like an Etch A Sketch tablet. One day someone turns your Etch A Sketch over and shakes it. There is no picture left. All my friends said, "Great! You have no past!" That might be great for some people, but what about being able to remember basic life skills like converting new information from short-term memory into long-term memory? What about not remembering concepts, how to solve a problem, or how to read and understand directions? I could not remember recipes, how to cook, drive a car with a stick shift, balance a checkbook, or ride a bicycle. Sometimes I forgot basic etiquette, like how to form a question when someone was talking to me. I would go blank. I would stare at people. I never knew what questions to ask. I never knew how to respond when someone asked me a question. Sometimes I just blurted out phrases with no thought of what I was saying. I just replied with anything. At times I experienced bouts of aphasia. I would call the toilet the tub and the stove the refrigerator. Still, there were greater challenges. I didn't know who to trust. I felt like a four-year-old — enthusiastic to learn but unsure what to do when people spoke, and I knew that it was not true or didn't fit what I thought they were talking about. I had no filters about what came out of my mouth. Life was not working!

In the beginning it was like I was deaf or dumb. My senses were acutely heightened. I could feel a car coming down the road long before it arrived. I became skilled at reading body language and facial expressions to understand what people were saying.

Only now, in the last few years, have I begun to learn how to form questions.

With encouragement from my friends, I returned to our RSE campus in Yelm. I wondered whether anyone would ask what happened to me. Will they welcome me? How will I be received? What if I can't remember anyone's name? What if I blank out on everything and everybody? I gritted my teeth and decided to start over. Quitting has never been an option for me. RSE was the only safe place for me. It was the only place where anything made sense. So I kept pushing through the winding maze of "Who am I?"

I registered for the Beginning 101 class. When I arrived, I recognized faces but no names. Nevertheless, I was shocked to see that the disciplines I had learned before were intact. I remembered all of them! But I didn't remember the finer points. When we were instructed to blow out three words during C&E® and then take the words to the name-field to do Fieldwork®, I could not remember them. I could not even remember that we were instructed to look for our cards on the top and bottom rails. Additionally, I was a terrible event partner because I was not able to hold a thought or repeat what the last teaching was, let alone discuss a concept that Ramtha had just taught.

My other challenges included hearing loss and having very little balance. Because we were blindfolded during Fieldwork®, I would get dizzy and fall over whenever anyone touched or bumped me. I had no point of balance. Also, if we were instructed to lie down on the ground, I could not, because I could not get up. I would lose my balance and end up stuck down there.

Just recently a huge change happened. At a current event we were told to spin and twirl before beginning our Fieldwork® focus. Before, it was impossible. Now I became a whirling dervish. I was standing clearheaded and ready to go again. "Just do it," I said. That was my moment of not accepting "can't." At that moment, I conquered fear.

In the last year, I have attended every event from the Beginning 101 class to the Assay event. During Assay, we were taught Analogical Archery®. This type of archery is done blindfolded. Where the arrow lands depends on our focus. When it was my turn, after a few arrows, my instructor came over and said, "You have focused intent. Now make it longer. You are too shortsighted." That comment changed me. At that moment I knew that I could change and create a longer vision.

When I was given the opportunity to engage The Tank® this year, I firmly decided to go. This was the first time I had gone to The Tank® since 1991. Once the decision was made, I was filled with fear. But I started out, made it through the name-field, into The Tank® field, and found the entry. In a moment I knew that I no longer needed other people's approval and that I was not a quitter. I am a doer!

Two and a half years after stepping foot back onto the RSE campus and engaging in classes, I can now remember the three items to blow out, three items to bring in, and my list for creating a new neighborhood in my brain. I can walk blindfolded. I have restored my balance. My hearing has partially returned as a result of relinquishing control to my Spirit. Now I am asked by other students if I would be their partner. What a change!

My confidence is being restored. The teachings from our Master Teacher echo in my mind. The soil has been tilled.

By the grace of my God within, I now understand instructions. I now understand words so I can build my knowledge. As all this has unfolded, I also looked at my body. I was carrying too much weight and showing signs of age. It was time to change and forgive myself.

It has been said that life is about finding yourself. What I have learned from my life experiences is that I am creating my life every day from literally nothing. Everything is my choice. I accept the destinies I create.

In 2000, I was told by my physician that whatever brain abilities I had at the end of five years following my surgery would be all that I could expect. It is now 2017, twenty-two years since my surgery. That shell of a person who came home from the hospital is gone. Today I have a blooming brain. My miracles stand on the shoulders of my previous miracles. My manifestations now belong in the realm of the miraculous. Yes! I wrote this story, all by myself, from the Glory of God within me, making known the unknown from the absolute nothingness of my mind.

HEALED IN A MOMENT

Bryan Liss

I had just returned from a short road trip with my wife Linda and daughter Sarah when I began having sharp pains both in my stomach and in the area above my groin on the right side of my body. The pains were so strong that I turned very pale and almost vomited. These excruciating pains continued for over two hours. No position — standing up, lying down, or sitting — gave me any relief. I also had to hold my hand over an inguinal hernia that was significantly bulging out of my abdominal wall. Since the pain was not abating, the three of us made a decision to get me to the emergency room at St. Peter Hospital in Lacey, Washington, as soon as possible.

After a very uncomfortable thirty-minute car ride, I very slowly, deliberately, and painfully hobbled into the emergency room. Within twenty minutes I was lying in an emergency room bed.

All during this three-hour period I could not think of anything else but focusing on relieving the pain in my body. I had to stay totally in the moment since the severity of the pain was such that it didn't allow me any stray thoughts or activities. While we were waiting for the nurse, I asked Linda for help in bending my legs to see if that would assist in pain reduction. It didn't help. Once the nurse entered the room, I explained my condition. While she was writing down all my relevant information, I unexpectedly and instantaneously, without any forethought, stood up, got out of bed, and onto the floor. I said to the nurse, "I am fine. I appreciate you, and I will recommend you for your healing miracles to everyone I know." These were my exact words and actions. It was as if a switch in my head had just been flipped. There was no lead-up to that moment of relief and change. One moment I was in a continuing three-hour ordeal of tortuous pain, and instantaneously in the next moment, it was as if a fog had lifted and I was back to my normal self and nothing had happened. There was no change in thought leading up to that moment. There was just a total switch in circumstances — from one second being one way, to the next second being another way. There was no thought that I had just healed myself or that a miracle had just occurred. The switch was as if nothing had occurred and I had always been my normal, healthy self, and of course I would get up and walk away from the hospital. Why not? As my normal self, there was no reason to be at a hospital. So I proceeded to walk effortlessly out to the emergency room reception desk and explain to the two attendants that I was healed and that "I am out of here!"

They both did a double take and shook their heads. They asked me to repeat what I had just said because just moments before, they had witnessed me slowly and painfully shuffling into the hospital and toward the emergency room bed. I had switched neighborhoods that quickly! So I repeated my farewell statement and exited the lobby out to my car in the parking lot. Linda and Sarah were both in disbelief and internally questioned my actions, both having witnessed me instantly returning to being normal after being a complete basket case for the previous few hours. Sarah mentioned to me later that she was asking herself, "Did that just happen?" And Linda mentioned to me later that her thoughts were, "There goes Bryan being Bryan again — just exerting his individual, willful reality without any concern, dialogue, or explanation to anyone and marching full-bore ahead with his unique perspective towards life."

I have been fine ever since. I still laugh when I remember this experience and will forever remember the moment when I went from a patient in pain in a hospital bed to a joyous entity jumping up, standing on the floor, and boldly stating, "See you! I am out of here! Bye!" It was all that simple and immediate in the moment.

I have attempted to understand more about how the switch occurred, but to no avail. The healing was just that immediate, clean, and clear. It was without any analysis or internal discussion.

I cannot say what exactly caused this miraculous, transformational experience. But what must have greatly assisted was my thirty years of being a student at Ramtha's School of Enlightenment (RSE), multitudinous Blue Body® Dance healing sessions, approximately forty Blu Room treatment sessions, and my daily, magical Neighborhood Walk® in which I create my life.

It has always been my perspective that even though I may not see immediate or direct effects of all these great choices I have made, I really do not know how I am altering my DNA or what health issues I have prevented. I have always viewed these great, willful choices in my life as "preventive medicine." Further, I know that my common thoughts of "I can do anything" and "Everything is attitude" greatly assisted in healing my malady. So in retrospect, I have been very happy to realize that my past thirty years of expanding my mind and developing a greater, more unlimited, perspective of reality has been more than worth all the effort. It has profoundly changed me. This healing was a testament to that.

THE FAITH OF A MUSTARD SEED

Judy Andrew

When Ramtha introduces a discipline, he expects us to participate to our best ability. Sometimes we do a discipline for a full event, and then never again. Such is the discipline I lovingly refer to as the "T-shirt" discipline.

In the summer of 1996 at Ramtha's School of Enlightenment (RSE), Ramtha's great school in Yelm, Washington, we were instructed by Ramtha to sit on our focus pillow outside on a field, as the sky darkened into the evening. We were clad in pants on the bottom and a T-shirt on the upper half of our body. We would then lie down and surrender to the elements around us. I did this discipline and did accomplish a peace, oneness, and detachment all at the same time.

Several years later, at a raucous and joyful celebration with our Master Teacher, Ramtha, I became filled with such exuberance that I lost my balance and fell, landing on my right shoulder. People quickly helped me up and when they turned their backs, I promptly fell again, landing on my right shoulder one more time!

The next morning the pain was excruciating! I could not move my right shoulder or arm. The only relief I could find was when I practiced what I learned from the "T-shirt" discipline. I became one with my pain and then could detach somewhat from it to fall asleep.

I continued with the event. A couple of nights later, we were instructed to do our healing Blue Body® Dance. We were asked to remember a fellow student who really needed healing as we were dancing and constructing our Blue Body®. Focusing on another person helped me transcend my pain. I passionately danced and could vividly see the blue webs on my shoulder and down my arm.

The event ended, and Ramtha turned and gave me a smile. I could not take down my tent because I still could not move my arm and was in excruciating pain. People helped me and somehow I drove myself home.

I never went to a doctor. In fact, it never even occurred to me. Somehow I just knew I would recover. I continued to focus. On the third morning after my event, I awoke and the pain was gone! My shoulder had full mobility and was as good as new! What a grand and blessed experience!

It is now 2016 and I heard Ramtha recently say that he would send his students a runner about having the faith of a mustard seed. This story is my runner. It is a reminder that the faith of a mustard seed is not something I have to attain but has been inside of me all along.

INSIGHT

Jenny Gifford

I was not born blind. But by the time I was twelve years old I was eighty percent blind — BLIND, I say. I would sit on my bed, alone in my bedroom, attempting to learn braille. I knew nothing of a loving God, a God I could trust and call on and talk to. I only knew of my own feelings of hopelessness, doubt, deep fear, and confusion about life. I knew only that God had condemned me for having been so bad. God had punished me for something I did that was wrong. I was lost. I had no understanding of what it was that I had done. The prospect before me of total blindness was devastating and HE had allowed it to happen to me. I was a very scared young girl. I was filled with nightmarish thoughts about myself and the world. How could I possibly reconcile a loving God with all of this?

Doctors the world over could offer no reason or solace for this progressive eyesight loss, only that I was rejecting my eyes. I was treated with huge doses of cortisone, an antirejection drug that blew up my body like a balloon. My body and face became misshapen. Although I tried to constantly diet and put on a brave face, my dating years were spent in endless sorrow and isolation. In my mind I was a freak, an outcast — excommunicated from the sweetness of the kingdom of heaven that I had heard about in Bible studies at school. My self-worth was crushed and utterly lost.

This desolation prompted my epic, worldwide search for the meaning of it all and finally led to the great alchemical journey within, which transformed and healed me.

In 1999 I attended an extraordinary event in South Africa. Ramtha, the great Master Teacher, had arrived in Johannesburg and was teaching the event. Those magnificent, majestic words the Ram spoke changed my life forever. Hope filled me up and leaped out of my chest. I was hooked deeply and passionately.

He spoke such words of *truth*. I knew it to be so. *Finally* I had found the being I knew could teach me and guide me and love me back into life.

I remember hearing Ramtha telling us that we have never sinned, you are God, conquer yourself.

Oh, my gosh, these words rang like giant beacons calling!

That was twenty years ago.

How do I even begin to describe this magnificent and textured adventure of learning and healing at this great school of the mind? This journey slowly but surely gave me back my love of self, my power, my worth, my kindness, my truth, my freedom, my reason to live, the SIGHT of the beauty of myself and others. It set me on a path forward to the future — A GREAT FUTURE.

I had found a school that taught me the truth about God. I had found my Master Teacher, Ramtha the Enlightened One. Only the genius of this Master Teacher could understand how to take a broken, ill, human being and inspire them to want to be whole again, to be beautiful again, and to help them to know and trust God again. He taught me that God lives within me — and all of us — and to remember the God that I already am.

He inspired me over and over again to become great. He gave me ideals to work toward. I was slowly but surely, lovingly and superbly, trained to reconstitute myself. I learned to be able to swing the sword of my mind and replace my fears with benevolent, life-enhancing thoughts. I started to open my self-enclosed prison state and replace it with beauty and wonder. I had been given the keys to the kingdom of heaven by an ascended Master who knew the pathway because this had been his journey too. This was wealth beyond measure. It was sweetness and majesty. It was benevolence beyond words. It was love and power in its most pure form.

I remember Ramtha always saying he cannot speak to us of the place we have to go to find God within. He can only speak around it and inspire us to do enough of the Great Work for ourselves to go there and to find it for ourselves — the quiet area, the multidimensional wellspring within us of our supreme greatness.

I yearned to be just like him — but in my own unique way — this wondrous being who is, and knows, all these things.

I never gave up, although there were times when my genes pulled me heavily backwards. But I did not allow it for long because I wanted a new way of life.

I know full well by now that this is a personal, inward journey of great change toward, and for, self-redemption. This is what I call radical responsibility for self. Piece by piece I have endeavored with all my might to apply myself to bring about my own change. I wanted to change the erroneous thought patterns I believed about myself. This was often tough. It was a battle — a war — to overcome my lethargy, my awful thoughts, and my emotional addictions.

As the years went on, I started to reap the rewards of my application. It was in the *doing* and the *risking* to step into the great unknown that I have rediscovered parts of me that started to show me LOVE.

I have been given great examples of SIGHT on many levels of my being. Below are some beautiful examples of the insights I have had into my own inner beauty and divinity.

I learned that *focus* creates reality. I fell in love with the discipline of Fieldwork®. I learned by drawing a simple card of my desire and then going out blindfolded to an area the size of a soccer field holding pure, clear, childlike focus for a period of time that I would be guided by my Holy Spirit exactly to my card. This was one of Ramtha's genius ways to teach us how to create our own reality. I have used this many, many times in my life and many times I have received the exact manifestation of what I had drawn on the card. I had been given the keys to creating my reality.

I attended a five-day "Becoming Christ Consciousness" workshop in which my focus was freedom. I wanted freedom from the past and my self-imprisoned state. As always, I did my best to stay focused for the duration of the event. I was high up in the mountains, in heavenly nature, doing my Neighborhood Walk®. Suddenly I was aware of eagles overhead. Nine tawny eagles were circling around me, unencumbered and free. I was one of them. I wanted to stay there forever with no past, with just pure magic and wonder. I had manifested in my reality what I really wanted to be. This was "INSIGHT" on how creating reality from within really works and how my focus had worked.

This was a profoundly loving, insightful moment for me. I was starting to understand that I was really the creator of my own reality. The mechanism for creating was inside of me. I was not a victim of a vindictive God.

On another occasion I attended a seven-day Blue Body® workshop. Ramtha has taught us in the great school that you can do anything, and the key is focus. He has told us that whatever we choose to focus on creates reality. My focus for that workshop was unconditional love. I wanted to have the experience of it. After five days of unwavering focus and repetition, I had such a profound experience of pure, unconditional love that it is hard to put into words. I became this state. Nothing except love was gushing forth from me. I was actually not sure how to handle it. My immediate response was to hug everyone. I had no judgment toward anyone. It was gone. This state stayed with me long after the workshop was over. I was changed forever. I was shown and given the SIGHT and a taste of the love of God within. I was in bliss.

Insights led me to more insights about myself.

I sold everything I had to have a private moment with Ramtha for myself and my daughter Dagmar. I wanted to learn more and more and more — more insights about myself and how to change. I wanted to learn how to be greater. I wanted to gain insights from an advanced perspective, from an advanced being that I completely respected and trusted. I wanted my daughter to have this precious moment with the Ram too.

I seized the opportunity, and my beautiful daughter and I had a private two hours with the Ram. It was a wonderful and magical experience. Ram guided us to see complex, deep, subconscious patterns in our entangled, codependent relationship. How did he know us to that degree? He spoke the truth to us, and although it was sometimes hard to swallow, I knew it to be the truth. In reality, it was the most loving and kind thing he could do for us. He told us it would save us lifetimes of entanglement. Ramtha was pure love in action. My daughter and I can now love each other in freedom. Today we have a beautiful, healthy, vibrant, independent relationship.

At one point, Ramtha sent a group of us students in his school to Kenya to learn humility. We sure did that.

A group of five of us spent ten magical days outside of time with the Maasai people near Mount Kilimanjaro. This is a place so remote that the Maasai people have existed there unchanged for thousands of years. Here, there is no war, no money, and no poverty. They live without competition. All life to them is sacred and revered. Each person had their own important role that adds to the well-being of the whole group. We slept under the stars and did our Neighborhood Walk® on the great red plains of Kenya. This was another aspect of my new SIGHT. This sight exemplified the beauty, diversity, and wonder of God.

I have also learned that I have been SEEN and known by God. This insight came to me when Ramtha unexpectedly turned and stared at me. He looked at me for what seemed like ages, seeing ALL of me deeply, and understanding more of me than I did of myself. At first I was uncomfortable. Then I knew he was helping me to let go of an old belief I had held. I believed that I was unworthy to be seen by God and that God does not care about me. This was a truly transcendental, eternal moment for me. I now know I am — as we all are — a precious and important being. I have had many magical moments such as this with Ramtha. Over the years these pieces of the puzzle have grown and fitted together, and I now know that I am God and that God loves me and always has. It was I that left God and not the other way around.

And so it is said that the lotus grows from the mud. The thousand-petaled lotus blooms one petal at a time, and each is a great pearl of wisdom formed from the "sins" of our humanity. Wisdom comes from our adventures into the unknown. These adventures are levels of the consciousness of God yet to be explored and discovered.

I now have entirely regained my eyesight.

As I have pieced together and understood more and more of who I really am and have SEEN who I really am, my eyesight has become stronger and stronger. The joy of regaining both my physical and my inner sight is beyond description. To me, it is wealth beyond measure. I am so excited to have these keys and, at long last, to have a taste of the love that grows with each new understanding and experience I have of another room in God's house. Along with that, I have just begun the grand adventure of learning what it takes to become a Master, a Christ, a God. This is my great goal. Into eternity I go with greater and greater realities to be experienced. My future now beckons strongly, wildly, and excitedly. LOVE is all there is.

CHAPTER 2: HEALING OTHERS

"Love brings you closer
to the greatest mystery of all — you.
When you love another, you love yourself,
you embrace yourself, you become passionate with self.
When you are in joy with yourself,
you are embracing God within your being, the principle,
and you are becoming a knowing force
that is awesome in its power."

– Ramtha

SAVING THE LIFE OF A COWORKER

Jacqueline Smith

I had been attending Ramtha's School of Enlightenment (RSE) for about a year and a half. One of the first teachings to be taught was the Blue Body® Dance and how to heal using ultraviolet blue. Little did I know that I would soon have the opportunity to use this discipline to heal a fellow coworker at 20th Century Fox.

That day I was working on the grip gang. Grips are lighting and rigging technicians in the filmmaking industry. We provide set-up and takedown support. At one point during that day we were on one of the sound stages taking down a set. We were using wall dollies and putting the walls away into storage. Bob — not his real name — was working with me that day when he hit his elbow hard on the crossbar of the dolly and collapsed.

Everyone was standing around staring at Bob. No one had a clue what to do. I knelt down beside him and shouted, "Call 9-1-1. Call 9-1-1!" He had urinated in his pants and I knew he had had a cardiac arrest. I put my hand on his heart and started running ultraviolet-blue energy through it while another grip knelt down, took his pulse, and watched for whether Bob was breathing. He said, "He's not breathing."

I suddenly had the strangest experience — everything went into slow motion. I felt like I was observing myself from a distance. It was like someone had traded places with me and had taken over and was running the show.

I watched myself as I struck him hard on his chest. He arched his back and screamed and became conscious. When he could talk, he said he had experienced being somewhere but just could not remember where.

The ambulance arrived and the paramedics questioned us about what had happened. We explained everything the best we could, and then they took Bob away on a stretcher.

The grips and carpenters were all standing and looking at me. One of the carpenters came over and asked if they could get me a Coke. They were telling me they would love having me on their gang any day because I just saved Bob's life.

As the day went on, I started getting calls from his doctor at the hospital wanting to know what had happened. The doctors could not find anything wrong with Bob and they wanted to know why I struck him on the chest. I could not tell them it was my God doing the work and I was just watching. I thought, "Oh, no! I am in trouble now for hitting him." Visions of lawsuits were dancing through my head.

I told them he had struck his elbow and passed out. I said to them if they had ever struck their elbow hard, they would have experienced that the pain goes right to the heart. I had found out that day that Bob's father had just died and he hadn't yet taken any time to grieve his father's death. I told them that Bob was carrying pain in his heart from his father's death and when he struck his elbow, his heart could not handle any more pain.

They kept Bob overnight for observation and released him the next day. When he returned to work, he came over to me where I was working. He gratefully thanked me and asked if I would please tell him what had happened. I told him all the details of the incident and told him that he had to take time to grieve for his father.

The doctors never did find anything wrong with Bob. And I knew why. It was because I had been running the immense healing power of ultraviolet-blue energy through him the entire time he was unconscious. So despite having a cardiac arrest, his heart had shown no signs of damage.

CLIFFORD

Terra Kram

It was Tuesday morning and, on a whim, I had decided to call Ramtha's School of Enlightenment (RSE) hotline. A message had just been recorded announcing that advanced students were being invited to participate in a Beginner's weekend event. After a brief consult with each other, the three of us students who lived in Berkeley, California, decided to stay to finish up the job that was going to provide us the funds in June to attend Boktau, the long retreat, where we would then join Blue College on the Yelm campus of RSE.

That evening we went out to survey the progress on our dry-set wall. On our way, we spoke briefly with a man and his son on their way to dinner at his daughter's house. A few hours later, on their way back up the hill to where their car was parked, we again briefly greeted one another. Moments later, we heard urgent cries of "Help, help!!" We dashed up the hill and found the man lying on his back in the middle of the street, his son over him. His son exhorted us, "He's had a heart attack! Stay with him! I'll call 9-1-1, and my brother-in-law is a doctor!"

RSE students have been taught that the most powerful position for healing is at the person's head, the second most powerful is at their feet, and next is being at their side next to their head. I was sitting at Clifford's head in a partial Consciousness & Energy® (C&E®) position, with his head resting on my calf as a pillow. My partner was sitting to my left. I had heard that the heart meridian went through the tip of the little finger of the left hand, and that pinching the fleshy part of the finger to the underside of the nail would stimulate the heart. I had a vice-grip pinch going on the little finger of Clifford's left hand. Now it was time to be with Clifford. My focus was to support him in any way possible. In my understanding, when beings are transitioning into or out of the body, the most important thing is maintaining an environment of love. I simply went analogical and focused on Clifford.

I focused on Clifford with my eyes closed and, in as purely an analogical state of which I was capable, I became aware that he had stopped breathing. I immediately had the thought, "We are not doing brain damage on my watch." Years of doing disciplines led by Ramtha and being analogical in the moment prompted me to command, "BREATHE!" Clifford resumed breathing. I continued focusing, and every time Clifford stopped breathing, the command would come.

Eventually the family came running up the hill. They got within about twenty feet of us, whereupon they slowed down, then stopped completely about fifteen feet away. I was very focused on Clifford so was only barely aware of this.

The paramedics arrived shortly thereafter. They dashed right in and started hooking up all of their equipment. I think they realized I needed a moment to get back to a normal state. Eventually I turned around and looked at one and said, "You need to get in here?" They nodded, and I leaned forward to Clifford to let him know "the pillow is moving." A fresh pillow was provided, and the first thing Clifford said to the paramedics was, "Now I don't want you telling my doctor about this." Ah ... no brain damage here!

This was on a Tuesday and we subsequently learned that Clifford was scheduled for valve replacement surgery Thursday morning.

About ten years later I had just gotten banded for an RSE event and was coming into the Great Hall through the main door when I felt a strong presence of Clifford. Clifford's new valve had gotten him another ten years, and when he crossed over, he came to check out the school that saved his life all those years ago.

BECOME LIKE A CHILD

Rosalie Saecker

We have all awakened from dreams to know that they were "only" dreams, meaning we know that we are now in a reality different from the dream. It is an amazing ability to shift from one reality potential to another. The acceptance of a little child makes it look easy but that does not make it any less miraculous.

This miracle happened when my son Akel was six years old. I was suddenly aware he was standing very quietly, slightly bent forward, gently holding his abdominal area. "Mommy, my tummy hurts," he said. It was midafternoon on a sunny, April workday. For the kids, the morning was filled with homeschooling, the afternoon was playtime. This particular day, I was working from home and his dad was at work. We were staying in a tiny tack room, part of a barn with four horse stalls and a large hayloft, while we waited to be able to move into the house we had purchased.

"Are you hungry?" I asked a little anxiously. As a mom, I always tried the easy solutions first.

"I don't feel like eating," he said. He looked uncomfortable.

"Why don't you try going to the bathroom?" I sent him off to the toilet, which was an enclosed space to one side of the "kitchen" — a shed attached to the tack room.

A short time later he came out. "It still hurts," he said, again holding his belly and clearly distressed.

"Okay. Let's do some healing then." In our family, we use a healing technique taught at Ramtha's School of Enlightenment called Blue Body®. He gingerly walked into the "living room" and I had him lie down on the couch that was located on one side of the room. On the other side of the room were the table and chairs where I had been working. As he lay on the couch, I sat on the floor next to him and placed my hands on his stomach. First, I felt different areas of his abdomen, trying to locate the most sensitive place. I am not a doctor, so all I could do was press on an area and ask if it hurt there. When I had identified the area of pain, I placed my hands over it, endeavored to clear my mind, and focused on healing whatever it was. Clearing my mind was challenging, as it wanted to race with possibilities. Is it just gas? Is it food poisoning? Is it an allergic reaction? Is it appendicitis or some other medical emergency? Being a parent is definitely not easy! I continued to lay my hands on his belly while I used my mind to send healing energy to him through my hands. When I asked him if it was better, he said, "No, it still hurts."

Needing to get back to work and feeling that I had not been much help, I said, "I have done what I can do. Why don't you talk to your God?" I then got up and went over to the table to continue working. At Ramtha's School of Enlightenment we are taught that everyone is divine. When I struggle with a problem, I reach a place where talking to God is really the only option left, so it seemed natural to me to suggest this to him.

I tried to complete the tasks I had brought home to do, but I was concerned. How much time do I allow before doing something more? Is it something serious? Do I need to call the doctor? There was no sound and nothing was moving on the other side of the room.

Ten minutes, then fifteen minutes went by and suddenly Sarrah, my eight-year-old daughter, poked her head in from the barn side door and said, "I want someone to play with!"

"Sorry, honey, Akel is not feeling well," I said.

Just then, a voice from the other side of the room said, "I am feeling better now."

Hmmm. "What did you do?" I asked, while wondering if perhaps he had just needed some attention.

He answered, "It hurt so bad and I really wanted it to stop. So I said to my God, "I am healed. So be it!" I could not see his face but the relief in his voice was obvious.

He paused, so I said, "And what happened?" Those are pretty powerful words for a six-year-old and I am feeling a little ashamed at thinking he might have been pretending.

"Then it just seemed like I woke up from a dream," he said. With that, he got up and went outside to play.

Ramtha has often spoken about how children do not analyze; they just accept. The moment Akel said that it seemed like a dream, I knew he had done something extraordinary. Yet what was important to him was that he could now go out and play. This ability to simply accept and change realities is what it means "to enter the kingdom of heaven."

WHAT DO YOU HAVE TO LOSE
BY SIMPLY TRYING?

Diane DuBuc

I visited Ramtha's School of Enlightenment (RSE) for the first time in the spring of 1995, looking for answers to the mysteries I had experienced since childhood. From a young age I had had visions of ghosts, multiple visions with or without people, and a near-death experience with sound, light, and the tunnel effect. I had known the state of nirvana, met my soulmate — and more.

In fact, it was the reading of Ramtha's book *Ramtha Intensive: Soulmates* that encouraged me to travel to Yelm to meet the Teacher face to face. I was skeptical, but I needed to address the urging of my Spirit to verify that this Teacher was real.

On my first visit in the spring of 1995, Ramtha arrived to teach us. I immediately felt electricity within my body, tears flowed, and I started to shake. Although I was staring at the body of JZ Knight, I was repeating to myself, "I know this guy. I know this guy." At the same moment I wanted to hug him in my arms like a mother meeting her son again. I was stunned!

I didn't understand most of the teachings because they were so different from what I knew. Moreover, I was very surprised by the discipline of Consciousness & Energy® (C&E®). Everything was new for me. I left after three days; I was not ready.

It was in October of 1995, after reading *Ramtha, The White Book,* and JZ Knight's autobiography, *A State of Mind*, that I came back to Yelm for my second visit. At that event I learned about the emotional body, Blue Body® healing, and engaged C&E®. All was going well until Ramtha spoke of healing others. Looking at him I told myself, "You just lost me!" and I started to pick up my things. Then I heard Ramtha say that those of you who desire to leave can do so, but what do you have to lose by simply trying? I put my things back down and realized that, truly, I didn't have anything to lose. Making the choice to stay proved to be incredibly valuable.

My first experience of healing someone else was in 1997, when my husband went three times to the intensive care unit at our local hospital for severe atrial fibrillation. During the last stay, the cardiologist told me that twice when I got close to my husband, his heart returned to normal. Then he said, "You want to tell me what you are doing to him?" I explained that I had been learning about healing and my presence carried a healing frequency which my husband's body was responding to. Although surprised, the cardiologist said nothing. He talked about a probable operation to insert a pacemaker.

The next day I asked my husband if I could try on him what I had learned at the school in Yelm. I spoke about it as a gift I had received from Ramtha and it was about healing others.

I felt shy when I told him, "What do you have to lose if you let me try?"

I performed Blue Body® on him three times that day. During the first session he had visions of something resembling a blue aurora borealis and at the same time his heart got regular. During the second and third times he saw a blue cone over his face and heard notes of music. To my husband's and my amazement and happiness, it was as Ramtha taught — my husband was healed. The doctors confirmed that his heart was normal and no pacemaker was needed.

The second experience I had of healing another person was when I met Samy, a young woman whose medical condition left her with virtually no hope of living. I met Samy's mother at *Book Fair 2000*. I had written a book and was sitting at my booth to sell and sign books when Samy's mother came up to me. She told me, "I don't know why, but I came straight to your booth. I know I need to buy your book."

Some weeks later, after reading my book, she invited me to visit her daughter. Samy was born with a malfunctioning heart. She had received her first pacemaker three days after being born. Samy was now sixteen years old, was very weak, and often had to stay bedridden. She had given up hope of living and had refused a potential heart transplant. Her parents had accepted her choice.

At the first meeting with Samy and her mother, I explained that I would try to help strengthen her heart. I explained how I would go about it and asked if this process was acceptable to her. The only thing she was worried about was if I would be reading her thoughts. I told her, "No! I will not read your thoughts and also I will not touch you." Samy asked my price. I told her I didn't want anything — that sharing this gift was all I wanted, nothing more.

This first Blue Body® session went well. At the end, I asked that Samy's mother give me an update on her daughter. The news came quickly. Shortly after I returned home, her mother called me and said, "Samy is smiling and she already feels a lot better."

At my second meeting with Samy, as I was focusing I saw the word "INFARCTION." I continued the Blue Body® work and then I spoke with her. "What do you spend your days doing, Samy?" I asked. She replied, "I go to school, ride my bicycle, walk, and meet friends." I explained to her that her energy was to be used for helping her heart. I told her, "You are presently in danger of having an infarction — a heart attack." I said, "I just saw that word in my head and I don't like it. So rest, rest, rest! If not, I will stop everything now. You can do slow and short walks while checking your pulse, but never exert yourself to the point of feeling any fatigue at all. Come now, I want to speak to your parents about that. Your cardiologist's opinion will be important too before doing anything else."

She listened well and gradually became stronger, her heart improvement holding. As time went on, this radiant young woman experienced real happiness. She fell in love. Her companion knew her precarious health condition and genuinely loved her despite her fragility. Because she now was in a relationship, her cardiologist was asked if Samy would be allowed to have sexual intercourse. He said it was allowed.

Two and a half years later, Samy's mother called me, very distressed. "Samy is at the hospital in emergency. She had a heart attack following intercourse. Can you do something?"

I knew from Ramtha that Blue Body® healing could be done remotely. Knowing how urgent it was, I stayed at home and immediately put myself in a position to do Blue Body® on Samy. All of a sudden, I found myself sitting on a hospital bed in the C&E® position. The whole bed was white, everything seemed motionless, and lying to my left, I recognized Samy. She looked like a chalk-white statue. She was covered by a white bedsheet all the way to her shoulders.

I received information on her state — she was dead. At first, I refused to accept it. The information continued, and all the while my God within was urging me not to judge the situation but rather to surrender and to continue Blue Body® healing.

Then looking to my right, I saw Samy in vibrant color, standing up, smiling, and looking at me. "What are you doing there?" I asked. She appeared to be calm and happy and full of joy. Then these words came to my mind — or did I hear them for real? "My mother is now free. She needs to think about herself. She needs to take very good care of herself. Can you tell her that?"

So Samy could see me too!

I then became aware of again engaging the Blue Body® discipline. Despite knowing it was the end of the body, I continued to focus on Samy with the energy coming off of my hands.

It was only after I left this state that I realized my mind had gone to the hospital and that I was out of this time frame. This allowed me to be in direct contact with Samy while my body was in my home, fifteen miles from her. It was amazing — in one instant I was in her presence. It was all a very special experience for me. I then knew the difference between the body and the mind and how the mind can journey separately from the body via thought.

For me, that one sentence that Ramtha spoke, about what do you have to lose by simply trying, changed not only my life but also changed the life of these two beautiful people — my husband and Samy. I am filled to overflowing with gratitude for my Teacher, Ramtha, for saying exactly the right thing at the right time to keep me in class so I could learn this marvelous knowledge.

Chapter 3: Healing Our Families

"The purest love, noblest love,
Mother/Father love of all emotion and feeling
is expressly given and earned
through that which is termed freedom,
when we can love one another freely
and let them express their truth."

– Ramtha

THE PLAN

Sophie Sykes

"I can and I will!" my father shouted into the telephone. "I am leaving hospice. I want to go back to my own home, live next to Helen, and live my dream. I can and I will. I keep telling your brothers that 'CAN'T' is not a part of my vocabulary."

At the time I didn't realize the importance of what he was speaking. Later, upon reflection, I smiled inside. For all these years that he and I have spoken and I have communicated the bits and pieces of what I have learned at Ramtha's School of Enlightenment (RSE), I saw in front of my eyes that my father was speaking his fierce determination to change. I listened as these teachings poured out of him passionately. The power of will and determination is what I had learned in my years at RSE. Here, now, was my father shouting back to me the exact same words that I had learned from my spiritual Teacher.

My father is ninety-one years old and had been in hospice for ninety days. Three months prior to this phone call, my oldest brother had contacted me and said, "Dad is in the hospital and we don't think he is going to make it. We just hope you get here before he passes." I rushed home from work, packed a bag, and raced to SeaTac Airport. On the flight to the Detroit Metropolitan Airport, I focused on the face of my father and prayed that my father would still be alive for me to say good-bye. I was longing to tell him some of the knowledge I had learned at RSE. I wanted to tell him about what happens when we pass this plane. I wanted to tell him about reincarnation. I wanted to help him create a plan for his future life, his next life — the same way JZ Knight had taught me about creating a plan for my next life. I wanted to give him the same hope JZ gave me.

I had been reared in the Midwest, in a Catholic Church, where I had never even heard of artichokes, organic broccoli, or the word reincarnation. We had spent Sundays in downtown Detroit, where my Uncle John was the parish priest of a church named Saint Elizabeth. Every Sunday we would all pile into our station wagon, drive to a shabby neighborhood in downtown Detroit, and march into a beautiful, historic church with stained-glass windows that smelled of incense and was lined with oak pews. Statues of Jesus, Mary, and Joseph lined the walls next to the Stations of the Cross. As a kid, I looked at these statues and figured that they were the reason why my mother always cried out, "Jesus, Mary, and Joseph!" every time one of us broke an arm or fell down the stairs and needed stitches. I thought it was Jesus, Mary, and Joseph who were the ones who patched us up.

My favorite part of the church was this little hallway where there was a statue of the Blessed Virgin. I loved to light a candle at her altar and pray. Long after everyone was in the car loaded up ready to go home, my brothers would come running back into the church only to find me kneeling at the feet of the Blessed Virgin praying for my redemption. I had no idea who or what God was. All I knew is that I loved God and that hopefully his mother would tell him.

My second favorite part of going to this church was that we were the only white people there and we were my uncle's family. Everyone else was cinnamon-colored or charcoal black. The women had big hips and big purses. The choir was made up of mostly women who sang like Whoopi Goldberg from *Sister Act*. They had a microphone and would come down from the altar and hand us their microphone. In our little childlike voices we would sing out, "We will raise them up" and "This little light of mine, I'm gonna let it shine!" These laughing, robust women would clap and squeeze us on our apple cheeks and hug us like they thought we were going to die. We loved it. We simply adored them. My father always said that my uncle was part black because he had rallied his church and marched with Martin Luther King from Alabama to the Capitol. Later I understood that my uncle walked with his people and was proud to fight for civil rights. All of this made a great impression on me. I continued to pray and love God. Maybe God was black?

My father, on the other hand, is a traditionally devout Irish-Catholic man. He loves twelve-year-old scotch, golf, drinking on Saturday nights, and going to church on Sunday. He believes in working hard and never once did he not provide for us. He started his own business and grew it year by year, working 24/7 to provide for seven children and our mom. He wasn't friendly or loving. He just worked. He didn't believe in helping with homework, spoiling children, or helping Mom with the house. But he did arrive home every night at exactly 6:00 p.m. for dinner. We all had our places at the pecan pull-out table with a bench that sat me, my sister Karen, and my brother Joe. My brothers Mark, John, and Jimmy sat on the other bench across from us and Colleen sat in the highchair. My dad would say grace, and if we grabbed for food before he was finished reciting grace, he would stab us with his fork and order us to wait. He was often impatient with our silliness or loud voices and believed that children were to be seen and not heard. If we cried too loudly he would say, "I will give you something to cry about!"

But no matter what, he always insisted on going to Sunday Mass every week and yelled at us to hurry up, get in the car, and get ready for Mass. He could not stand it if we rebelled in any way. When I refused to go into the dark and musty confessional box to report my sins to Father McNamara, my father threw me headfirst into the confessional box commanding, "Go now," which, of course, I did. I confessed that I hated my father. I confessed that I didn't believe in sins and I thought I was pretty fine the way I was. The priest gave me five Hail Marys to perform.

In 2005 I attended RSE and learned that there is life beyond death. I learned that we can reincarnate. I learned that at the moment of death I will go through a tunnel, become a ball of light, and can — and will — have adventures that I have never had before. I can choose my next parents, come back as anyone, and create my life in any shape, color, or form that I desire. I could make a plan! This information was so freeing for me that I could not wait to pass this along to my father who was now dying. To give this information to my father was my deepest desire and what I imagined might be the only gift I could give him before he passed.

Armed with my new knowledge, I flew to the Midwest. My brother picked me up at the airport and drove me directly to the hospital. We got into the elevator and he tried to prepare me for what dad looked like. "He's lost a lot of weight. His kidneys aren't functioning and he has end-stage renal failure. He's refused dialysis and his breathing is labored." I walked into the hospital room and saw my dad. He was frail-looking, pale, and was sleeping. I walked up to his bed, touched his hand, and he opened his eyes. He began to cry. "I am so glad you are here," he said. "Your brothers really need you." I began to laugh and cry all at once. "Really?" I said. "How are you doing?"

All of us were hovering over his hospital bed ready to say good-bye to a man we all had mixed emotions about. He didn't say much but said that he was ready to go to heaven and that Mother Mary was coming for him. I thought that maybe this was my moment to talk about the afterlife. But I stopped because my brother was standing in the room with me and was signaling me that it was time to go. I figured it would be better to wait until the morning when I would be alone with my dad.

The next day he was moved to hospice and the prognosis was not good. "He has three to five days at the most," the doctor said. Because all my brothers and sisters needed to go to work, I started taking the morning shift with Dad. I would arrive about 8:30 a.m. and stay until someone else showed up at 2:00 p.m. It was during our morning visits that I began to talk with my dad about what I had learned that happens when you die. I told him that someone would be waiting for him at the end of the tunnel. He would wave his hand and say, "Yah, yah, yah, I know all that." He continued to tell me about Mother Mary standing at the end of his bed. Slowly and nervously I began to talk about some of the things I knew. I talked about reincarnation and making a plan. I told him that he could return again and live a wholly new life filled with excitement and joy. For the first time since I had arrived, he looked fully awake and alive.

Nevertheless, we were all sure he would pass. We were all getting prepared. Every night we would go home and put out our clothes on the end of our beds to make sure we would be ready to jump into them and run to the hospice room when the nurse called. Every night we said, "Tonight he will be gone." Every night I lit my candle and focused on peace, love, and joy. We said our prayers. My brothers had already decided what Bible scriptures would be read at his funeral and what priest would say the Mass.

Well, he didn't die. By day two when I arrived at hospice I found Dad sitting up and drinking coffee. "You look great." I said. "I am feeling better," he said. "Let's have a wee bit of scotch." I laughed and agreed. When someone is dying, what do a couple of scotches matter?

The days passed and every day my dad got better. He started eating again. He ate oatmeal for breakfast. By day five he was eating breakfast and lunch and had convinced the hospice nurses to look the other way while we all drank scotch every day at 5:00 p.m. This was his cocktail hour. He would pour us all a shot and then he would drink several fingerfuls for himself.

Twenty-one days later he was sitting in a wheelchair, going to the cafeteria for breakfast, and walking outside in the courtyard to get some fresh air and sunshine. On the twenty-first day I woke up and looked at my brother and said, "I need to go home. I miss my home, my garden, and my friends. Dad has decided to live."

It is now two years later and my father is alive and well. He travels back and forth from his home in Michigan to his condo in Florida. My sister Karen is dedicated to caring for him in Florida. In Michigan my brothers lovingly care for all his needs.

When I talk with him, he always says, "I am living my dream. All I know is that I can and I will."

We all have coined my father the "Miracle Man." How anyone can live with hardly any kidneys and drink six scotches a day is a mystery and miracle to all of us. We shake our heads and give thanks for "Life is a Gift." His new life has been a great healing for our entire family. We have all witnessed his change and experienced forgiveness. We have all seen that one can reincarnate again. What I had not imagined in my journey with my father was that we can live again in *this* lifetime! After all, is not that what I had wanted to tell my father that I had learned at school? About reincarnation? About The Plan? About moving to a new neighborhood in his mind? Somehow I had accepted that he would die and had no thought that he would be "born again" in this life. But he has. And so can I. He is a new person and we are a new family. Is this what Jesus meant when he said we must be "born again"? We must die to our past to live again? Is it that we transmute our past into something new — something wonderful?

For my sister Karen, my dad has given her the opportunity to give and know him in a way she has never known. For my brothers, they have lived through his fiery ways into peace and compassion. And for me, I have garnered a grand knowing of living again in this life, with a new neighborhood, and an understanding of what it means to be "born again" with wonder and self-love. Without being born into this family, none of us would have had these godly lessons. Dad's life and near death have been a healing for our family. We are no longer victims of tyranny, hatred, and prejudice but proud survivors of God's strong "Will" and "Can-Do."

ORCHIDS FOREVER — GOD IS A WHISPERER

Karla Broschinski

In 2001 my husband and I moved from Europe to Yelm. The move allowed us to attend Ramtha's School of Enlightenment (RSE) on a regular basis and to start a new life — a life which was not about the past but about the future.

After a few years, my visa status changed and at that point I was not able to leave the country and come back again. So I stayed. That meant I was not able to visit my parents in Germany.

For one of my mother's birthdays, I sent her a big orchid. For several years the orchid flourished and bloomed. As it turned out, every time my mom and I spoke on the phone, it was orchid season. She would always excitedly tell me how many buds were on the orchid or how many blossoms had opened. She always had something to tell me about this orchid and how she loved it. I am sure it was a lifeline from me to her.

At age eighty-four, my mom decided to visit. "If you cannot come to me, I will come to you!" That was her clear decision. She had never been outside of Germany or on a big airplane, but she bravely made the trip. And, needless to say, we had an amazing time together, filled with love and laughter. A few weeks after returning to Germany, she passed away without any drama. She just slipped from her chair onto the floor and passed, moving to the other side of this life. She had fulfilled her last dream — visiting me.

My friends Giorda and Margarette Elie brought me an orchid with a condolence card, and I placed the orchid on my table in the living room. I have to say that I do have a green thumb, but only with plants that grow outside. Growing plants indoors is not my interest. I have little space to put indoor plants on window sills or elsewhere around the house. And because our house is in the middle of nature, nature is all around and I see it all the time outside our windows. There has never been a desire for me to bring nature inside.

I had no idea about how to take care of an orchid. The only thing this little orchid got from me on the material level was water. Yet this orchid kept blooming and blooming. When one blossom spike finished blooming, another new spike was already up with plump buds ready to start its display of new blossoms. And this went on and on. I was impressed and loved this constant, beautiful display.

Close to two years after my mom's passing, I was in the middle of candle focus. The candle was on the same table as the ever-blooming orchid. I suddenly got this flash of knowingness which brought me to tears: my mom is communicating with me through this orchid! She is helping it blossom continuously for close to two years, trying to tell me how much she loves me and that she is fine. I could not believe that I didn't understand this much earlier. The joy my mom received from the orchid I gave her as a gift was beyond words. Now she was on the other side and was doing the same for me in return. It took her nearly two years of making this orchid bloom continuously until I finally recognized it. I was overjoyed that at last I understood.

It is not surprising that this little orchid died very shortly after. My mom's mission had been accomplished! Eventually, I Googled how to care for orchids. I discovered that orchids had a number of very specific requirements, including dormant periods during which they collect energy for the next round of blooms. All those countless spikes being produced one after the other, blooming without stopping, was not possible. My orchid only got water and never took time out for a dormant period.

But this was not about growing orchids. This was about love — love without boundaries and beyond the death of the physical body. I remember my beloved Teacher, Ramtha, saying that God is a whisperer. And I know now that when we are quiet and listen, that is when we can hear God's whisper of love.

MY SISTER UNDERSTANDS LIFE BEYOND DEATH

Marian Clements

Our story is simple and profound. We came together from very different life choices to an understanding of each other and to a greater understanding of life, death, and beyond.

My sister Annette and I grew up in a small Midwestern city, in the nurturance and consistency of a devoutly Catholic family. Our parents loved us sweetly and sacrificed to send us to Catholic school. As we reached maturity, she stayed in our hometown working for the local newspaper, marrying a high school sweetheart, and raising her family of six children. I fled to a university — a Catholic one — never to return except for occasional visits. I finally threw off the restrictions of religion in my thirties after experiencing its lack of a connection with God. Soon thereafter I found my Teacher, Ramtha the Enlightened One, and my way to a true sense of myself and my Holy Spirit. In my spiritual studies and disciplines I found the meaning of my life and an understanding of the afterlife.

Annette and I were some years apart in age so that we did not share the same interests growing up. However, we were friends. She looked out for me, the younger, and I admired her big sister accomplishments. That is how our relationship unfolded over the years as we reared our families and went about our own lives, visiting each other infrequently and sharing occasional letters, birthday calls, and holiday gifts.

In May of 2013, Annette lost her beloved husband Darryl after fifty-nine years of marriage. I also had experienced widowhood and understood how difficult this would be for her. So I began calling her often, semiweekly at first. I just listened, loved her, and was there for her at least by telephone and eventually by Skype. We gathered a few lovely threads from our past together as children and developed a satisfying relationship.

It eventually became clear to me that my sister was quite preoccupied with death. She was beginning to think about her own death, questioning the details of life after death, and anticipating a reunion with her husband and a daughter who had passed at the age of twenty-one. She came across a book on near-death experiences and started talking to me about these phenomena. That led to conversations about reincarnation and opened a door for me to share with her some of my own experiences of reincarnation — knowing several people in two separate lives and receiving messages from the beyond from loved ones. She knew I was studying with the entity Ramtha and strongly disapproved, hoping that I would eventually return to the fold of the Catholic religion. However, she also seemed to respect my knowledge on the subjects of so much importance to her. So we talked and talked! ... and talked some more. I began to realize that even though she was greatly saddened that I had "fallen away," she loved me and listened to my ideas. Through our conversations she allowed me to coax her out of her spiritual box, at least a little.

Gradually we got to the topic of heaven. I learned that her idea of heaven was just "being with God and being happy." She had no other substance for that scene and so was interested to hear my understanding of the Plane of Bliss. Again, my experience of contact with several beloved people who had passed and communicated from the other side was important. And of course it was inevitable that a discourse on the Plane of Bliss would lead to talk of "The Light" and "to go there or not go there and why." This was a very delicate area for her, as she fully expected to be reunited in heaven with her husband and daughter. So I took a page from Ramtha's methodology and dove in. I shared the illusion of the light and then simply asked her to not go there but rather to go to the Void, the darkness — to go directly to God! I reminded her of this in various conversations. By this time I had already asked Ramtha to be with her whenever she passed.

Annette asked me many questions, such as why is there so much evil in the world? And why are such terrible things happening? I just did my best, giving her my opinion as gently as possible, knowing that I was "fingernails on the blackboard" to her very devout, religious paradigm. We also had lots of laughs together and much reminiscing about our lives and our children's lives. I blessed her again and again for her open mind on the tough subjects.

In May of 2016, her otherwise healthy and vigorous body suddenly became critically ill and she was now facing her own death. It was a summer of fear and pain for her, and our conversations changed to brief murmurings of love and encouragement. I did make a request of her. I asked that after she was on the other side to please come back to me and say good-bye one more time. She said sweetly, "I will if I can."

She clearly intended to leave quickly, as she had no desire to continue in pain and confusion. So on a Friday morning in mid-August she slipped away, sooner than we expected. Now my new journey with her began.

With my tears flowing, my first act was to create a picture. I drew a symbol of the two of us with a very weak, thin, and broken veil between us. That evening after dark I stood beneath the big tree by my house and called Annette to come as an Orb and appear by my left shoulder while my husband David took photos. She did indeed show herself, a small white Orb by my shoulder, the same way in which our father had come some thirteen years before. I was pleased and not surprised. The next evening my husband David and I had our own special memorial to Annette. We lit candles, played music, turned on the Ghost Radar, and began conversing with Annette and about Annette. Ghost Radar is a computer application designed to detect paranormal activity that shows us words on a screen. The first word from the Ghost Radar was "SISTER!" I knew it was she. And the more I pondered the appearance of the word, the more certain I was that she was speaking to us. I was thrilled to know she was present as we celebrated her life. Yet I was deeply grieved. After all our years of being casual in our relationship, we had finally truly found each other in a deep and intimate kind of conversation.

Now she was gone.

About ten days later I was engaging the Twilight® discipline taught by Ramtha. I was deeply in this state of Twilight® when her name "Annette" came to me. Then I heard her speak to me: "Now I understand what you were telling me." I burst into tears and wept deeply and joyfully. It was the culmination of our beautiful journey together.

CHAPTER 4: HEALING OUR ANIMALS

"All things, master,
grow into life
and fight for life and maintain life
and are never distraught with life
if left alone."

– Ramtha

HORSES AND THE POWER OF C&E®

Dr. Louie Enos, D.V.M., B.S.

I have been a practicing equine specialist veterinarian since 1977. I began with a successful equine surgery practice in eastern Washington State. Since coming to see Ramtha at Ramtha's School of Enlightenment (RSE) over thirty years ago, I have been able to evolve myself personally and to understand the knowledge of true healing. Because of Ramtha's teachings, I now know that all disease is ultimately created by deep-seated, and often unconscious, attitudes. Based on this knowledge, I have healed many of my own attitudes and diseases.

Ramtha's wonderful knowledge ultimately fostered in me the creation of an equine healing practice. I left traditional medical beliefs behind to create *Equine Manipulation Through Mind*. I have centered my practice on the teachings and personal experience learned at RSE. Through twenty-five years of practice, traveling coast to coast in the United States as well as in Europe and South America, I was often faced with healing worst-case scenarios. But as long as there is a breath of life and a will to live in an animal, I know it can be helped and healed. My passion has always been to be a Master Healer. This story of a remarkable healing is a true example of the power of what I have learned and passionately applied.

In the fall of 2012, I received a frantic phone call from a new client claiming that her horse, called Cowgirl, had both serious spinal problems and severe behavioral problems. The owner said she had been told by three chiropractors to put the horse down but she was told by a fellow horse owner that I might be able to help. She said, "You are my last chance!" I said, "Don't put her down! I can help you and I can come right over." Before we hung up, she nervously gave me more history, indicating the mare had been injured at a boarding facility in

California. They told her they didn't know what happened. From the California facility, the owner took Cowgirl to a large equine veterinary clinic in Arizona but was given no definite diagnosis. She then brought the horse to the Oregon State Veterinary Hospital. There they examined her extensively but again could not give a definitive diagnosis. Cowgirl was put on antipsychotic medications and was brought by the owner to Tenino, Washington, where both the owner and horse would reside.

Because I live nearby, I was able to immediately drive to the facility where the horse was boarded. As I arrived to meet Cowgirl for the first time, people began to gather. The owner was relieved and happy that I had come. We walked over to the stall. The mare was lying down, very depressed. We asked Cowgirl to get up and she did so, but with much difficulty. When she finally stood, she was wobbly and staggered into the aisleway. I began to assess her. She had a contracted, compressed neck, fear in her eyes, a dropped back, and a very sharp-angled pelvis. She appeared rigid throughout and was not able to move her neck. Her health was generally poor, with loss of hair on certain areas of her body. She could not shake her head or move it up or down. She was essentially frozen.

As I began to gently approach Cowgirl, she began to panic. She scrambled backwards, totally uncoordinated, and almost went over backwards. I slowly brought her forward and began to apply quantum healing by placing my hands slightly above her to emit the specific electromagnetic frequency of ultraviolet blue. This was Blue Body® healing as taught by Ramtha. I had many times applied this healing knowledge and knew its power. She started to quiver and then exploded backwards again. But this time she could stop herself and she came forward. When she did this, it was obvious she had a little more control and was able to walk better. The audience who was watching also saw this. I then took her slowly into the arena off the concrete aisleway and continued treatment.

I began once again to apply Blue Body® healing and Cowgirl began to accept, with only brief moments of panic.

Maintaining focus, I gently touched her poll, allowing her to express her emotions and slowly release the neck. She started to respond by slightly relaxing her severely contracted neck. It began to open up slightly and lengthen. I continued to change her and relieve her extreme fear and anxiety. As I proceeded through the rest of her spine, I was able to have her release some pelvic blockage and fears as well as help her to open up and have relief through her topline. As I continued to methodically work with her, she became calmer and was walking better as I let her explore the changes in movement.

After about three hours of working on her, Cowgirl was able to walk steadily with a better gait and was more focused and calm. She was put in her stall, and the owner as well as the audience were thrilled to see the changes. Because I am able to read a horse's history through the horse's expressions and emotions, I was able to give the owner information about her horse's past and what happened. In addition, the spinal system and body provided their own information to me.

Even though the owner said the horse had been a quiet mare, I told the owner that Cowgirl had repressed traumas before the California boarding incident. When the boarding facility incident occurred, the brain unleashed all its past emotional traumas adding to the recent traumatic experience. This caused the horse to react even more. I knew the past trauma was that Cowgirl had gotten herself caught in some physical structure or by the halter, had struggled and fought excessively to the point that she went over backwards. This is extremely traumatic for a horse and causes severe fear, anxiety, and panic. She fought and stretched herself out like a rubber band and then contracted back, misaligning and disturbing all the muscle groups and spinal nervous system. The result was much pain, suffering, and fear.

At this point in time, I had the owner start to wean Cowgirl off the antipsychotic drugs that I knew were compounding her very reactive, emotional state. The owner and I kept in close contact, since it would take a lot more treatments and healing to get Cowgirl back to mental and physical health. She wrote me about a week later and said Cowgirl was much better and, as her owner, she was thrilled to have answers and solutions. She wrote most kindly and said:

"I wanted to THANK YOU again for coming out to see Cowgirl. And I DO believe you have a gift. I know you have put a lot of work into research and learning. But what's amazing to me is that you have the gift of being able to bring together all the different approaches as well as having the gift of remarkable knowledge. Not all of us have such a gift and it's nice to see people using the abilities they were given to help so many others. Again, THANK YOU so much!"

After hearing from the owner and being very appreciative of her report, I decided to see Cowgirl and treat her once again. This is sooner than I usually see a horse for retreatment but in this case, due to the extreme nature of Cowgirl's problems, it was necessary. I saw Cowgirl and it was evident to me there was a change in her attitude and movement. She still showed some expected anxiety and there was still much in her physical state that needed progress. She also expressed some fear, which was important to release. In addition, I needed to help her release the spine/body encapsulated traumas. Happily, there were signs of evident improvement — a change in gait and a noticeable relaxation with her neck. It was longer and she was able to use and stretch it as she walked. Her hair had begun to return. Overall, Cowgirl had become healthier in appearance and began to show an improved conformation. She had a personality returning and wanted to interact and show affection. I again treated her a few weeks later and then gave her time to heal.

Shortly after, the owner wrote me with great excitement:

"Soooo, Dr. Enos, Cowgirl has just been doing AMAZING! Get ready to sit down! Cowgirl actually nodded her head UP and DOWN like saying "YES," in a VERY pronounced way! She was irritated because I had her in her pen and didn't get her grain yet. She was pawing and then nodded her head UP AND DOWN about five times! She has had hardly ANY cramps at all this week. I have taken her for walks and have also put her in the indoor arena and let her loose, with me walking beside her or behind her and making her walk fast. She got into a trot once, but not since. She is starting to shed all that weird hair and is getting a new coat! She is really doing well this week! She seems really happy when I work with her and take her for walks. I am thinking she really wants to get back to work and a normal life."

After this wonderful report, I talked with the owner a few days later. Then a month later, the owner said, "I know you told me not to get on Cowgirl yet, but she seemed so personally available and doing so very well. I jumped on her bareback and rode her to the barn. She loved it, moved well, and showed no symptoms! Wow! So pleased!"

I continued traveling across the country, as I often do. I hadn't heard from Cowgirl's owner for two or three weeks. It was now almost the first of November, so when I returned from my trip, I wrote the owner to see how everything was going. She finally wrote and told me about her last, big experience with Cowgirl. She wrote:

"I was going to call or text you the other night about Cowgirl but then I got busy and never did. I had gone to get her around 5:00 p.m. She had been in the rain all day and was just soaking wet, so I took her into her stall and dried her off with some towels. At that point I thought I would walk her around the indoor arena. I took her in and just let her loose. Cowgirl immediately DROPPED and ROLLED! She got up and did it about five more times! Then all of a sudden she took off running and bucking! She ran to one side of the arena bucking and then suddenly stopped and just stood there kind of freaked out — like, 'OH CRAP! I don't think I should have done that' — and kind of moved her head around, slowly walked a few feet, then turned, looked at me, and RAN back to me. It was like she was making sure she didn't hurt herself on the first burst of energy. When she got up to me, she was breathing HARD, like she had run 10 miles, although it had been just a short distance. Cowgirl had her ears back and a slightly uncomfortable look in her eyes and I thought, 'Great — she hurt herself.' She stood there about five minutes and again moved her head back and forth and up and down. Her eyes softened, her body relaxed, and she started walking herself on the rail of the arena. She walked around two times and then she ran a few feet, trotted, stopped, and did a quick rollback and turn, as well. I just let her feel herself out and see how she did. But NOT ONE cramp, NOT ONE issue. So I thought, well, I will see how she is tomorrow. I am sure she will be a train wreck. But NO, she has been GREAT!"

Cowgirl continued to develop and eventually returned to being totally sound in mind, brain, nervous system, and all other functions. She is in complete health. She is ridden and being used for all the needs of the owner as well as her needs as a horse. She has more spirit and willingness to live and thrive and is greater than she has ever been. I most sincerely thank the owner for this amazing opportunity to heal her horse back to a new life. I celebrate the owner for not ever giving up and knowing there has to be help, answers, and solutions somewhere. I am honored she found me!

THE FROG, THE CAT, ... AND ME

Jan Ferrari

The Frog

It was early spring when I had been admiring a little, green tree frog that had appeared in the center of a deep-red dahlia that grew in my garden. I thought that it was one of the loveliest things that I had ever seen — green with copper highlights. It stayed on my dahlia plant, moving from one blossom to another as the blooms came and went. I checked on it regularly and it was always there.

One morning I went out on my porch to discover one of these little frogs squashed flat on the deck. I suspected that my dog had accidentally stepped on it. I thought to try to heal it but didn't want to touch it. However, I had been a student of Ramtha's School of Enlightenment (RSE) and had been studying the discipline of Blue Body® healing. In this work we study a discipline using ultraviolet-blue light to heal ourselves and others. As I looked at this little, squashed frog, I remembered Ramtha telling us to take every opportunity to heal and not to be repulsed by anything. I put my hands on the frog and blew a few breaths. My teapot began to whistle at that point, so I headed back into the house.

At RSE we had been trained to see the person or animal as whole and healed, so as my hand reached for the door, I saw in my mind the little frog hopping across the porch. I poured my tea and walked back to the porch. There was the little frog — whole and hopping across the porch. What wonder!

The Cat

Several weeks later, I was driving home from work looking forward to relaxing with a cup of tea on my porch. As I drove down my road I noticed a cat in the middle of the road. It was bleeding. I pulled to the side of the road and walked toward the cat. It had defecated and there was blood coming out of its nose and mouth. It seemed to be struggling to breathe. I sat down next to it and was about to engage the discipline of Consciousness & Energy® (C&E®), that Ramtha taught his students, when a man carrying a rifle walked out of the trees. He said, "Someone has run over my cat and I am going to shoot it."

I remembered the frog, and I said to the man, "I am a student in Ramtha's School of Enlightenment and I am learning how to heal. Would you give me ten minutes with your cat?" The man didn't blink an eye. He just turned and walked back into the trees to his house. I began C&E® and in my mind saw the little black-and-white cat running through the bushes along the road. After a short time I heard a funny sound and opened my eyes. There was the little cat sitting up, purring. The blood was gone. The feces were gone.

Stunned, I scooped the cat into my arms and walked to the man's front door. When he answered, I handed him the cat. He stared at me and said, "You sure fixed that cat!" I remembered Ramtha's advice about what to say to people when we had accomplished. I said to the man, "It was not me who did this. It was the God within me."

... And Me

About four years ago during a summer break from work, I went to my doctor for a regular, annual physical exam. It included an electrocardiogram. At the end of the visit the doctor told me that the test showed some unusual results. It appeared that I might have had a small stroke and that an area of my heart was damaged. She referred me to a cardiologist for further tests. The electrocardiogram was repeated at the cardiology clinic and showed the same ambiguous results. I was scheduled for a third set of tests at a later date. These further tests were conducted but the cardiologist was out of town on vacation after the test. It was several weeks before my follow-up appointment was held to discuss the new test results.

During that waiting time I was not concerned about my health and continued with my regular disciplines, always including radiant health. It never occurred to me that I had a serious problem, so I never worried about it or even thought about it much. When the day came to discuss the test results with the cardiologist, I was sitting in a little room waiting for him to arrive. I was looking at a blank, white wall and saw a blue web sitting there. I heard a voice in my head say, "There is nothing wrong with your heart." Thirty seconds later, the doctor walked in saying, "There is nothing wrong with your heart, and I am so glad that I don't have to prescribe any poisons for you."

I walked out of his office floating on air! How magical is that?

DOGS, A CAT, AND MIRACLES

Elizabeth Axe

In the summer of 2007, my husband Mike and I had two wonderful dog companions called Ursa and Tao. They were brother and sister, and a great combination of Chow and German shepherd. Tao, the male, looked like a large red Chow with a longer nose and Ursa looked more like a collie dog, still sporting plenty of red, silky fur but with a white tummy and socks. They were both beautiful, highly intelligent dogs who got many compliments from passersby on our daily walks. They were ten years old, very fit and healthy, eager to go out for their daily walk, and rabbit chase.

As the summer wore on, we became aware that Ursa was slowing down. She no longer ranged out in front of us flushing out rabbits from the hedgerow, and she seemed to have lost her enjoyment in our walks. There was nothing obviously wrong with her. She ate well and in all other respects seemed fine. So for a while we wondered if she was just slowing down due to her age, or maybe she was bored. However, Tao was not slowing down at all. We tried taking them to different places and, yes, Ursa would perk up briefly but then start lagging behind again. Because she was happy in every other way, we put it down to getting older and took it no further.

In the fall of that year, our oldest cat Shadow, who at fourteen had already used up more than her nine lives, was once again offering us the opportunity to practice Blue Body® healing. This is a discipline Mike and I learned at Ramtha's School of Enlightenment (RSE) and experienced its power to heal many times.

It was a Sunday, and Shadow woke us up in the middle of the night screaming in pain. We rushed downstairs to find her on the floor next to the bed she had just jumped down from. Her back legs were paralyzed. We lifted her gently onto the bed, and

Mike and I lay down on either side of her with our hands on her and started to do the only thing we could think of to help, Blue Body® healing. Within a few minutes she quieted down and dropped off to sleep. Mike and I stayed there all night, each of us with one hand on her, sending her ultraviolet-blue energy as we drifted in and out of a light slumber. She never moved.

In the morning I desperately needed the bathroom but was jammed up against the wall with the cat and Mike between me and relief. I tried to maneuver without disturbing them but Shadow woke up. She got up on all four legs, then jumped off the bed. I was amazed and excited. She had a pee and I noticed blood in her urine, which was not a good sign. She then curled up in a ball in a corner behind the living room chair and went to sleep.

That morning we immediately called the vet but could not get an appointment until 5:30 that evening. Shadow slept all day without moving. Mike and I utilized Consciousness & Energy® (C&E®), another discipline that we learned from Ramtha, to send her more healing, and then went about our day.

When the vet examined her that evening, he found no kidney stones, no bladder infection — nothing — and said she was perfectly healthy. He said he didn't know what had caused the paralysis, but she was fine now. We were very happy. Shadow showed her gratitude by peeing all over his hand.

That night we decided to do the Blue Body® Dance, another discipline of healing learned from Ramtha, just to make sure Shadow was okay. Mike and I put on our blinders and began. In the middle of the dance, Ursa came into my mind and I switched my focus to her. Suddenly my vision was inside her body. It was all blue and I could clearly see her skeleton, especially her backbone. It was an extraordinary experience, as I was completely detached, observing it as if watching a movie. Ursa's body began to animate and the skeleton began to move as if she were running. The spine rose and fell in a smooth, flowing movement. I felt enormous joy for life as she ran and ran until the music ended and I came back into the awareness of my own body.

The next day we went out for our usual walk. Ursa was back to her young self, ranging out front searching for the rabbits she and Tao never caught!

The power of the trained mind is unlimited, and both our animals were the beneficiaries of the disciplines of Ramtha's school that trained Mike's and my mind so well.

CHAPTER 5: HEALING OUR DNA

"The God who I love,
who be indeed the essence of my being,
who be the ongoingness of my being,
be one that in the totality of its existence
permits all to be in spite of all that is
through love."

`– Ramtha

CONFRONTING PREDETERMINED DNA

Juliet Eichorn

I grew up in Australia during the Second World War and as a very young child I can remember having vivid nightmares. My dad was the only one who seemed to understand. He would stay by my bed, hold my hand, and stroke my brow until I was able to sleep again.

After the war ended, my father, a bank manager, helped the local farmers reestablish the Bega (New South Wales) cheese and butter factory so that his bank could redeem the loans the bank had made to the farmers.

I was thirteen years old when a bushfire began threatening these dairy farms. My father joined the firefighters in an endeavor to protect these properties. The fire was so great that the town and the whole Bega valley were immersed in black smoke. I remember that breathing was extremely difficult for us. As I saw the eucalyptus trees exploding in the heat, I became increasingly concerned because my father seemed to be gone a long time. When he did come home, I saw that my father's behavior had radically changed. He was no longer the gentle, loving dad that I knew.

We found out what happened.

He had witnessed the burning to death of two young girls who were my sisters' friends. As the fire crew — my father among them — attempted to save the girls, they were surrounded by the fire with no obvious means of either saving the girls or escaping the fire. Miraculously, just as it seemed there was no hope, the wind suddenly changed and the men found a way to safety. But they had not been able to save the girls, and the girls perished in this terrible way.

From that time on, my father was highly agitated and inconsolable. He seemed indifferent to the family and kept up a constant angry conversation with himself. A doctor was called and he confirmed that my dad had suffered a severe mental breakdown, triggered by his experience in the bushfire.

Dad's brother was called to take him to the nearest hospital three hundred miles away. In his confused mind, he believed that his brother was trying to poison him with the sedation medicine. As this state of paranoia overwhelmed him, my dad suddenly jumped from the moving car and was gone by the time my uncle could safely park. When my uncle and the police found him an hour later, he was dead from a self-inflicted throat wound.

Along with the grief, my usually fun-loving, stable family was about to go through a devastating ripple effect from my father's sudden and violent death. During the next ten years, my brother and two of my sisters began to display aberrant behavior patterns. Their erratic behavior episodes, devastating for each of them and the whole family, eventually led to hospitalization and electroshock treatment when antipsychotic drugs didn't work.

One of those sisters began to display disturbing behavior after the birth of a child. She believed her healthy infant baby had died and, being a nurse, began to prepare him for burial. Fortunately, her husband returned home and was able to restrain her in time to save their son. Sometimes she would regress into physical rigidity and eventually into a catatonic state.

By the time we sought medical help, she was not recognizing our family. She was taken to a mental asylum, and during a six-month internment she received electroshock treatment. These did not help and she had recurrent episodes for the rest of her life.

I then began noticing that my nieces and nephews were beginning to display a more extreme form of psychosis than their parents, and at a much younger age. And so the recessive gene was being passed on.

My own experience with psychosis, which was diagnosed as schizophrenia, was triggered after a stressful divorce, the unusual complexities of which created posttraumatic stress disorder (PTSD).

At first my symptoms manifested as voices in my head that were informative and complimentary. The voices seemed very real — each voice had a different emotion and attitude. Later, I started to experience phases of mania, during which I had difficulty sleeping. When I did sleep, I had terrifying nightmares of torn-apart bodies like the images depicted in the paintings of Hieronymus Bosch, the fifteenth-century Dutch painter.

I believed the voices were coming from outside of me, as Nobel Laureate mathematician John Nash experienced. Eventually the voices repeatedly tried to convince me that the only way out of my dilemma was to commit suicide. At these times I remembered and empathized with my father. I could feel a much broader and deeper connection with his experience. But I still refused to get help because I was afraid that I would be given electroshock treatment like my family members.

Over the years, some of my terrifying experiences included being at the height of irrationality and hypermania, or at the nadir of depression. The most pivotal moment occurred when multiple voices menacingly began shouting obscenities at me. That cacophony left me holding my ears and shouting at the voices to stop. I realized I was not able to control my own mind. I was going mad.

In desperation I went to my sister, who began to visibly shake when she saw my disheveled and anxious state. For a brief moment, I snapped back into rationality and I saw her fear. She was afraid of me. *I was afraid of me!*

Against my will, my family had me committed. In the hospital, I witnessed the more violent patients being dragged off to be given shock treatment and I feared I would be next. I remembered looking into my sister's eyes after her shock treatments and not being able to find her. There was no light or life there. Through sheer will, I was able to manage my behavior enough to avoid my worst fear.

After many months in the hospital, in a moment of clarity one day, I was able to convince the doctors that I wasn't hearing the voices anymore and I was discharged.

I was able to recognize some associated dysfunctional symptoms related to the psychosis. My psychosis expressed itself as hallucinations, nightmares, obsessive behavior, paranoia, depression, hypermania, and delusions of grandeur. I was unable to make coherent decisions, and later I learned that this inability was due to the lack of activity in the frontal and temporal lobes of my brain.

After much introspection, and what now seems to me like divine intervention, I was blessed to be able to haul myself out of my sense of worthlessness. I said to myself, "There must be another answer."

It was then that I came across a video of Ramtha explaining how unresolved attitudes, expressing as a genetic dysfunction, could become more concentrated with every successive lifetime. I heard him say that it was as if the soul is pressing us more urgently each lifetime to resolve our debilitating, genetic imprinting in order to evolve. Then I got it! Until this time I had not been able to cry. Suddenly the dam burst and I sobbed and sobbed throughout the viewing.

That night I had a dream which revealed to me that the voices were not outside of me. Indeed they were the result of unresolved attitudes of my lives past. Within this understanding there came a moment when I could no longer deny my soul's persistence. I felt the most compelling urge to change myself, that I would be free to evolve. Ramtha's teaching had interrupted my own rigid mind track and set in motion a sequence of events that I never could have envisioned.

The question of how I could accomplish this kept pressing me. Ramtha's teaching about unresolved attitudes resonated so deeply within me and gave me such strong inspiration that I knew my questions could be answered if I went to study with this enigmatic being.

Against my family's wishes, I moved to Yelm, Washington, where I could study with Ramtha at Ramtha's School of Enlightenment (RSE). I was still in a very fragile mental state when I arrived. In the early days of the school, the classes were all taught by Ramtha. From him I learned that some of the knowledge he would deliver was about taking responsibility for my attitudes and actions and the way I express and live. I learned and experienced that I am responsible for creating my own reality with my own thoughts, and have always been doing so, albeit unconsciously. With that knowledge, I could begin very consciously to change my thoughts and thus change my life.

So I began my training at RSE. I initially experienced many set-backs, which often exacerbated my symptoms. My nemesis was my personal doubt, but something was always urging me forward. And I never gave up!

I experienced that Ramtha's method of teaching was to deliver knowledge and then have me engage the disciplines he taught to gain personal experience of the knowledge. The next step was to have me consciously engage life, armed with my new knowledge, training, and experience. I saw that it was in this way that I could gain my own wisdom through personal experience of Ramtha's teachings.

The first discipline that I learned was the Consciousness & Energy ® (C&E®) discipline, a powerful tool that helped me to temporarily quiet the destructive voices. That brought some relief. Later, when I learned and correctly practiced the Neighborhood Walk® discipline, the voices were further diminished.

After that, I learned the discipline of self-correction and the voices became even more remote. My mental and emotional balance improved.

I was taught at RSE — and science supports it — that new stem cells are being generated by my brain's hippocampus every day. Stem cells are undifferentiated neurons, which can become mature neural pathways with consistently repeated new thoughts and speech.

I learned that if I stimulate and nourish these stem cells by speaking these new thoughts and words every day, a new neuronet will be formed. And if I persevere, these new neuronets will eventually become hardwired, and the unwanted thoughts and neural pathways will disconnect. I know this is how I was able to erase the voices, which were old, hardwired, neural networks in my brain. I actually rewired my own brain with new pathways of mental stability.

I have learned that sometimes the brain is unable to filter or quiet the unwanted, irrational thoughts from the more rational ones. The resultant "noise" can result in sensory overload, confusion, and irrationality. At these times I actually see a disturbing, undulating screen or veil that affects my thinking and my equilibrium. This is my signal that I could be about to descend over the edge of the abyss into uncontrolled madness!

Despite these challenges, I no longer feel overwhelmed by a mind-altering disorder, having discovered a mind-altering alternative! I have chosen to take responsibility for the way I think, instead of giving my power away to the voices. I have consciously constructed specific narratives and self-fulfilling statements to create new neurological pathways and neuronets. For example:

"I have always had a calm, clear, neurochemically balanced brain."

"I now activate my progenitor, alien DNA into a healthy, youthful, future longevity."

"I always choose the state of agape."

"I have forgiven myself for my dark thoughts and my misdeeds toward others."

I will always be eternally grateful to my dad for his genes that gave me the opportunity and the challenge that inspired my change. I know my soul will no longer have to intensify previous beliefs that reflect the recessive flaws of my DNA. In the broader perspective, my future selves will be the result of a well-intentioned, self-empowered focus, *free from past encumbrances*.

Out of nine of my family members, five developed debilitating mental disorders. I was the only one out of that five that successfully conquered that condition.

CHAPTER 6: HEALING OUR COMMUNITY

"Being Christos is being you.
It is liken to whatever be you.
It is grasping whatever wish you to grasp
and holding onto it.
It is formulating the brilliance of ideas
and seeing them through."

– Ramtha

ZEPHYR

Michelle Horkings-Brigham

Zephyr's regal posture on her last day took my breath away. Her black fur glistened in the sun as she sat poised for action. In retrospect, it's as if she already knew her fate and wanted to spend those few precious hours enjoying her favorite pastime — retrieving rocks tossed into our pond. That same afternoon, without warning, two gunshots rang out as I tugged on stubborn weeds in the garden. Zephyr collapsed moments later in my arms and died from the wound inflicted by our neighbor. He and his family had long been dealers in marijuana before it was legalized in Washington State. Records showed law enforcement had raided their property in 2008. I wondered if he was stoned to be so cruel to shoot Zephyr, our Australian sheepdog/German Shepherd mutt. This neighbor swore to my husband that a distant neighbor had done the deed, yet there was no way that was possible. It took Zephyr just moments to return home and be comforted through our tears as she passed.

Although recreational marijuana production and processing — now legal in Washington State — is providing millions of dollars in additional tax revenue with the noble intent of supporting education at the same time, not all residents with homes close to these facilities are faring well. Some are forced to live with the situation; others are having to move away. And some, like us, have spent thousands of dollars fighting the intrusion through the legal process. Having endured and fought at length against our neighbors' pot activities situated less than one hundred feet from our property line, my husband and I know all of these impacts for a fact.

When can you bulldoze acres of hillside and then grade, level, tier, and berm a large area without permits? Our neighbors did. How many have paid the penalty for such environmental abuse? How can you call your business "Organic Harvest" and then on your property burn piles of toxic materials — household garbage, plastic chairs, Styrofoam, and construction debris? But our neighbors did, repeatedly, even during a burn ban. You can't grow over a thousand marijuana plants without a license or land use permit, with photographic evidence taken from the air, and not be held accountable. At least you would think so. *But they did.*

Through many sleepless nights I wrestled with our dilemma. Every morning, as I walked our forested path creating my day, I contemplated strategies to defeat this Balrog, the formidable monster in *The Lord of the Rings* trilogy. It became more than a personal fight. I realized the landscape could be overrun by large-scale operations if the marijuana ordinance continued to allow production and processing in rural residential and agricultural zones of the county. I have seen such areas in Eastern Washington. During a break at one county marijuana planning meeting I attended in 2017, I heard an official proclaim, "Thurston is growing faster than anywhere. We'll soon be the next 'Pot Silicon Valley!'"

Realizing the implications to our future, we couldn't remain silent victims as this hell broke loose. Despite concerns of retaliation, we prepared our arguments and did our best to inform county and state officials, firmly believing in authority, regulations, and government oversight — until even that we began to doubt. Thus an environmental enigma, neighborhood nightmare, and unbelievable battle began in 2014 that occupied our lives almost daily for nearly four years.

Not long after Initiative 502 passed, legalizing recreational marijuana in Washington State, I experienced a life-threatening tumor that with focused determination I healed in six weeks. However, my doctor had warned me that the cancer could reactivate within the year. "You're healed," he said, "but there is still a window of time when it could all come back." While regaining my strength, I knew that with each passing month my life depended on mastering stress and the sudden panic attacks that would overwhelm my body in the middle of the night — intensified when our neighbors began degrading the land next door to produce and process industrial-scale, commercial marijuana. Theirs wasn't the hippie ideal seemingly lost with the '60s. It was the opportunist's greed, no matter the environmental or neighborhood cost.

Landlocked behind this unpermitted development, we observed beside our driveway three acres of hillside deforested and leveled into two large tiers. Our valley had always been peaceful, a safe space to be immersed in nature where quail, bald eagles, pheasant, deer, trillium, butterflies, and so many exquisite creatures had thrived according to their niche. Even a snowy owl had once fledged its four young in an old snag in this valley. So we were shocked as the rural character of our neighborhood was drastically transformed. How could such behavior be allowed? Why hadn't we been asked, or even notified, about their intentions? Weren't there regulations to prevent this kind of environmental abuse? A few hundred feet below the site lay acres of wetland with a central creek that meanders across Yelm Prairie to the Nisqually River. Wasn't it the role of government to mitigate degradation to the environment and such neighborhood loss?

When one is left alone to walk the edge of personal and family safety because bureaucratic agencies have failed to enact adequate regulations, one's perspective is changed. County Commissioners, the Governor, and our legislative representative would hear about this. I no longer cared. They were going to hear this until someone ultimately responsible for our neighborhood safety would act.

Beginning in early 2015, I visited officials and attended public hearings on county marijuana regulations. Because my neighbor had shot Zephyr, I was afraid of retaliation, so I was cautious in my testimony on the issue. In November 2015 a Thurston County review board, having heard testimony from me and a handful of others regarding the negative impacts we were experiencing, requested an in-depth review and subsequently changed the Interim Marijuana Ordinance to no longer allow large-scale marijuana operations in rural residential or agricultural zones of unincorporated Thurston County. They were hearing the same story repeatedly — large-scale marijuana facilities were causing negative social and environmental impacts to neighboring residents. Such potentially hazardous operations were only suited to commercial or industrial areas.

Yet despite this change to the ordinance, and my efforts in reporting the illicit activity, in July 2016 my husband and I were devastated when I learned from a government aide that Seattle investors had received a first Washington State Liquor and Cannabis Board (WSLCB) license on the next-door property, without a Special Use Permit (ASUP) as required by the county. I was terrified. How was this possible? Fighting drug dealers AND government officials was unfamiliar territory. We didn't know any longer who we could trust or where to turn. Only days before the license was issued, I had spoken for hours with employees at the Thurston County Planning Department and the WSLCB. I had shown them photographs of the hundreds of unregistered marijuana plants being cultivated on our neighbors' property. The shock of this seemingly betrayal of trust by government agencies was beyond my comprehension. I finally realized we were involved in a situation much larger than ourselves, especially when WSLCB records later stated that no one had submitted a complaint prior to the issuance of the marijuana license. In my intense fear at the time, I had left a scribbled, handwritten statement with a WSLCB officer. Therefore, my complaint was disregarded. As a result of that experience, I knew I had to conquer my fear or all would be lost. I also knew we needed an attorney.

Although tempted to hire the legal representative familiar with marijuana issues with whom I had spoken at length about our situation, my husband received a "runner" — a person or experience that brings important information — at Ramtha's School of Enlightenment (RSE) where we are both students. We decided to pursue the runner. The first attorney was later hired by our neighbors to fight our appeal and managed to cleverly stall our legal action. The attorney we chose, well known for his ethical behavior, remained stalwart and guided us brilliantly through the two-year process of appeals and interventions. Had we not chosen this attorney, I believe our neighbors would already be in full operation.

Since 1988 I have been a student of RSE and for almost two decades an employee at the school. Throughout these many years I have observed JZ Knight never back away from a challenge. If it wasn't right, JZ took it on. I knew what we were dealing with wasn't right, and the example I saw in JZ's courage, often under extreme adversity, drove me to take this on. Fighting alone, I also found support in Ramtha's words on a Lofty Thought card displayed on my desk:

"Your trials are according to your strength.
You are never given more than you can handle.
How do you expect to embrace the unknown
if you are full of fear?
If you are fearful of trials, they will pass you by.
But how will you grow?
The greater the trial, the greater you are."

Throughout this adventure, I applied Ramtha's disciplines of focus to build my courage and to turn the situation around. I was determined to find the key to a solution. I knew I had to conquer both my fear and, at times, my intense feelings of hopelessness. I had to empower myself to continue on when the journey seemed nearly impossible. I had to keep going, not understanding why this was happening, or how to find resolve. Many times it seemed we couldn't succeed. One government official wished me luck. "You can't beat this," she told me. I refused to accept that outcome. The greed sweeping our neighborhood was not going to destroy my life, my family, or the harmony with nature we had worked so hard to achieve. Just as I had focused to heal the tumor, I walked through our forest to heal the cancer spreading in our environment. As rats, attracted by our neighbors' garbage and marijuana, infested our property, over and over I declared the fight already won. At RSE events, again and again, I overlaid the reality with a new dream.

In 2016 I decided to rent a small plane. I wanted to document the hundreds of unregistered marijuana plants I knew were hidden in the forest and unpermitted site area on my neighbors' property because I could smell the intense, skunklike odor. Flying at an altitude of 800 feet, Thurston County is magnificent. The undulating hills are still mostly forested and the stalwart presence of snow-covered Mount Rainier enhances the scenic beauty. As the wind blew and further intensified my adventure, I witnessed and photographed the large wound in the landscape and the hundreds of illegal marijuana plants growing behind my garden. "How can we allow this beauty to be destroyed by an industry that doesn't seem to care a whit for the environment?" I wondered. I was heartbroken as I saw my precious land next to the ugly tear in the landscape. Greed! How could such inconsiderate behavior be allowed to prosper? My neighbor once told me that his business would be worth five million dollars. "Why wouldn't I do this?" he asked me. I responded, "If you do, it will consume you," and drove away thinking, "At what cost to the entire community?" It became obvious that if I didn't find a solution, my neighbors would only become more empowered. They had already jeered at me repeatedly. The torment would never cease. I couldn't accept losing everything my husband and I had worked to accomplish on our land for twenty-eight years. I refused to be forced to move and start over.

Following my memorable flight over the county, I engaged in a panoply of activities to defeat this monster. I slept on the porch to observe the clandestine behavior. I noted the rented U-Haul trucks moving out plants immediately before a county inspection. I tried not to arouse the many free-roaming dogs — brought onto their property as guards that would bark at the slightest disturbance — as I photographed the illicit activity. I wore headphones to be able to tolerate the din of industrial greenhouse fans and at least three generators running simultaneously to water the undocumented marijuana and power two households. I visited multiple government agencies: the Washington State Department of Ecology, the Washington State Department of Health, Thurston County Resource Stewardship, the Thurston County Commissioner's office, a State Representative's office, a State Senator's office, the Governor's office, the Olympic Region Clean Air Agency, the Washington State Department of Natural Resources, U.S. Fish and Wildlife, Thurston County Public Health and Social Services, Yelm City Council, local law enforcement, and the Thurston County Sheriff's office. I spoke with a variety of other government appointees, including an assistant to the State Attorney General. I invited a former Thurston County Commissioner to see for herself what we were dealing with and helped her climb a ladder to photograph the unregistered marijuana being produced behind our garden. She apologized to us saying, "We just didn't realize the difference between marijuana and agriculture when the first ordinance was created." After that visit, the Commissioner tried her best to help neighboring residents by increasing the setback to adjacent properties. The increased setback was then negated in the next Interim Marijuana Ordinance.

In the fall of 2016 the Narcotics Task Force became interested in the situation. Detectives quietly observed the marijuana hidden behind my garden. Yet due to confusing regulations at the time, they could not override the power of the WSLCB. Although a raid was scheduled in October, it was suddenly canceled that morning. "If we damage any of the plants," I was informed after waiting hours on my porch for the drama to unfold, "law enforcement could be held liable." Instead, that same day our neighbors were approved a *second* WSLCB license that would allow an additional 30,000 square feet of marijuana plant canopy, *again* without any special use permits from Thurston County, and ignoring the fact that two marijuana operations could *not* be licensed on the property.

There are times in your life when you can hardly believe the reality you have become part of. "How did I create this?" I often asked myself. "Can't officials see the obvious? Doesn't anyone care?" Friends and professionals who visited our property knew this was wrong. It was an obvious social and environmental injustice and they couldn't understand the WSLCB or county's position in allowing the licenses. Staying above the fray and not succumbing to hopelessness are a challenge in any battle. But I resolved that when all doors seem closed, find another. If need be, tear down a wall.

As public hearings continued, I became bolder — and wiser. I had to make this known. When an official stated that the county had only received one complaint regarding zoning in rural residential areas prior to revising an Interim Marijuana Ordinance during the fall of 2016, I decided to raise an army to take them on.

During that September and October, others joined the march and, through letters and public testimony, we stopped the proposed return of marijuana production and processing to rural residential and agricultural zones of unincorporated Thurston County. Few citizens had realized what the zoning of commercial marijuana operations in such areas could mean. Only a brief notice about the hearings appeared in local papers, and newspaper reports never accurately explained the real social or environmental issues involved. I knew from our experience and my research that outside investors would eventually flood the forests and transform the landscape into that potential "Pot Silicon Valley." Instead of the perfume of Douglas fir exhaling in the cool summer evenings, the countryside would reek of skunk, the signature odor of marijuana. So I took out an ad in the *Nisqually Valley News* and tried my best to inform local residents.

Although we won that battle in 2016 and prevented the return of marijuana zoning to rural areas of the county, my fight was not over. Despite misrepresentations of fact, unresolved land use violations, unlawful marijuana cultivation, and expansion way beyond his original application, our neighbor's ASUP to produce commercial marijuana on his property was considered vested by the county because of the earlier ordinance. I continued to protest.

During Ramtha's 2016 Capstone event, the opportunity arose to speak at another public hearing. Snow was in the forecast. Regardless, I created my day and headed to Olympia determined to critique the vesting of marijuana operations in rural areas where inadequate regulations had failed to protect innocent neighborhoods. I spoke for three minutes to the Thurston County Board of Commissioners. The weather remained clear until I arrived back in Yelm. I lay down for a quick nap and awoke to find a blanket of snow covering the RSE campus. That evening Ramtha delivered one of the most profound teachings on courage I had ever heard. Deeply inspired, I made it my business to win "Master Courage," the auctioned apparel placed on the snowperson that students had created in the name-field that night in honor of Ramtha's teaching.

After speaking at that public hearing, and listening to Ramtha's Capstone teaching that same evening, I finally understood that the fear of dying was what I had to conquer. I found my courage when I realized that only by speaking truth without fear of consequence could I defeat my necromancer. My RSE training, my education at the Evergreen State College, and my God were all tools I had used to overcome and strategize throughout the years of challenge. But it was only after letting go of intense fear that my mind was strengthened and I could wield a sword. Ever since that Capstone event, a "Master Courage" substitute, dressed in the auctioned apparel, has remained beside my bed.

Throughout this journey in learning to master my fear, there were times when I could barely move beyond the contempt building inside of me toward my inconsiderate neighbors. I was angry with officials who would not stop the abuse. Everyone seemed to be pointing to everyone else as accountable. Again,

Ramtha's teachings and the disciplines came to my rescue in overcoming the hate that was growing like a poison within me. I began to understand that it was all right not to like what my neighbors were doing, but if I succumbed to hating them, that energy would be mirrored back to me, intensified, and the cancer would return. I worked hard to conquer this destructive emotion because I understood that indulging in it would only result in more pain. Through engaging Ramtha's Consciousness & Energy® discipline, I blew out my anger and replaced it with joy. I busied my mind with a new vision, and I forced myself to get up and do my Neighborhood Walk® during times when all seemed lost and I didn't want to face another day. I knew my hate had been transformed when I attended another public hearing during Ramtha's Reunion event in 2017 and found myself locked outside the courthouse with my neighbor. "Michelle hates me," he said to my friend who was also locked outside. I held up a large photo of his unpermitted pot activities that I had prepared for the hearing and sincerely responded, "I don't hate you. I just don't like what you and your family are doing."

My neighbor spoke before me at that hearing and stated that he was in the review process to produce marijuana "on about an acre of his ten-acre *flower farm,*" (my emphasis added). His words were printed the next day in The Olympian. The only "flower farm" on about three acres that he could be referring to on his property was the unpermitted marijuana. For the first time I broke down in tears in the courtroom. It was just too much. What I hadn't realized was that the County Sheriff had been observing our testimonies. He handed me his card and told me to call.

The week of Ramtha's 2017 Reunion event at RSE was the first time I accomplished all the disciplines of the event: I found my card during Fieldwork®, hit the Analogical Archery® target, and made it to the Void in The Tank® — all the result of an intense focus to overcome my adversity. At the same time I took several trips to Olympia to testify and counter what had been reported in The Olympian.

A short while later, and after a meeting with the Sheriff, small yet significant changes began to occur. My husband and I had spent years, and thousands of dollars, battling this multitiered monster — our neighbors, wealthy outside investors, shadow marijuana production, government regulations, clever attorneys, noise, dogs, traffic, fear, greed, abuse, and power. We refused to give up. The wisdom gained has been worth the heartache, yet I would never wish others a similar experience. This story could become anyone's story. The enigma is what my neighbors were able to hide and get away with through loopholes, misrepresentation of facts, confusing applications, minimal information, lenient policy, a secluded location, and a cartel to move around plants. Until you go through such an experience, it's difficult to fathom that so little government support would be given to private residents or toward a community's well-being. "It's all about the money," as one Commissioner told me.

In July 2017, aware that unpermitted marijuana was still being produced behind my garden, I again decided to rent a small plane. Early that morning, while walking through my forest, I heard the arrival of a semitrailer and quietly observed my neighbor unloading more than a thousand marijuana plants, presumably untracked and unregistered. The synchronicity of having booked a flight that very morning was astounding. I knew we were approaching the eleventh hour. Despite all the evidence of wrongdoing and abuse, the county appeared to be moving toward granting our neighbors' Application for Special Use Permit that would allow them to produce and eventually process industrial-scale, commercial marijuana that could mean ten thousand or more marijuana plants and potentially employ more than a hundred workers, as indicated by the WSLCB. We seemingly had nowhere left to turn. I knew the timing of my flight during this delivery was the miracle I had asked for and hurriedly drove to Olympia airport, excited to capture aerial photos. On arrival, I was told my 8:00 a.m. booking had been canceled. I refused to accept that reality. Determined to find a pilot and a plane, I demanded to speak to the pilot at home. He agreed to change his schedule and we finally lifted off at 10:20 a.m. This time I never saw the stunning landscape. I only had one agenda. The timing could not have been more perfect — a second delivery allowed me to photograph hundreds of untraced, unpermitted marijuana plants being unloaded at my neighbors' property. Those photographs, on a borrowed camera from the Evergreen State College, were immediately sent to our attorney, the Sheriff, and a few days later *The Seattle Times*. It was a turning point in this epic adventure of confronting shadow marijuana production, greed, and deception. A few weeks later the long-awaited raid finally occurred. Shortly after, my husband and I sat beside a creek at Unity, Oregon, and watched the moon pass in front of the sun in total eclipse. The moment was profoundly symbolic of our conquest. We toasted to "out with the old" and to entering a portal of restored peace and harmony at our property.

Following the raid, Thurston County reversed their support of our neighbors' activities in late 2017 and denied the application for special use to produce and process marijuana on the property. Our neighbor appealed. We intervened. The case went before the Hearing Examiner in February 2018 and lasted the whole day. She ruled in our favor. Again our neighbor appealed. On April 4, 2018, the case went before the Thurston County Commissioners. They too ruled to deny our neighbors' Application for Special Use Permit on Friday, April 13. One month later the fight was over. Our neighbors did not appeal the Commissioners' ruling. We had made it to the Void!

On November 8, 2018, during a public hearing to renew the Interim Marijuana Ordinance for the 13th time, I submitted my Master's Thesis, *Cannabis, the Conundrum*, to the county. One month later, on December 11, 2018, the Commissioners approved Thurston County's final marijuana ordinance restricting marijuana production and processing to industrial and commercial areas of the county. That same day, law enforcement served a letter of Cease and Desist to our neighbors due to their continuing disregard for county regulations and production of marijuana on the property. "How was any of this possible?" I have asked myself time and again. It's possible because the WSLCB refuses to acknowledge or take responsibility for the dangers they have invited to residential neighborhoods.

Being jeered at, being denied access by our neighbors to the electrical power grid to be able to install our own security, and being bombarded with endless hours of generators and industrial fans to produce illicit marijuana, drastically shrank the enjoyment of our beautiful property and home. Enduring skunklike odors and toxic fumes permeating the landscape, being observed on cameras and by strangers for years as we moved to and fro, being robbed of the dream for the future of our land, being invaded by rats from the garbage, knowing our family was at risk, and spending more than $70,000 in legal fees, had at times been exhausting. Being dismissed as NIMBYs ("Not-In-My-Backyard") by government representatives had not been easy. I wrote research papers. I enrolled in the Masters of Environmental Studies program at the Evergreen State College. I did what I could to raise public awareness. I formed a nonprofit called N.O.P.E. (Neighbors Opposing Pot Environs). And, most importantly of all, I applied Ramtha's teachings to never give up, because he had taught us a determined mind could accomplish anything. Another of Ramtha's Lofty Thoughts was a constant reminder:

"Miracles always happen
for the faithful,
pure, and knowing."

My doctor informed me a year after my healing that any danger of the tumor recurring had passed. He reminded me that my disease could have been fatal. Others my age had not fared so well, he told me. Despite this long ordeal, I would vote again to legalize marijuana for the sake of all who might benefit from its medicinal comfort. Had my journey with cancer taken a different path, I may have chosen marijuana's solace over other painkilling drugs. Perhaps we would have fared better as a society had marijuana never been banned at all. My hope is that should it become legalized around the United States, the disruption to families and property will diminish because the illegal, shadow activity that has long surrounded this extraordinary plant will be a thing of the past. However, I strongly believe regulations should only allow marijuana production and processing in zones *away* from rural residential and agricultural areas. Perhaps Zephyr, whose name meant gentle breeze, would still be with my family today if that had been the case. Throughout this ordeal, nature has been with me in some of my darkest moments. I know Zephyr lives on. I also know that it is time for the worldwide abuse of power through drugs — where the world is ruled by money and greed — to come to an end. Ethical behavior and concern for the welfare of all must become the new mandate in our business and private affairs if we hope to preserve the pristine, natural environments, and even our very planet, that we all consider our home.[5]

---

[5] This essay is a compilation, in part, from the book: *Cannabis, The Conundrum: Medical Mystery; Environmental Enigma; Neighborhood Nightmare,* by Michelle Horkings-Brigham.

TZEDAKAH

Steve Klein

I was born and reared in the Jewish community, but I have been on a lifelong quest to garner more knowledge. Because of this, I have expanded beyond religious theology. So I say I was born a Jew, but now I say I have become greater than that.

However, one aspect of Judaism that has stayed with me in a very deep way is "tzedakah." The direct translation is "charity," but it means much more. It means giving. It means listening. It means having an ear for others.

Tzedakah is instilled from birth in every Jew everywhere in the world. It is not a tithing, as is practiced in the Christian religion, where a plate is passed around the congregation to give money to support the church. Tzedakah is giving from your inner being — from your soul. Some people give from their soul, some people give out of their pocket, and some people choose not to give at all. But since early childhood, it has always felt right to me to give.

In addition to being brought up in tzedakah, in my ninth-grade civics class I was taught that the United States was created as a constitutional republic. We are called a democracy, but if you look at the actual definition of the word, this country was not founded as a democracy; it was founded as a constitutional republic. And in any constitutional republic we are required, indeed demanded, to participate in our government. Wherever I have lived, I have done just that. I think that is the only way a constitutional republic can stand — if the public is involved. "We the People," the first three words of the Constitution, speak directly to us. And it has been my mandate to be in service to "The People." The elected officials of the city of Yelm have taken an oath of office to uphold the Constitution, not only of the United States but of the Constitution of Washington State.

For me, that is the same mandate that we have as citizens in the process of being governed.

I began my journey of participating in the Yelm, Washington, community when I moved here on September 21, 1988. Before that I worked in the airline industry and was constantly being transferred from city to city. Because I was taught that wherever I live I should be of service to the community, I have always gotten involved. I made my mark in Miami, San Francisco, Houston, New York City, and San Diego by giving to those cities in a number of ways, based on my personal interests.

My first project in Yelm was the Children's School of Excellence — now called The Phoenix Rising School. The Children's School was a private school in Rainier. I was asked to be an adviser to the Board as it was being created. I also gave a significant financial donation to help bring the school into being.

Secondly, I have always been interested in the arts. I think the arts are important, not only for entertainment but also as an avenue for children and adults in the community to come together and express themselves on the stage. The fear of expressing in front of an audience is people's greatest fear besides the fear of death. I have always felt that if you can get the public involved in the arts — get them to confront themselves and their fears — you can build a great community of confident, expressive people. Consequently, I supported Nancy Hillman's work in the Drew Harvey Theater, including making a major monetary donation. The theater began performing plays in Yelm under Nancy's direction and has flourished ever since.

I also took a great interest in the Yelm Library because I love libraries and have spent many hours in them. When I first moved to Yelm, the library had space for 27,000 volumes. It was housed in a very small room of what is now City Hall. Eventually, the library Board knew it needed to expand and I became very involved with them in looking for a new library facility.

When the new facility opened, the library doubled its space to hold 54,000 volumes with extra space available for future expansion of library collections. At that point I took the opportunity to make a proposal to the library Board about creating an area that would house everything that had ever been published by Ramtha's School of Enlightenment (RSE) — all audiotapes, CDs, videotapes, and books.

The proposal was enthusiastically approved, so my wife Yael and I donated $25,000 to purchase the materials. As a result, the Yelm Library came to house the entire RSE-recorded collection that was available at that time. This made the material available not only for RSE students that were arriving from overseas, who didn't have easy access to the materials, but also for the community at large. Now the people of Yelm could gain understanding of the knowledge being taught at the school by reading firsthand what Ramtha was teaching.

In 2003 I was invited by Kristin Blalack, the head librarian, to fill an opening on the Citizens Advisory Committee Library Board. I accepted and was appointed by Mayor Adam Rivas, several years later becoming elected by the Board as their Chair.

When I first came to the Board, the library was five years into a lease on the current library building. I knew the lease would be up in five more years and thought the city needed to begin to plan for a city-owned building. According to the Timberline Regional Library's (TRL) charter, the city must supply the library facility; TRL manages everything else. My wife and I sat down with the TRL Foundation and spoke with them about forming a fundraising group to generate funds for a down payment on a new library facility for Yelm. I spoke with all of the principals — the library director, staff, and Board — and made specific proposals regarding fundraising. Additionally, the Yelm Library Board saw the problems inherent in the current leasing agreement, and because we took our fiduciary responsibility seriously, the Board unanimously agreed to make a presentation to the Yelm City Council regarding the problems with the current lease and about fundraising for another facility.

Despite identifying the problems with the lease and presenting realistic proposals for fundraising, the Mayor and City Council did not show interest.

When I moved to Yelm in September of 1988, it was on the eve of the city of Seattle buying 22,000 acres in the Bald Hills just outside Yelm to use as a toxic sludge dump site. To stop this from happening, JZ Knight, the sole channel of Ramtha the Enlightened One, formed a march on the Capitol in Olympia, along with her friend Linda Evans, also an RSE student. They succeeded. Then there was a push to locate a jail here. That was also defeated due to people being mobilized. After that was an attempt to allow NASCAR to build a racetrack not far from the downtown core of Yelm with all the attendant noise, oil, gasoline groundwater pollution, and horrendous traffic. That was also beaten back by mobilizing citizens who opposed it. I was integrally involved in all these efforts. So healing a community often means stopping harmful things before they become a disease to be healed. That is part of a citizen's mandate.

In the summer of 2004, Ramtha met before an event with the comrades — a group of students chosen by Ramtha to meet with him for certain instruction. He began talking about the Yelm city elections coming up the following year. He said that the comrades should be getting involved in the community whether we lived within the city limits or not. He told us that we had no right to complain about the situations in the city unless we participated. Then he turned and challenged me. He told me I was in a perfect position and should run for mayor. I didn't hesitate. The first thing out of my mouth was, "I will." He then gave me some counsel on how to proceed.

For the next year and a half I went about campaigning for mayor. First, I developed my vision and a detailed platform which addressed the major issues facing the city. Then I brought together a campaign committee that included people from a wide cross-section of the community. They were people who were deeply committed to my vision and what my platform advocated. This was a true highlight of the campaign for me — gathering people together who shared my vision and platform. Yet even more important to me was using my campaign to inform the community on important issues. As I campaigned, I saw that many people deeply appreciated receiving more in-depth information about city issues and having a chance to see proposed solutions.

One enormous issue facing the city was the long lines of traffic clogging the main street of Yelm at rush hours, Fridays, and weekends. For many years the city accepted what is called LOS F — Level of Service F. This was the lowest level of service that a city can accept for streets in a downtown core. I wanted to get the City Council to understand this was not acceptable, that the citizens deserved better than this. I was the first person to introduce the concept of roundabouts in Yelm. Further, I proposed creating one-way streets as thoroughfares through the middle of town to help alleviate the long lines of traffic. These solutions that I had previously offered to the City Council now became part of my platform.

The city also had a water issue; in fact, they still do today. When I was running for mayor, I wanted to bring that important issue to the forefront. I spoke at great length about Smart Growth, a Washington State program wherein growth is managed within the parameters of a city's vision and infrastructure. Despite an in-depth presentation made by my campaign chairman, Bill Hashim, they were not interested in pursuing this concept further. The City Council and Mayor had not heard of Smart Growth based on their responses. They thought their intelligence was being questioned. As I continued to campaign, I met with every City Council member, large business owners, and county officials. I clearly outlined what my platform was and why I was running.

This was my first time running for an office. I wasn't savvy about what it takes to campaign against an entrenched mind-set of those in positions of power. I discovered that there would be a good deal of adversity.

Some of this adversity came about from my purchasing a home within the city limits in order to meet the legal requirements for running for office. There is a law that requires candidates for city office to live within the city limits. In the summer of 2004, my wife Yael and I were living just outside the city limits. So before I announced my candidacy, I went to the Public Disclosure Commission and identified the requirements for running for office, which were that I had to live within the city limits for one year prior to the election and be registered to vote. So we purchased a home within Yelm city limits and I began living there in time to meet the election rules. I lived there four days a week.

During my campaign I was intensely criticized by many sectors of the community because I bought a house to reside in to be able to qualify as a candidate. They said I didn't really live there, even though the majority of every week was spent there. The criticism didn't let up. Prior to the November 2005 election, on a Friday in September, about 4:00 p.m. — and I was at my home in Yelm — a Thurston County Sheriff arrived at my door and served me with a summons. The former police chief of Yelm claimed that I had not registered properly to run for public office. I called my attorney in Seattle and he contacted the former police chief on Monday. It turned out that the chief had misheard something that was said in the County Auditor's office and based the summons on that. But by then there was a newspaper article published about me and the summons. Of course the police chief had to retract his statement to the newspaper and invalidate the summons, but the damage was done.

The mayoral race was over in November of 2005. When the voting results were in, I lost. But I had garnered respect from a lot of people and had learned an enormous amount. I now possessed in-depth experience about accessing public records and what to look for in those documents. And to this day I am proud to have offered the community a choice in the 2005 mayoral race. It was the last time until 2016 that Yelm had a choice in electing a mayor. My opponent, Mayor Ron Harding, had no challengers in the 2009 and 2013 elections and abruptly resigned in the middle of his third term to take a city manager job elsewhere. Interestingly, not long after I lost the 2005 election, Ramtha told my wife and me that the mayor-elect would not finish his mayoral term. This shows Ramtha's long sight into future events. A month after the election, Ramtha made a suggestion to Yael and me to show my platform in the newspaper for the whole community to view. So we took out a two-page centerfold at that time. Recently, I gave my platform document to the newly hired Yelm city administrator. Seeing that platform now, twelve years later, shows how prescient it was.

A few months after the election, in March of 2006, I got a call from a person who was a big supporter of my campaign. He said, "Steve, now that the election is over, there is no news from you. There is no in-depth information, no knowledge, no feedback that the public is getting about important local issues. You have too much knowledge and important information that is not being shared." He said that he was a web designer and suggested that I do a blog. I asked, "What is a blog?" He explained and said, "You don't have to post every day. I will set it up for you." Without any hesitation, I agreed to do it. So at the end of March 2006, the Yelm Community Blog got started. Now the governor, our congressional representative, the Yelm community schools, the county, the city, and the newspapers are all followers of my blog.

To me, the blog is a great tool for healing. Why is it healing? Because I don't put anything on the blog without providing supporting public documents that back up my statements. The public can read everything for themselves, think for themselves, and draw their own conclusions. They can share their opinions with each other by posting comments for everyone to see. To maintain a constitutional republic, the people have to have access to clear, trustworthy information and be able to have a civil dialogue. Only then can the citizens make intelligent choices about their lives and their government. My blog is healing because it puts forth factual knowledge, and this promotes the health of a community as well as a country.

My blog began in March 2006 and has been ongoing to this day. Even when I am on trips away from Yelm, I publish the entries before I leave and they are automatically posted daily and updated. I want to ensure there is a consistent flow of information to the community.

Beyond my blog, one of the actions I took that I am most proud of occurred in the fall of 2008 when the Thurston Highlands development project was being proposed. It was the largest planned development in the state at that time. The proposal was to build 5,000 homes in the Tahoma Terra Thurston Highlands, an area near Yelm High School. It would bring 15,000 to 20,000 people into this town. At that time Yelm was a town of only 4,492 people. This development was going to quadruple the size of the town if it were built.

I started hearing and seeing some things that gave me pause. I went to the state Department of Ecology and they confirmed there might be a water issue. I decided to do extensive background work. So I drove over to the Thurston County Courthouse in Olympia and pulled records on all of those properties. I found that every single property had a lien against it, which meant the properties were in foreclosure.

By the spring of 2009, I took my next step. I went to City Hall to gain access to records under the Freedom of Information Act (FOIA). I ordered all of the billings, all of the payments made, and all of the checks. I ordered every record that related to the Thurston Highlands development. I had to be relentless, but I eventually got the records in hand. Through these records I discovered the property owners were behind on their taxes and fees for over a quarter of a million dollars, all of which was owed to the city of Yelm.

I put everything together in document form. My decision to make this public meant that I had to have an impenetrable defense. I knew there would be huge blowback, so every one of the documents I put together had to be utterly unassailable. In May of 2009 I came out publicly with all of the damaging information. The documents showed that Thurston Highlands had been in default since the previous September and that the developers had left the city of Yelm and their taxpayers holding the bag for over a quarter of a million dollars in unpaid taxes and fees. The documents also showed that the properties all had liens against them and the water rights were in dispute.

Every news media in Puget Sound carried the story — the Nisqually Valley News, The Olympian, the Tacoma News Tribune, Seattle's TV stations: KING-5 (NBC), KOMO-4 (ABC), KIRO-7 (CBS), KCPQ-13 (FOX) — all of them. In light of all the things I had done in my life, I felt this was my proudest moment. I brought public attention to the default of the Thurston Highlands developers and, further, that the city of Yelm had failed in their duty to act in the public's interest by not disclosing this bankruptcy to the community and not placing liens on the properties for over a quarter of a million dollars in unpaid taxes and fees. I brought this out so the people of Yelm could see how their city had betrayed their trust.

I faced a lot of adversity as a result of this exposé. But when you have the public documents and you speak the truth, there is no risk. It is irrefutable. There is only risk to your image. Taking a stand will always lead to polarity, so one must prepare to be disliked by some citizens. When I have the public documents that prove my point and I know it is the right thing to do for the public good, I don't care what people say about me. I accomplished this exposé because I did the work to find out about it. Anybody can do it if they do the work and have the courage.

What is my point then? If you are speaking your truth, you don't have to be afraid. There is really no adversity then. There is only a problem if you have to sacrifice your morals, your backbone, and your principles. I would not do that. If you can see the greater good in having the experience, then you reap the invaluable fruit of your work and courage. The greatest thing is to deliver knowledge to help people make a decision for themselves. In the end, that is the greatest thing you can do for yourself and for the health of a community.

"WHERE TWO OR MORE ARE GATHERED..."

Carolyn Chew

"Look up!" my bird study partner shouted, excitedly, upon her arrival early in the morning. Above us we counted forty-one large, black-colored birds in a "bird herd." We thought maybe they were turkey vultures, but we hadn't seen any in the past three months of our survey time so we were not positive. I said to the birds, "You could be a flock of large ravens or turkey vultures."

A couple of minutes later, two of these birds flew directly over us and circled our heads in close proximity. Wow! They came to visit us! Continuing to look through binoculars and being a novice birder, I said to them out loud, "I still need to see your heads to make a positive identification." At that moment one of the two birds tipped itself in midair to the side and showed us its red head! Yes! Turkey vultures!

Clearly these raptors were picking up on my thoughts and were responding to them. They were helping us and acknowledging us. They seemed to know of our continued intention over the past year and a half to keep the local sheep farm free from a cell tower so that the abundant wildlife in the area, along with its human inhabitants, would continue to thrive.

This local saga began in August of 2015 when engineering schematics were submitted to the Thurston County Resource Stewardship to erect a one-hundred-fifty-foot monopole cell tower. The proposed tower location was within four hundred feet of a Washington Department of Fish and Wildlife (WDFW) designated Priority Habitats and Species (PHS) and within six hundred feet of a one-hundred-ninety-four-acre wet meadow on the Deschutes River floodplain owned by the cities of Olympia, Yelm, and Lacey. These are currently being restored to native wetland habitat as required by the Washington Department of

Ecology to gain water rights approval. In addition, the tower would be located four thousand feet to the west of Lake Lawrence, another WDFW PHS waterfowl concentration area and eight hundred feet north of the Deschutes River.

The above areas contain a lot of wildlife territory. There are priority species habitats, many line-of-sight flight paths for our flying friends, waterways, marshlands, and many beloved trees. Across the field there is also a pristine view of Mount Rainier that is photographed year-round by locals and tourists alike. There are people living at the sheep farm and dozens of others who live across the street. Many of us, including myself, who live in this area have a great love of nature and value both our relatively pristine environment and our health. We each chose to live in a rural neighborhood for various reasons, not the least of which is to be close to trees, clean water, and wildlife for our health, hearts, and sanity. It is well-documented that being constantly exposed to sustained radiating microwave energy can intensely stress lifeforms of all kinds and can have deleterious and even morbid effects. The sheep ranch is not a location for another cell tower.

My friend Alison got wind of this project by noticing a tiny sign on the sheep farm fence post announcing the intention to erect a cell tower. This kind of notification is required by law. At Ramtha's School of Enlightenment (RSE) we both had learned to make focus cards to create reality. I found an image of a smiling sheep with a little piece of hay sticking out of its mouth looking through a gridlike fence. We focused on this card at the proposed cell tower site five mornings a week for two months for the farm to remain free of a cell tower.

We also learned in our school that like minds with like focus is a powerful force. We informed many others in our community of the proximity of the proposed cell tower and of the health ramifications to humans and wildlife. If we all focused on the same sheep symbol, it would enhance the power of our combined mind for an outcome we desired — no cell tower at the sheep farm.

Alison's home is very near the proposed cell tower site, so she was committed to stopping this project. She has had many experiences where she was adversely affected by extreme, directed microwave energies. Although I live a little further away, I already had personal experience with the energies of excess microwave and radio frequencies. They were so debilitating to my health that I was admitted to the hospital with heart palpitations, dangerously high blood pressure, dizziness, and feeling like I was plugged into an electric socket! It was an intense, frightful experience that lasted several days. I could really relate to Alison's concern about living near a tower that radiates nonstop microwave energy.

We birthed a loosely knit, like-minded community called the Deschutes Neighborhood Group (DNG). The majority of the DNG was comprised of students of Ramtha's School of Enlightenment. The remaining balance was made up of concerned, aware citizens. By going door to door and by talking to patrons shopping at two local businesses, a handful of us gathered hundreds of petition signatures to be submitted to Thurston County in protest of the cell tower placement. Eventually, it was the DNG that appealed Thurston County's decision to allow a cell tower. They issued a Determination of Nonsignificance (DNS) that basically said wildlife would not be adversely affected. Verizon attempted to obtain permission from other homeowners in the area to place a tower on private property, but once the homeowners were apprised of the health risks to human life and wildlife, they declined Verizon's offer of monies in exchange for the right to place a cell tower in their backyards.

The DNG core group of seven, composed of very different personalities from all walks of life, worked toward the common goal of stopping the cell tower from being erected on the sheep farm property. It was gratifying to witness how the strengths and talents of each person were critical at different times to our success in accomplishing our goal. What a heartfelt, intelligent, focused group of people! I am grateful to all of them. And, yes, we also had our strong differences and two core people left, but somehow, as differences unfolded, they were resolved because of our common goal. In many instances we set aside our personalities for a greater purpose.

It surprised me that I was even involved in this project because being seen, being a voice, and being "out there in the world" was not my modus operandi. The manner in which I interpreted my life experiences led me to make myself innocuous — sort of invisible — so that, in my fallacious thinking, I could stay out of "harm's way." I am vigilantly defusing this program because it keeps me looking around the corner for something to get me, harm me, or trick me. In a nutshell, this program had been telling me that life was not safe. I was not safe! I believed it and unconsciously lived it.

Going door to door, talking with people I did not know, and asking for their signatures was a stretch for me. In addition, the DNG had meetings about what we were going to do and how we were going to do it, which involved legal language I knew nothing about. However, I did learn and it was even fun. I remembered my Teacher, Ramtha, telling his students that when opportunity presents itself, walk through the door! I heard him say that we were to make known the unknown through experience. I was not an activist. I did not want anyone to confront me or yell at me. I was shy, but I recognized that it was really fear. So walking through the cell tower door gave me many opportunities to experience that which my little personality thought it did not want. Thankfully, what I got instead were runners to reveal my fear and then bring about the courage to change. Until I was challenged to change and grow in rather pointed ways, I did not know of the fear that subconsciously ran me nor did I know who I was deeper inside. What kind of person was I under duress? Who was I? Why was I doing this?

Many times throughout our work on the cell tower, Alison and I experienced being targeted with microwave energies. We felt our brains and bodies overheating — like we were cooking from the inside out. Dr. Matt, a local chiropractor, said that being in water was very helpful in mitigating the effects of microwave energies in the body, so we took long showers and baths. Being a student of Ramtha, Dr. Matt also gave us a statement related to our protection to add to our daily Create Your Day® list.

Alison and I, on one particularly intense day of "being hit" with microwave energies, drove to Olympia to Dr. Matt's clinic. He took one look at us and said, "You are both glowing and not in a good way. Be careful!" I grumbled back, "How?" irritated at being "fried" once again. He said, "I guess that is hard to do in war." It was like a war in many ways.

During my first experiences with seeing black helicopters closeup, I was almost frozen with fear. I questioned the wisdom of my participation in working to stop this cell tower. My life was being threatened and, to say the least, I was not happy about it. Alison did not seem as freaked out as I was by what was happening, so that helped me to moderate my fear. I was grateful that one of us was more neutral.

Many times I wanted to stop my active involvement, yet there was a part of me that knew I needed to walk through this experience. My fear of death was being revealed to me in an obvious manner. So quitting was not really an option because I wanted to confront this, knowing it was an ancient program in my subconscious mind. Finally, after having repeated experiences of helicopters and directed energies, I realized that my fear had brought on these experiences and actually made them more intense. Instead of just observing the presence of the black helicopters, chemicals of fear coursed through my body confirming that they were, indeed, something to be feared. However, over many months' time I began to have less and less fear until eventually I could laugh at it.

Meanwhile, as a community, the DNG's first hurdle was to raise $1,750 needed for filing fees to appeal Thurston County's DNS. Thurston County had agreed with Verizon that the proposed cell tower site would not have a significant environmental impact on wildlife, waterways, or land, which would allow a cell tower to be put up immediately. Verizon's environmental impact study (EIS) basically said there was no wildlife of any concern and no waterways or marshlands — all of which was not factual! There is wildlife of concern and not just "a few songbirds and a couple of deer," as Verizon had portrayed it. Since it is against federal law to protest a cell tower for human health and safety reasons, we focused on demonstrating the negative environmental impact it would have.

I took it upon myself to set up a "GoFundMe" account to receive funds from donors. A friend helped me put together the slideshow that GoFundMe requires, and I recorded dialogue to accompany it. At the time I wished I did not have to use my voice because it has always been difficult for me to have attention drawn to myself. Later, I realized it was the discomfort of feeling unworthy and insecure. After the GoFundMe site was up, I felt more secure in myself and had a feeling of accomplishment. It was a small step in the right direction.

Our attorney's fees for the appeal totaled close to $30,000. Our community participated by contributing monies both directly to the DNG and through the GoFundMe site. I had never had to raise funds before and it was awkward asking for money from people. However, we had donations from people in our community anywhere from $10 to $300, and the DNG group together paid a good portion of the fees. We were grateful for the community support that we garnered both in focus and funds. The rest of the fees were paid off in payments by concerned individuals that live across the street from the proposed cell tower site. We as a community paid for the appeal when no one person had the funds to do it on their own. A common focus brings people together and no one was alone.

It was throughout this almost two-year process that I was required to do more and more. Each time there was something I needed to do, I said, "I can do this," as a way of encouraging myself. All of these experiences were helping me to get out of my self-made, tiny box. I stood up at the Thurston County hearing and talked about the health ramifications of being in close proximity to a 24/7-radiating cell tower while being negatively affected by an individual who had intent to prevent my testimony. He stood within a few feet of me at the podium and I found myself suddenly struck with a fear that came out of nowhere. I was allowed the standard three minutes to speak. Despite this, I used my will and mind to speak to the hearing committee while, inside, my heart was thumping wildly and my throat was tightened. I felt like I was shouting over the fear so my voice would work. After the hearing, a person said to me, "We did not have any trouble hearing you!" Great! I overcame, rather than bolting out of the room.

After twenty-two months of cell tower work, I knew I was more focused and sovereign in myself, because that which used to knock me off center, I was now able to take in stride. I was not nearly so emotional and afraid, and most of the time I was able to calmly observe a situation when there was an accusation or confrontation going on. This was a big change for someone who could barely stand a raised, angry voice as a younger person! Instead, I now reflect on the person's anger that was directed at me: What was my part in creating this drama? What was my responsibility? These were questions we learned to ask ourselves in Ramtha's school to reveal the programs that subconsciously run us and cause us lack, doubt, and insecurity.

The cell tower is representative of a much larger agenda that is being foisted on humanity. As I researched the cell tower industry, the rabbit hole became deeper and deeper. I became aware that cell towers were not really about cell service. I saw that it was about keeping track of each individual via a cell phone. I saw that it was about the militarization and weaponization of cell towers to mind-control humanity.

I discovered that frequencies can be used to incite riots and cause people to fight each other. The constant bombardment of strong microwave energies can wreak havoc on our bodies and brains. Long-term cell phone usage has been shown to be highly related to glioma tumors in the brain, DNA changes, neurodegenerative and cardiovascular diseases, migraines, and allergies. A sick population is easier to control, and sick people spend a lot of money on their way to the grave. The new 5G is microwave frequency on steroids — many times faster and potentially more detrimental than the older versions. It is capable of severely disrupting the human body as well as birds, bees, and all wildlife. With all that I learned about the cell tower industry, it was also a great learning to be constantly exposed to what I thought might harm me and learn to change my knee-jerk reaction of fear by being present in the moment. I found that if I had an even attitude, my experience would be more even and chemical fear in my body was significantly diminished.

It was not that those of us in the DNG were against all cell towers. Cell phones are used by many people who enjoy this technology. It was that we did not want any more towers in our local, rural, wildlife-filled neighborhood. Many of us prefer less impingement by electronic frequencies to enjoy relatively more peace and quiet and freedom in our lives. Nature is healing.

In May of 2016, Thurston County remanded the Determination of Nonsignificance. The DNG won a partial victory. That meant that after reviewing all of the research and information presented by the DNG, Thurston County's Hearing Examiner agreed that a cell tower in the area would have a significant impact on wildlife! It was, however, only a partial victory because the door was left open for Verizon to submit another environmental impact study (EIS) and to reapply for a Special Use Permit to erect a cell tower.

Approximately nine months later, upon receiving the notification that Verizon did indeed decide to do another EIS, the DNG decided to conduct its own community-driven bird study while Verizon was doing theirs — January through April 2017. The Black Hills Audubon Society graciously donated time to give a basic class on bird surveying to our volunteer birders. We made laminated, colored, and bound bird-identification books for our volunteers. For four months, about two dozen of us armed ourselves with binoculars, bird identification books, compasses, and pencil and paper and surveyed every Thursday in three-hour morning- and three-hour evening shifts. We could not have done the bird study without all of the help from our wonderful community volunteers. To this day those volunteers tell me how much they enjoyed doing the survey and really miss, like I do, being with the birds.

To involve and inform the larger community of our citizen scientists' bird study, I set up newspaper interviews with the *Nisqually Valley News* and *The Olympian*. The reporters that came out to interview us and take photos were delighted with our project, and we received really nice coverage. See the news links below:

> "Southeast Thurston County residents and volunteers turn their eyes to the sky to document the birds that move between Lawrence Lake, the Deschutes River, and a small, unnamed pond that is bustling with wildlife," by Tony Overman, *The Olympian*.

> "Bird lovers help residents fight Verizon cell tower in rural Thurston County," by Andy Hobbs, *The Olympian* April 21, 2017.[6]

> "Citizens use bird study to take on Verizon. Group's weekly tracking could be used in effort to stop proposed cell tower," by Andrea Culetto, *Nisqually Valley News*.

At one point during the bird study, I ended up at an observation point by myself for three weeks running because volunteers were not available. To top it off, I saw only a few small birds here and there. I was disgruntled, so sort of ranting at the sky I said, "No birds, no action, no nothing!" Needless to say, I had an attitude! Delightfully though, nature heard my call and put on a show that I will never forget! Out of the blue, instead of a sky devoid of birds, I saw a small flock of seven

---

[6] http://www.theolympian.com/news/local/article146108419.html

crows and eight bald eagles flying together, weaving and soaring around each other a short distance above the tree line. They were sky dancing for me! It was amazing to see. I was so excited! Then, for a finale, two bald eagles circled several times in close proximity over my head. Shortly thereafter, two red-tailed hawks followed suit. I was beside myself with joy! I so loved being connected with the birds! Not only was there community involvement in this project for keeping the sheep farm free of a cell tower, nature in the form of birds was also giving us her vote! From these experiences I know clearly that nature hears our thoughts and that our mind fields can mesh if we allow it. I grew to more deeply love nature and its responsiveness. I just had to take the time to look and listen.

Reflecting upon my experience with the cell tower, I saw that I do indeed create my reality by my own thoughts, beliefs, and programs. Nature, through beautiful birds, taught me that my thoughts are heard and nature responds in kind. It was a gift that I saw so clearly. My internal reality is not created by things external to me — not by people, places, things, times, and events — but by my mind and how I choose to view reality.

With all that is going on in the world in 2018 — the time of this writing — what really became crystal clear to me was how much of my life was spent looking out for the next thing in my environment that was going to somehow harm me. Feeling unsafe was a big part of my life. Because of this belief, I experienced all sorts of challenges throughout my lifetime. I would put out one fire, and then another, and then another. My "box" became larger when I became aware of the global elite's agenda of global depopulation through air and weather manipulation, genetically modified foods, water contamination, medical industrialization, mind-control psy-ops, and on and on. I learned a lot and I saw my belief that life was out to get me. I realized that was what I was focused on. What a victim! Through my disciplines, however, I finally began to realize that I create my reality no matter what is going on around me. The birds showed me my perception of life is what I got and that what I perceive is simply my perceptions through my own colored glasses. Everything "just is." I was the one who ascribed meaning to everything. Do I choose rose-colored, or gray, or purple, or colors I have yet to imagine?

I can say that my heart expanded and I embraced life in a different way after my experiences with the birds. I love their free-flying nature and their beauty of form and song. I am looking to do the same as the birds — to fly free and to dream of realities I have yet to imagine and experience.

It is obvious that, for me, the bird study was the highlight of the saga of the cell tower. I call it a saga because it is still ongoing even though our community, through its efforts and consciousness, has held the tower in abeyance since September of 2015. As expected, Verizon has reapplied for placing the cell tower on the sheep farm. We will continue on this journey. We have all gained in experience and wisdom through this last adventure and will continue to do so.

Life is such a beautiful opportunity for all of us to experience ourselves and to unveil ourselves to greater and deeper unknowns! What an exciting adventure it all is.

"Living by faith includes the call to something greater than cowardly self-preservation."
-    J.R.R. Tolkien

LET NOTHING IN YOU HIDE YOUR LIGHT!

Diane Dondero

After 25 years working as a caregiver, I was ready for change. I wanted to do something different with my life, but nothing presented itself before my last job ended. My life seemed to be going nowhere — no new adventures, no new horizons. In April 2013, I manifested my focused intent of attending a private audience with Ramtha. My conversation with him cleared away my past, righted my ship, and opened the door on an unexpected adventure.

My anger was aroused when I learned about a new proposal for increased penalties on property violations. Title 26 is a grouping of ordinances under one heading purported to simplify the code for public consumption. Applying civil penalties across the board, however, eliminates variation, increases penalties, and streamlines enforcement.

As I dug into this issue, I learned about the United Nations Sustainable Development Plan, known colloquially as UN Agenda 21. I downloaded the 351 pages from the Internet and read them front to back. I learned that one of our Commissioners had signed Thurston County up under the Voluntary Stewardship Program (VSP). After reading this multipage document, I realized the VSP was a vehicle for implementing UN Agenda 21 into local government.

UN Agenda 21 is a plan of action that employs specific guidelines for sustainable growth and development adopted by 180 nations around the globe. In her book *Behind the Green Mask*, Rosa Koire connects this globalization of sustainable development to the *new language* of environmental protection, increased property restrictions, new taxes and fees, increased enforcement, and restructuring countywide policy. All of this is implemented under the guise of managing our "carbon footprint." The goal to concentrate and conserve energy and resource consumption is designed to steer rural residents into city neighborhoods.

Globalization poses grave consequences for Thurston County taxpayers by privatizing the Nisqually and Deschutes River watersheds, forcing new rulings on mineral rights, compelling new septic tank ordinances and fees, adopting egregious measures to protect a gopher, adding $20 to all vehicle registrations. Globalization changes the language of "advise and consent" to "must" and "have to" while intentionally reducing funds for road repair and services to rural areas.

Hoping to awaken rural residents to these ubiquitous activities, I researched and wrote letters to the editor. For the first time, I went door to door with fliers and was humbled by the warm welcome I received. Often shaking in my boots, I willed myself to speak openly about my concerns to the Commissioners at the Tuesday public meetings. I understood their power and I was determined to speak fearlessly to that power. For two years I fought these issues and my anger festered.

In March I walked into my doctor's office with a growth the size of a purple grape on my forearm. When she came into the room, I pointed to the growth. "See that? That's my anger and I want you to cut its head off." She came to my side, gingerly inspected the disease and said, "That's just what we'll do." When the tests came back benign, I had proof it was the end of my anger.

Two Commissioners announced their retirements. At the time, I was taking a multilevel course on the Government with a buddy of mine. The course was known as CSG or Center for Self-Governance. I broached the idea with him of me running for Commissioner in District 1. I later wrote him an email sharing my deeper thoughts:

"I would suspect that getting elected to the Commissioner's office is a far reach. However, in running a campaign a lot of truth can be spoken. I would look at it as an opportunity to expose the county's shenanigans by challenging government secrecy and overreach.

"I am no one special, nor do I have credentials. My best qualification is that I can translate the county's actions into real life effects on common people because I have lived this all my life. The only power I possess is personal, and I have had to fight the good fight to reclaim it. Nothing could happen in this regard without a grass-roots effort. I have not deluded myself in thinking I could win a popularity contest. And I would never deny my participation in Ramtha's school.

"I feel the mood of the nation. It could be the right time. The last election saw a group of people with military backgrounds get elected. Why not someone from the backwoods like me this time? Is it possible? Can we do it? Do we want to? I don't take it lightly. If there is a better person to support, I am all for that too."

In early April, a group of supporters gathered on my patio to talk about my potential run for Thurston County Commissioner in District 1. Important jobs needed to be filled and I hoped to sign up volunteers. My CSG buddy was reluctant to commit when I asked him to be my campaign manager. "Summer is the busiest I am all year. I just don't have the time." Everyone enjoyed the food and wine and said my candidacy was a good idea, but they all left without committing to help with my campaign. I called another potential supporter the next day. She had run for the local legislature twice. After talking for only a few minutes she said to me, "You're not committed. Call me back when you decide," and hung up the phone!

Running for public office is an alone journey. Even with the financial backing to hire a campaign manager, winning is all about selling an image with three talking points! I was passionate about making a difference for rural residents. Not one of the members on the Board of County Commissioners lived rurally. For me, it was a matter of insight and perspective.

The momentum for change sweeping our nation at the time was inspiring. I wanted to be a part of it. If an RSE student was ever going to get elected to public office in Thurston County, surely it would be in 2016, I thought. The flux was there. People were clamoring for change. I also knew most of the people in my community would not be able to vote for me in the primaries because they lived in District 2. However, *they could vote for me* in the general election. I trusted the spirit of the American people and their desire for change. I decided to run on that trust.

I had been a Democrat for years but I could no longer recognize myself in the current platform of the Democratic Party. However, I was aware that Jim Cooper was the District 1 Commissioner's pick as her successor. He would be the only Democrat opponent. The other three candidates were running as Independent Republicans. I decided I would run as an Independent Democrat.

For ten years I suffered from a painful psoriasis on the palms of my hands. I focused on healing them for a long time. Sometimes the sores would go into remission only to crack open again. I was embarrassed to shake hands or put out my palm for change. Within a few days of making the decision to run for District 1 Commissioner, the remarkable happened. My hands completely healed! I knew I was on the right track for my greater learning. I was no longer indecisive!

Healing my hands was humbling, and that humility was exactly what I needed to accept and allow everything, no matter the appearance. The weight of my decision sunk in right away. People around me who were saying, "You should do this!" were now saying, "Oh, sorry, I have got other stuff to do." I hoped the people from CSG would come on board, but most of them chose to support one of the Independent candidates. Actually, the constitutionalists treated me like the Democratic Party did. It was two months into my campaign before anyone invited me for a "meet the candidate" night.

Thurston County hosts a candidate workshop designed to teach the rules of campaigning. When I attended, I discovered having a treasurer was more important than having a campaign manager. My neighbor who is an accountant agreed to volunteer when I asked for her help. She attended the second workshop that was all about the money. My CSG buddy agreed to write my bio for the campaign. He did a great job of turning my "nobody story" into a "somebody candidate" worth voting for. I never did find a campaign manager to recruit.

Thank God for seasoned activists! One woman I knew was politically involved locally and regionally throughout the years of our acquaintance. She literally took me by the hand and led me door to door, despite my shy reluctance. I fell in love with the American people that day. Humble and inviting, the people were warm, sincere, and lovely — interesting and engaging: "Would you like a glass of wine?" "We're having a barbecue. Come out to the patio." "Let's sit on the porch and talk about it." "You look tired. Would you like a glass of water?"

This activist and I went to all the heavily concentrated Democrat neighborhoods first. I had no idea the people living in Olympia, Washington, chose their homes according to their neighbors' political bias. We covered a lot of territory together, but there were so many more neighborhoods! I was told I had to reach 10,000 people if I wanted to win. I was so grateful when an ex-U.S. Postal Service delivery person volunteered. She was well-practiced in going door to door.

One afternoon while campaigning, I stepped off the porch of a house where no one was home. Two middle-aged women came walking up the sidewalk toward me. With leaflets in hand I approached them. They looked up, saw what I was doing, and waved me off. "We don't need any campaign material. We're voting for Diane. And she better do a good job!" I filled with the joy of knowing I was supported without them even knowing I was Diane.

My first donation for $25 came from a fellow RSE student. The second, for $50, arrived anonymously in the mail! And they just kept coming. A few weeks into my campaign, something wonderful happened. I received a donation that was nearly one third of my total budget! Now I could buy campaign banners, signs and brochures, and schedule my launch party. The support I received in dollars was remarkable to me. I had great respect for this money coming from individuals. Gratitude filled my heart and the love fueled my campaign.

Attending meetings with different groups and organizations, listening to people express ideas, was a great learning. I gained knowledge about the broader issues, got freer and more confident in expressing my views, and stronger in my political position. People talked about a new building for the County offices. Should we build downtown in Olympia or in Tumwater? Should we drain Capitol Lake or build out the estuary? Where do I stand on the pocket gopher issue? How about property rights, regulations, the environment, wetlands, growth management, eminent domain, land use, zoning, housing, economic development? What about the budget?

I had a lot to learn, but I saw this as a good thing. County staffers would have a lot of research to do if I were elected — to satisfy my voracious hunger to learn and make sensible decisions. I was candid when challenged. "When it comes to creating the budget, Diane, do you think you have enough experience for that?" "Oh, I'll just hire my opponent here," I said, pointing to one of the Independent candidates. "He'll do that job for me." He smiled at me and nodded because he knew I wasn't entirely joking. *I would have hired him.* In my opinion, he knew more about the Thurston County budget than any of the people on staff.

I turned a previously developed website into my campaign site on the Internet. I set it up to receive donations and used it to blog about my campaign experiences. My family and other volunteers helped with preparing campaign leaflets and distributing signs. My son mounted all five hundred signs on stakes. He was so proud of his mom, he didn't care that he lived in District 2 when he planted twenty signs in high visibility along the bank in front of his house on Vail Road.

The local candidate campaigning for Commissioner in District 2 wasn't too pleased. When I saw him at our next mutual event, he joked halfheartedly with me. "Hey, I see you have some signs up. You know that's not your district; right?" he queried. "It looks really great. But now you need to pick them up and move them along to the next site." He laughed and I smiled, but I knew it wasn't a prank. "Sorry," I said. "That's my son's home." It was the only place on Vail Road where my campaign signs were safe. All others were removed or destroyed.

Tenino was entertaining a corporate venture with an investment group. The plan was to build a local food processing plant as an incentive for area farmers to grow organic vegetables for the Seattle market. The Chamber of Commerce invited me to a luncheon along with the local candidate from District 2. When it was my turn to speak, I told them that the idea was good, but I also challenged them. "If the people of this town still have to buy produce from China when you're done, then you will have not served the very people you plan to extract this wealth from." The candidate from District 2 cranked his neck suddenly and looked at me aghast.

While attending the Democratic Caucus in Yelm as an observer, hoping to meet potential voters and make new contacts, I spontaneously gave my first campaign speech to a crowd of five hundred! The suddenness of the unexpected invite from the District 2 Commissioner made my heart race. Glancing at my talking points printed on my name badge, I started writing. Just before I stepped to the podium, the Commissioner realized I was running in District 1, not District 2, but it was too late.

I was calm, centered, and prepared. I focused on speaking slowly and clearly, and probably a little too seriously for that excited crowd. But I did my best. What I said was heartfelt and it had an impact. I was surprised to receive applause after nearly every statement I made. WOW! I was speaking to District 2 — my community!

The Democratic Convention in Tumwater was like the alien side of the moon by comparison. The people didn't know me when I got up to speak on May Day. All the candidates spoke before me and they all commented about the holiday. I started with a little history. "Did you know May Day is our original Labor Day? It is celebrated as Labor Day all over the world except here in America, its birthplace. It was a political decision to separate our working-class struggles from the rest of the world." I didn't finish that last sentence because the convention chairman started bellowing, "Cut the mic!" The people yelled back, "Let her finish!" I shouted over the discord giving my website information and called for their support before I was intimidated from the podium!

When my activist friend grabbed me again, it was to attend the Gay Pride parade in downtown Olympia. I hadn't even thought about parades. This is why a candidate needs a campaign manager — to get the candidate to events! She and I walked both sides of the street along the parade route speaking to voters. We must have passed out four hundred fliers that day. I had already missed several other parades, but I did make it to the Tumwater parade. That turned out to be a crowning moment in my campaign.

There I was, standing behind the cab in the back of a friend's really nice pickup. Several hay bales were placed around the truck bed for friends to sit on and wave. Blue-and-gold-star, helium-filled balloons floated in the air around me. Long campaign banners draped the full length of the truck bed on both sides. I was campaigning 1950s-style, calling out to the people.

"I am the people's candidate. I am a retired, in-home care provider. I have served Washington families for twenty-five years. And now I am stepping up to take my turn to serve all of you — but only for four years. Then it's your turn," I teased and pointed at someone in the front of the crowd. People laughed and waved. Smiling faces were everywhere.

"We can no longer afford business as usual. Now is not the time for more taxes and fees. We can't build an economy on retiring baby boomers like me — or on service jobs, wounded veterans, students burdened with debt, and the homeless. I want to use the law to roll back misuse of the law and create a renaissance in mom-and-pop shops. I want to see you thrive."

I went on, repeating my message of hope over and again as the parade moved from a block off Trosper Road, down Capitol Way, and on to Israel Road. "I love you. You are my neighbors. You are my friends. You are my family and I want to see you do better. I am the people's candidate." The words kept pouring from my heart, as my chest expanded in joy. I was speaking my truth and it changed me.

At one point, I looked over at my friend sitting on a hay bale. Tears were streaming down his cheek. He looked up at me while wiping his eyes. "It's because I am in the past, I know," he said striving to self-correct. "No. You are here campaigning with me. If what is happening here touches you, it's okay to cry. Now is the time." When the parade was over and we rolled to a stop, the men in the cab shyly admitted that they too had teared up. What we did together that day was heartfelt, and it touched me that the men felt it so deeply.

Tenino held a Candidates Forum. After the questioning was over and folks were wandering around talking, one of the Port Commissioners came up to me. "I saw you at the parade in Tumwater," he said. I brightened to attention. "We don't do it that way anymore," he chided. Remembering the stream of all the candidates gliding by in fancy cars just waving at the crowd like celebrities during the parade, I said, "Well, I guess I do!" He was taken aback and walked away, as I let the criticism roll off like water on a duck's back. What people thought about me may have been vital to getting elected, but its importance no longer mattered to me. It is what it is.

When the primary votes were counted, I did not win the nomination, nor did I feel like I failed. I was 882 votes away from being the nominee. But I knew if I could have run for office in District 2, I would have beaten this margin and had a better chance of getting into the general election. I thought of all the wonderful people I had talked to going door to door — all those people I trusted who wanted to experience real change. People *say* they want change, but I know they are frightened by the unknown. I was the unknown candidate in District 1.

A grass-roots campaign inspires hope. That hope opens a conduit for the flow of passion that energizes community toward change. People get excited about self-governance and, like me, find opportunities to be involved in tangible and meaningful ways. Politics can be an easily corruptible undertaking, but it also provides a meaningful platform to hone and polish the Spirit of God within.

My 1935 edition of Webster's dictionary defines freedom as: "Beloved; to love and be loved." The real fight for freedom starts with loving self. When we can get to the emotional core of our fear, our doubt and shame, and just say it as it is, we now know we can trust ourself to let our inner light shine. That is real freedom. As Ramtha said to me in the private audience, freedom is not what we want. It is what we unburden that gives us freedom.

Throughout my campaign, my capacity for acceptance, allowing, and gratitude shifted with every new experience. Gradually, I redeemed myself to trust again. I hope my frankness inspires others to always trust in themselves, to live fearlessly, and do the unexpected.

Let nothing in you hide your light!

MY DEAL WITH RAMTHA

James Brigham

In October of 1987, I purchased the Ramtha books *Change: The Days to Come* and *Last Waltz of the Tyrants*. The information in those two books rang true to the core of my being. It seemed like something I had always known. Reading these books explained to me why, eight years earlier, I had suddenly short-circuited my budding professional career in Los Angeles and announced that I was moving to the Pacific Northwest within the next six months. To me it was important to never forget that Los Angeles was a desert and that any man-made or natural disaster could cause it to revert to barrenness, making millions of people homeless and confused. And everyone's food was trucked in. What would people do if the trucks couldn't make deliveries?

I knew I had to go to a place where the natural environment was supportive of life, and the Seattle area fit the bill. It had clean water, rain, the climate never got too cold or too hot, and if there were a disaster, I thought, you could always catch salmon and eat blackberries to survive. So when I read Ramtha's words, I knew I had made the right decision and moved to the Seattle area. Eventually I moved to the small town of Yelm, Washington, to be close to where Ramtha's School of Enlightenment (RSE) is located.

After reading these books, I decided I should put up food straightaway. This took a while to figure out, but in February of 1988 I jubilantly packed my first buckets of beans and survival grains. It felt like a celebratory moment. "What should I do?" I thought.

As I had done many times throughout my post-1960s college adventures, I decided to smoke some marijuana to celebrate my new achievement. But after doing so, something felt wrong. I could not put my finger on it, but something seemed incoherent about celebrating putting up food for survival by smoking marijuana. It wasn't until several weeks later, when listening to a Ramtha teaching on audio cassette called *Drug Addiction: The Curse,* that I heard Ramtha speak about marijuana, as he referred to a man in the audience who had joints (marijuana cigarettes) in his pocket. He told the man that marijuana destroys the brain and takes away one's joy. Then Ramtha told him if he quit now, he will heal his brain, but if he ever goes backwards, he will bring it back to him a hundredfold.

"I'll take that deal!" I exclaimed out loud, even though I was home alone. And not knowing whether Ramtha's words extended to me or not, I disposed of all my remaining marijuana and smoking paraphernalia. Suddenly I realized that this was the understanding I was missing several weeks earlier. I was celebrating my survival preparations yet had not felt any joy. In addition, I now recognized I had been losing my joy for years but hadn't been aware of it.

From that point forward, I have never smoked or ingested marijuana again. I was done. However, I still remembered the seeming camaraderie of marijuana smokers and the social support they implicitly gave to each other in the '60s and '70s.

One year later, after returning home to Yelm from an event at Estes Park, Colorado, I was crowded in the arena one morning with a group of students as Ramtha led us through a session of Consciousness and Energy® (C&E®). There were no seat markings or aisles in those days, so everyone crowded as close to the stage as they could get. During one of the songs, while blindfolded, I suddenly felt a hand pressed against the back of my head for several minutes and realized it was Ramtha. He was healing my brain, keeping his word from the audio teaching I had listened to on drug addiction.

Ever since that day, my joy returned.

Because of my previous experience with smoking marijuana, I could never bring myself to tell the authorities that my neighbors were growing marijuana illegally, nor actively oppose them when I thought their operations were not extensive.

My wife, however, was adamant that they needed to be stopped because, unlike me, she could see where things were headed. She had investigated the available public records and understood the deceptions occurring. I kept reassuring her that based on my professional work with land use regulators in numerous counties in the Pacific Northwest, there was no way our neighbors were going to be allowed to continue their deforestation and grading work without permits. "Sooner or later they are going to get red-tagged," I kept telling her, "which means a county order to cease and desist unless the proper permits are obtained before any further work is performed."

Months went by and their operations continued getting larger and larger as the scar on the environment grew greater and greater. In addition, like us, they were off the grid. Their constant operating of four generators to power their two homes and several marijuana facilities filled the air with exhaust fumes and noise. So one day, in an effort to help alleviate the situation, I offered to collaborate with the individual neighbor I was dealing with on extending the power line to both our lots. He agreed, while informing me that he had already put in an application. I immediately called Puget Sound Energy (PSE) and took the necessary steps to file a parallel application for power to be installed to our property. I explained to the power company that this would take place simultaneously with our neighbor, per his and my agreement. However, I was unaware at the time that my neighbor's application was to provide commercial electric power to run six large greenhouses to grow marijuana on an industrial scale and power two or more separate commercial marijuana growing operations.

Several months went by, and when passing him on our shared easement I would occasionally ask where we were on the process of putting in power to our properties. He would always reply that it was several months off but that things were progressing. I heard nothing further until early October 2016 when he excavated a trench along the shared easement from his marijuana growing operations to the connecting transformer located on the adjoining neighbor's property. As I had not heard from PSE for several months, I immediately called my contact and asked about our application and my request that both properties connect concurrently. After some searching, they located my application and said it had a different project manager but they would notify him of my request.

When the PSE project manager called me several days later, we agreed to meet on site and go over the route. When we met, he immediately advised me of my neighbor's plan to install six commercial greenhouses to produce marijuana and that would take all the available power from the line and not leave any excess to power our residence or to our neighbor's other two residences on his property. I was incensed and explained that this was a residential neighborhood and that commercial business operations were not allowed. In connecting to PSE, I had hoped my neighbor would now power his entire property and finally turn off the noise and fumes from his constant running of multiple generators that we had lived with for almost a decade.

PSE's initial response was, "Well, you can run another line up to the street." But the distance of an additional one third of a mile would cost over $30,000 based on an original estimate in 1998. I couldn't believe it. I explained the agreement with my neighbor and my 2015 application submitted to PSE and that this was not in accordance with that agreement. I also understood why my neighbor had not notified me. His plan to exploit the remaining power in the line for his commercial endeavors would leave no power remaining to connect his multiple residences or anyone else's property along the easement.

The PSE representative called the next day and informed me that after consulting with his supervisors, and due to the early date of my application, PSE would make an exception and allow us to hook onto power after all. However, our neighbor's two private residences would still have to be powered by generators. I immediately scrambled to place the required conduit in my neighbor's open ditch. He did not appear to be happy about this.

I informed him I would contribute our fair share of the cost for our agreed-upon residential line and that if PSE was willing to make an exception for my hookup, then they might make an exception to power the two residences on his property as well.

After extending the conduit to our property, I was required to leave the end exposed at my neighbor's open junction box for a period of several weeks prior to his hookup in November 2016. Although I had capped the end of the buried casing for the cable — and requested several times to PSE that they run the wire to our property at the same time they extended the wire to my neighbor's property — they refused to do so until our transformers were in place, which occurred approximately six weeks later. We were finally able to schedule our connection to PSE for the end of January 2017 after investing more than $8,000 in a conduit, two transformers, and a meter box.

In the meantime, I had been intently negotiating with the outside investors from Seattle, who were funding our neighbor's marijuana operations, to determine our fair share in connecting to the power line. The morning of the hookup they finally agreed to my offer but never responded to my subsequent email asking where to send payment. That same morning, the PSE crew informed me that our conduit was blocked somewhere near the junction box inside my neighbor's boundary and they could not install the power cable until the plug was cleared.

The following weekend I determined that the blockage was within five feet of the junction box located just behind the locked entry gate on my neighbor's property. Since I had no equipment, I took a shovel and began digging by hand at the determined blockage point to expose and clear the blocked conduit. Shortly after I started digging, my neighbor showed up and informed me that I was trespassing and would have to leave. When I reminded him that we had made an agreement with his Seattle investors, he said that he and the investors had had a falling out and that any previous agreements made between us were no longer in effect.

227

During this brief conversation I asked him how he could say his marijuana business was organic in his application with the county when there were piles of trash visible everywhere on his property. He informed me that the organic operation was limited to his fenced, production-site area and that anything outside that boundary was not his concern. He also stated, "My lawyer said you haven't helped me so why should I help you?" and informed me that the large driveway ruts we had complained to the county about were entirely due to my wife speeding in her Prius and not caused by his large dump trucks and frequent worker and construction traffic.

I finally realized that greed and exploitation were my neighbor's true intent and that any of my assumptions regarding his basic decency and honor were in error. I also understood that the camaraderie I had always assumed was present among marijuana enthusiasts was a figment of my imagination. My neighbor was intent on exploiting anything and everything to further his financial well-being at the expense of nature, basic regard for others, and anything else that stood in his way. He would manipulate the truth to achieve his goal, as had been revealed through public records. His word could never be counted upon, yet I had been lulled into trusting him. His actions reminded me of the character Worm Tongue in *The Lord of the Rings*.

I knew in that moment that the only honorable thing to do was to stop his unpermitted activity and his intent to destroy our once safe and peaceful neighborhood. That is when I became willing to engage the expense of hiring an attorney and do whatever it took to end this abuse. I now realized that this was war, but I refused to hate him or his deceit because I also realized that this was all he knew, and his mistreatment of nature and others was bound to come back on him, just as hate would be mirrored back to me if I allowed myself to go there.

My wife had been telling me for years not to trust our neighbor's words, but it wasn't until this incident that I realized the devil was at our door and I needed to proactively join her in this fight. I became furious with my complacency. My naive assumptions from my early experience as a consumer of marijuana had caused my blindness to his true intent.

Together with my wife, I attended county public hearings and testified to the Commissioners about my neighbor's intent to rob our property and easement from access to the power grid. I became disillusioned with government officials for allowing my neighbor's unpermitted land use violations to continue to this extent due to seemingly insufficient enforcement. I began to focus my intent on obtaining power, despite my neighbor's obstruction and halting his misplaced enterprise. As an aside, I have worked on several marijuana facilities in my professional career for tribal enterprises. All of them are located in industrial areas which have the infrastructure necessary to support these enterprises, so I am not categorically opposed to marijuana growing operations, except when located in rural residential areas. Such large-scale operations are not appropriate to the prevailing land use or character.

This attempted exploitation of power is an example of the potential abuse to a neighborhood environment motivated purely by financial gain. My neighbor doesn't live on the property, yet we were being forced to tolerate the traffic, noise, odors, and degradation to the environment his two unpermitted marijuana operations had introduced without our consent. To turn this situation around I began to utilize Ramtha's training in C&E®, the Neighborhood Walk®, Fieldwork®, and The Grid®.

My wife arranged a meeting with the Thurston County Sheriff, and he acknowledged that abuses were going on throughout the county with no one willing to tackle the problem. Meanwhile, I continued to hold my focus while pursuing all options available to counter my neighbor's industrial-scale marijuana operations. Several months later my focus was rewarded by a raid on my neighbor's property that revealed hundreds of unregistered marijuana plants being grown, despite the absence of required county Special Land Use permits.

A month after the raid, PSE informed me that a new project manager would be taking our case. When we met her on site to go over the situation, she acknowledged the difficult challenge we had been facing and finally offered an unusual workaround to avoid our neighbor's property and give us access to power.

Although this situation is still going on, the tide has now turned. When I reflect upon this experience, I realize that one should never give up and that no matter how seeming impossible it appears, anything can be changed through focused intent. But you must be a doer. You must act.

I am reminded of a poem by Shel Silverstein that I used to read to my daughter when she was little:

"Listen to the MUSTN'TS, child,
Listen to the DON'TS
Listen to the SHOULDN'TS
The IMPOSSIBLES, the WONT'S
Listen to the NEVER HAVES
Then listen close to me —
Anything can happen, child,
ANYTHING can be."

Like the labyrinth discipline at RSE, life is about experience. We all take the wrong path at times and rely on our personality to get us through. Thankfully, there really IS such a thing as divine intervention. Without the opportunity presented by my Master Teacher, Ramtha, I could easily have taken a path similar to the one my neighbor had chosen to pursue.

I am thankful for the inner voice that allowed me to engage the runner of healing my brain that my Teacher so freely offered, and I am deeply thankful for Ramtha's example of unconditional love taking me along the path to an incredible future.

A TRIBUTE TO A WATER HERO
Sara Foster

Sara Foster is presented in this chapter because of her efforts and willful determination to correct and implement ways to ensure community water rights without exploiting our environment. Here you can read Sara's letter to the editor in 2014 and her subsequent success and tribute as a result of her dedication. She is truly one of "The Radical Few."

Nisqually Valley News
Letter to the Editor
June 10, 2014
By Sara Foster

Dear Editor,
I am concerned regarding my water rights. On June 3, 2009, I paid $50 and filed an appeal to the City of Yelm regarding their statement that the pumping of water out of our aquifer was 'non-significant to the environment'. I was appalled.

At the same time JZ Knight and the Squaxim Indian Tribe also filed an appeal with the City. Knight went forward and pursued this appeal, all the way to the Supreme Court. I was personally grateful for that.

As the years went by and that court case was won, the City of Yelm quietly bought up some water rights and reapplied to DOE (Department of Ecology) for their new water right application. I have been following up on the water case for years.

Once again, I was amazed to find that Ecology had rubber stamped the same old Mitigation Plan that was rescinded years ago and they were about to issue the OK for Yelm to pump enormous amounts of water out of our aquifer.

I again filed an appeal . . . hoping that the Squaxim Tribe or JZ would again file . . . but no one did. Who will stand up for all of the folks with wells? Who will be there to pay for the digging of a deeper well, as Yelm pumps out all that water for new development? That is who I am.

What have I got to gain from this? Simply the right to my water.

What is now known as the 'Foster Decision' states that the Department of Ecology can no longer issue water rights that might deplete river flows. After losing in two lesser courts, I won in the Supreme Court of the State of Washington.

For all of my work throughout this case and my overall water activism, I was awarded the Ralph W. Johnson Water Hero Award at CELP's (Center for Environmental Law and Policy) Celebrate Water event on June 7, 2018.

DIVERSITY IN UNITY

Jayne of The Triad Theater

The Triad Theater was conceived in the quantum field of Ramtha's School of Enlightenment (RSE). After hearing Ramtha live at one of the Blue College events, I made a focus card to open an arts theater in Yelm, Washington. My intention was to unite the community, which seemed to be fractured at the time. I believe that art knows no boundaries and, believing that, I felt that creating an arts hub was the best way to bridge a diverse community.

I had done this same thing in Las Vegas and Boulder City, Nevada, and knew the challenges ahead. I knew the time that would be needed to create and nurture such an endeavor. I knew the money it would take — which I no longer had after selling my real estate. But I marched forward. Ramtha said this town was filled with genius people in the arts and there should be a home for them. He said that Yelm could someday be a mini-Paris. I spoke a little French and I love Paris!

I made the card for Fieldwork® with three mountain peaks and a slash of quantum light behind it. The light represented Mount Rainier — Tahoma. The mountains looked like triangles representing the "triad," a most profound illustration by Ramtha of how an unlimited potential comes down through the levels of a triangle of frequency, until it pops out at the bottom of the base of the triangle as a solid manifestation in the Hertzian field. If ever this theater were to become a reality, it would be a perfect example of this teaching that I loved so much.

If I found my card blindfolded among the hundreds of cards on the fence, I would know this was something I was supposed to do. But since I rarely got my cards during Fieldwork®, I smiled with satisfaction that I would not get it and therefore had a great excuse that I wasn't supposed to take on this project.

You can only imagine the shock I felt when I was pushed right into the fence and the only card on the fence was MY CARD. Instead of screaming in glee as many students do upon finding their card, I was dead silent and then whispered to myself, "Oh, no." I went to the Red Guard who was conducting Fieldwork® and he taped the card to my chest. He was excited for me, but I was elsewhere thinking, "Oh, Lord, what have I done?"

I finally accepted that this was a sign from my inner being or from divine interference due to the shove I had felt going into that fence, so I accepted that the game was on.

So in April of 2011, I contacted the landlord of the theater building. Of course the theater had to be named *The Triad*. The rest is history.

The first information that appeared about The Triad in the local newspaper came as a letter to the editor from someone who said, "This person" — that being me — "is NOT welcomed in our community! We don't need her kind!"

I wasn't sure what "kind" that was. Was I the wrong color? The wrong sex? Wrong religion? Too "out there"? Was it my political beliefs? My musical taste? Or was it that I wear dark fingernail polish, cowboy boots, and long skirts? Since my list of "not belonging" was endless, it seemed futile to try to understand anything except that the person writing the letter was afraid of me. The town that was reading this was getting their first taste of what it's like to have Jayne in their midst.

I saw the only way to resolve the fears and issues of local people accepting the flux of diverse people moving into Yelm was with an arts theater to unite everyone under the name of "Diversity in Unity." So I made sure the theater represented most styles of art to include everyone's taste. I felt this would create buy-in.

I brought in conventional speakers and unconventional ones, lecturing on a plethora of topics that expanded the mind. The Triad Theater hosted Captain Randy Cramer on the Mars Mission; the Mount Rainier Superintendent Randy King; Chief

McCloud of the Nisqually Tribe; Coast to Coast guest Andrew Basiago; the time jumper, Laura Eisenhower, granddaughter to President Dwight D. Eisenhower; medical doctors on fasting, longevity, and nutrition; James Gilliland from the ECETI Ranch; Michael Tellinger; JZ Knight; and Dr. Miceal Ledwith, all best-selling authors and internationally acclaimed speakers.

I booked a variety of musical groups to expose the people to the different styles and moods of music to expand their hearts. Some of the performers included Claudia Simpson-Jones, who brought in the Olympia Chamber Orchestra; a show featuring local teen rock-and-roll bands; the Great Antics Blues Band; and a Joe Bongiorno piano concert.

The Triad was home to SRO Productions, the best, live theatrical production company on the West Coast. They put on jaw-dropping performances like *Spamalot, Arsenic and Old Lace,* and *Young Frankenstein.* I also organized art gallery shows, poetry nights, and town hall meetings — discussing major issues from both political party perspectives on everything from cell towers to gophers living in the Yelm Prairie. Nancy Hillman, a famous director of live theater, taught classes to young people and would perform every season with a fantastic children's show production. Sonia Pena, operatic soprano and voice teacher, would do biannual musical recitals with her students that were wonderful.

The Triad took part in the local Prairie Days parade two times a year, providing the color and fun needed in a parade that was mostly business advertisements.

We held a Kumbh Mela festival; an alternative medicine health fair; a racecar exhibit; an animal communicator/healer; and old-fashioned, musical Valentine's Day shows with local singers performing favorite crooner love songs of the '40s, '50s, and '60s. I thought I had covered it all.

But I realized that we still had a long way to go before the town would accept the theater as a genuine part of their community.

The Triad Theater needed a fundraiser to help us financially and the town needed something to help bring in people to our community for business. We already knew from our UFO lectures at the theater — as Frank, our techno-genius, reminded us — that the first flying saucers were reported while on a mission close to Mount Rainier. I had heard over and over that Thurston County, especially Yelm, was teased by the other counties as the "woo-woo" place because of the strong counterculture that had settled in the vicinity of Yelm to be close to Ramtha's School of Enlightenment (RSE). RSE brought people from all walks of life and all parts of the world who got to experience the lovely prairie town and who decided to settle here. A lot of people who wanted to get away from cities in California migrated up North to this area, as well as many people who were very environmentally aware. Mix that with the local homesteaders, farmers, and ranchers, and you have quite a mélange!

There were those living in the town who thought UFOs were a joke. There were those that knew that UFOs were a reality. Others were curious and just wanted to dip their toe into the information. And I knew many people liked a good, summer outdoor concert where they could hear the top bands of the Pacific Northwest, eat great food, and drink "Alien Beer." So for me to come up with the idea of a UFO Fest was a no-brainer! It was going to be a festival for all. It would be a festival that allowed Yelm to make fun of its reputation with a light heart and at the same time provide important cutting-edge information from the space industry and highlight cosmic disclosure issues. This Fest would be a cultural and scientific exposé with a spoonful of sugar via the live bands, delicious food, and vendors galore.

Our first UFO Festival brought in 4,000 people! James Gilliland, the internationally known UFO pioneer from the ECETI Ranch here in Washington State, kicked off the festival. We had a varied collection of bands from blues to the Fabulous Downey Brothers, Altai, Robert Corl doing Opera to the Stars,

Clinton Dogger, and many more. There were documentaries on crop circles and secret space programs. All of this was topped off with the Anarchestra Marching Band!

Of course a genius is merely one who has crazy, invincible thoughts and can hold focus long enough for others to jump on board to help manifest the dream. I would not have made the Fest happen without the help of my sisters, my awesome volunteers, the *Nisqually Valley News,* Yelm Prairie Park Inc., Steve Craig, Steve Klein's Yelm City blog, Bettye's Newsletter, the City of Yelm, the Chamber of Commerce, and so many others who spread the word in their own special way. We did this all with no wages, no salaries, and very little financial support other than my own money and some assistance from a few friends and family. There were a lot of glitches, stumbling blocks, and fumbles, but if you wait for perfection, you often miss the boat of opportunity. We grabbed the moment and made it happen! The first annual Yelm UFO Fest brought together a grand "Diversity in Unity." Success!

THE REAL MESSAGE OF JESUS

Míċeál Ledwith

The number of really great Sages and Teachers known to us from the entire history of humanity can be counted on the fingers of one hand. There may well be some others who were wise enough to remain hidden, but be that as it may, the grand total of such magnificent beings is very small. However wildly different were the historical circumstances and times in which they appeared, they all had one thing in common: the belief that a great power existed within the human being, and that our supreme purpose while here on this Earth is not to work out our salvation but to learn how to bring that power under our conscious control. When that is accomplished, it gives us the ability to create whatever reality we wish to experience. Those few great Teachers all called that process by different titles that fundamentally all meant the same thing. Jesus summed it up in a memorable utterance that has the dubious distinction of being one of the best known, yet most misunderstood and ignored, of all his teachings: "You are all Gods."

Within a few years we will be commemorating the two-thousandth anniversary of when Jesus launched his mission. There could not be a better time in which to decide to sort out for ourselves what his mission was really about and to start to distance ourselves decisively from the massive distortions of his teachings that for now, close to two millennia, have been masquerading as the real thing. The price for embracing those colossal distortions has been tragically high. The most obvious result has been a disempowerment on a truly grand scale which has placed us further away than ever from being able to control that enormous inner power which all the great Teachers through the ages have told us we can achieve. The scale is different, but the condition of the mind-set of humanity is very much the same today as that which confronted Jesus at the start of his ministry.

For most of a century now, research of the highest quality has drawn back much of the veils of ignorance in which the story of our past has been shrouded for so long. For instance, there is a consensus among scholars that the first five books of what Christians call the Old Testament — and in Judaism, the Pentateuch or Torah — were not "written" in the normal sense of the word but rather emerged over the course of several centuries. It is further pointed out that many of its central themes — such as the great Flood that destroyed the world, and Noah's Ark — are borrowed from much older Mesopotamian sources, such as the Enuma Elish, the Epic of Atra-Hasis, and the Epic of Gilgamesh. If we are alert when reading the first chapter of Genesis, we will notice that it states the creation of mankind was apparently done twice, as the two creation accounts in Genesis 1:27 and Genesis 2:7 show. This is an obvious indication that Genesis was copying earlier accounts of the creation from more than one source and did not feel at liberty to drop one of them for the sake of a unified and coherent narrative.

Needless to say, many scholars with vested interests to defend have spent rivers of ink proving only to their own satisfaction that no such dependency of Genesis on Mesopotamian epics exists.

In these ancient Mesopotamian sources, we are told that the early members of our race were in contact with advanced humanoid beings whom they regarded as "Gods." But those advanced humanoids apparently had far more than their fair share of very typical human failings. They were prone to take offense quickly at real or imagined faults and become angry or jealous and anxious to exact retribution from those who "sinned" by transgressing their edicts. These ancient interactions from the earliest levels of the history of our race have percolated very effectively in our DNA down through history. They still profoundly color the ways in which we think about God or anything to do with the transcendent. Needless to say, if such convictions are deeply held, it makes it extremely difficult for any humans to put into practice what those enlightened Teachers of long ago told us about directing a great power lying within. Instead we take it for granted that humans are by nature fallible, sinful, powerless, and unworthy. We always envisage humans as dependent on currying favor with an "outside" God to gain anything they might wish to have, and that is the end of the story. Fortunately, according to the great Sages and Teachers, including Jesus especially, that is far indeed from the truth of the situation.

But the message of Jesus teaches us that normally we are profoundly conflicted when we try to manifest reality in the way the ancient Sages all taught. Until those inner conflicts are resolved, we are going nowhere in this adventure. To put the matter in contemporary terms, we must ensure that all levels of our conscious and subconscious minds are in harmony and completely aligned when we attempt to create reality out of the quantum field. In practice, those levels of mind within us are normally seriously at odds with one another and consequently manifest only varying forms of chaos — to which the course of human history tragically bears eloquent witness.

Experts tell us that the electromagnetic field of the heart brain, which operates largely in the subconscious, is about sixty times greater in amplitude than the electromagnetic field of the brain in the skull. If I fervently imagine in my conscious cranial brain that I am financially abundant, but at the same time have an acceptance in my subconscious mind of the heart brain that I am a misfortunate, penniless victim, then it is not rocket science to figure out what will manifest for me out of the quantum field because of the quality of the information in the electromagnetic radiation I have sent out to it.

Another helpful illustration is to observe what happens when we pray. Jesus taught us that when we pray, what is required to create the manifestation we desire is to profoundly accept *at all levels of our being, conscious and subconscious, that* whatever we pray for is already ours. If we can manage to do that, then it shall be so. That might seem to us to be wishful thinking and self-deception, but it is in fact the magical key to manifestation.

However, when we pray, we normally do the direct opposite of what Jesus taught. We pray for help to pass examinations, to ensure the success of business ventures, or to get a good job. We beg, we beseech, we implore a human-style God, or some venerated saintly figure in the beyond, to help us get *what we do not have*. So we have reversed the message of Jesus on prayer. Instead of firmly believing it is already so, with all our conscious and subconscious levels of mind lined up in harmony and transmitting a unified and harmonious energy into the quantum field, we emphatically proclaim in prayer our unworthiness, confusion, but, above all, the lack of what we are trying to manifest. We are proclaiming to the quantum field that we do not have what we are asking for, so it is hardly surprising that the quantum field will deliver to me what I have put before it if I am praying like this — the lack of what it is I desire. Tragically, in the most profound sense, prayer is always "answered," because the quantum field is responding in kind to those convictions we hold at the deepest level. In short, such "prayer," as most believers practice, only makes matters worse. To put it bluntly, prayer normally creates trouble for us out of the quantum field, for it usually centers on what we lack and engenders a process within us that generates more of the same lack. For those reasons, prayer as we normally practice it should be avoided like the plague.

Jesus did not come here to die for our sins, but neither did he come here to teach us how to create out of the quantum field. Every human being who has ever lived and possessed a mind has been doing that since our race began — and normally with extremely unhappy results because we haven't cleaned house first. What Jesus came to teach us was how to harmonize the multiple levels of mindful intent within us and thus be successful in creating desirable things from the quantum field. He had refined that skill himself to the level where he could heal the sick, feed multitudes out of nothing, control nature, and raise the dead.

As we contemplate these issues more and more, it should dawn on us that Jesus did not do "miracles" in the normal sense in which we understand that term. Normally, miracles are understood as events that can't be accounted for by the laws of nature and are generally thought to be due to some form of divine intervention from on high. However, we now begin to see that they are the result of a powerful and unified focus from all levels of mind in the human person. The interaction of such a force with the quantum field produces what was actually focused on by the general intent of all levels of our minds. In short, miracles are not outside the laws of nature. They are due to the functioning of a level of nature which we know about but do not yet fully understand. That is a matter of major importance.

It is easy to realize at this point that we can never function as the "Gods" Jesus said we were until we have dug up and harmonized all levels of intent within us. In this way we will avoid creating havoc for ourselves from the quantum field, which is what we normally do.

This area is one of the dimensions within us that stands most in need of healing at the deepest level, for it is in this dimension that the roots of all our suffering, woes, lacks, unhappiness, sickness, and diseases come. To realize what is really at the root of our everyday trials, tribulations, and lacks can be a very sobering and humiliating experience. None of us welcomes the dawning realization that we have for millennia very effectively been our own jailers and the creators of our all-too-doom-laden condition.

For a long time, the center of the Christian tradition's focus has been on the last three days of the ministry of Jesus. As a result, the picture of Jesus that has emerged to dominate the Christian tradition for two thousand years is a very false one. Those final three days were followed the next day by the sacrifice of the Paschal Lamb on the altar of the temple. It was the central ceremony of the major Jewish spring festival,

Passover. The blood of the lamb flowing down the stone of the altar symbolized the washing away of our sins in the sight of God. So it was that Jesus became seen as the quintessential Passover Lamb, who died to wipe away our sins and thus save us from the vengeance of an angry God.

This tradition of Jesus as our Suffering Savior soon came to dominate the history of Christianity. That is a tragedy, for the mission of Jesus had nothing at all to do with any such thing. The type of images that have come to dominate popular piety, such as the Crowning with Thorns, the Scourging at the Pillar, the Hill of Calvary, and even wearing the Cross as a symbol of his suffering, have nothing at all to do with the real mission and message of Jesus. It is not that these images don't have much to do with what Jesus was about; they have nothing at all to do with it.

In short, if Jesus had vanished immediately after his Last Supper with the Disciples on Holy Thursday evening, nothing at all in his message would have been damaged nor would anything have been left incomplete. The so-called "Passion" of Jesus had, and has, nothing whatsoever to do with his mission and message. Yet in the minds of so many today, the Passion is seen as the very heart and core of what Jesus and his mission were all about. When will we come to realize that cherishing such a belief system not only does not honor Jesus, it demeans him?

What is even worse, in a sense, is that it also demeans humanity by exalting the consciousness of guilt, sinfulness, and suffering and repentance as spiritual ideals.

By no stretch of the imagination did Jesus come here to suffer and die for our sins. He came with the singular purpose of teaching us how to create desirable realities out of the quantum field. That requires a major amount of cleaning out of our psyche and an enormous amount of healing at the very deepest level. We know from modern research how powerfully subconscious programs can disempower us. Seeing Jesus as our Suffering Savior is not a dutiful religious attitude. It is an atheistic belief masquerading under a pious guise, for how could a being who desired the sacrifice of his own innocent son ever claim to be the God described in the New Testament? The notion of the Suffering Savior has generated one of the most malevolent and disempowering subconscious programs which we all carry.

Nowadays we are well aware of how difficult and sensitive a matter it is to attempt to remove the influence of a subconscious program. It is pointless to try to kick it out, for that only strengthens it, since the first duty of any subconscious program is to ensure its own survival. But there is a technique that will do it. It is to that difficult process that my recent book, *Saving Jesus*, is dedicated. We have to investigate thoroughly the roots from which those subconscious programs grew originally and then calmly assess if they were justified by the facts or not. That involves examining the roots of all we know about the mission of Jesus and his teachings, evaluating if the popular conceptions about him do him justice, or do they rather turn his message completely on its head? It is a slow and difficult task, and unfortunately not for dilettantes! For the deprogramming to work, we must do this personally, for it won't suffice for someone else to tell us that it is so. We must see the evidence firsthand for the subconscious program to start to loosen its grip.

Concluding Reflections

Science, more than religion, has always shaped the ways in which we think about God, and self-proclaimed agnostics and atheists are often revolting against the Church's caricature of God rather than against belief in some form of Supreme Being. Our awareness of the world today is at the opposite pole to the one described by Isaac Newton, often called the father of modern science. It was a predictable, observable world, for which Galileo, Copernicus, and Kepler had laid the foundations. It began to dominate thought in Europe around the year 1600 and eventually it completely replaced the old medieval mind-set of an unknowable and mysterious universe, presided over by a mysterious and remote God. This mysterious God, for reasons best known to himself, placed mankind, the pinnacle of his creation, on this planet Earth, which was the center of the entire universe and around which all other heavenly bodies were located. So obviously humans were at the center of everything as well. Even as late as 1920, the world's top astronomers still believed the Milky Way galaxy was the entire universe. In a companion belief, many religious groups still believe the human race is unique in the cosmos. Evidence from the Hubble telescope today tends to suggest there may be two hundred billion galaxies in the universe.

The scientific views that dominate the time and place where we are born automatically infect our ideas about God and where everything else exists in relation to him. These fundamental ideas function like programs, and as someone once commented, they act like wallpaper that we don't even notice until it begins to peel.

The new views that began to permeate around 1600 certainly began to peel away a lot of cherished belief systems and replaced the old mysterious God and his equally mysterious universe with what can probably be best described as an extremely complex Clockwork Universe, presided over by the Great Clockmaker himself. This is the mind-set that created the distant and remote God so familiar to most adults from childhood and which we have always assumed is the real thing.

But if the prevailing scientific views of an era tend to produce their own flavor of God, surely it is time— well over a century since the advent of quantum physics — to move beyond the Clockwork God and his Clockwork Universe in which so many still seem to be entrapped for security, like flies in a honey pot.

Newton studied an observable world, made up of phenomena that were predictable. Quantum physics revealed to us that the world in which we live is unseen and devoid of predictability and that everything, not just humans, exists in a fully conscious whole. Obviously, this has profound consequences for our understanding of the Source of all that exists and the role for which we were placed here, which is poles apart from the traditional world of the Clockwork God.

At the start of this section, I noted that the few great sages that have appeared in very diverse times and places on this Earth could be counted on the fingers of one hand, but they all agreed on one thing: There is an enormous power within the human person and our purpose on this Earth to bring it under conscious control. That will enable us to create the reality that we wish to experience instead of endlessly producing from the quantum field what mirrors our own sense of victimization, worthlessness, and fear. Jesus expressed it by stating, "You are all Gods," and taught us we can create reality only by already being it in our minds, in our hearts, and in our souls. When we have accomplished that profoundly altered state, then the process of the physical manifestation starts to occur. The advice of Jesus to say we are already what we desire is not hypocrisy. What we are stating is that at an energy level above the physical, we already are or have what it is we desire to manifest, which is a prerequisite for the physical manifestation of our focus to appear.

When we "pray," on the other hand, normally we contradict the teaching of Jesus, for in praying we are stating that we do not have the reality we wish for, and we are asking God or Jesus to give it to us. We should hardly be surprised when such prayer makes matters worse instead of better, but we can hardly deny that it was our own expressed wish to the quantum field that created more of the same. We are indeed Gods, not in the Clockwork Universe and its God that we inherited from Galileo and Newton but rather in the energetic state of the quantum field, which shows a radically changed paradigm for thinking of God and our role as cocreators in this physical universe. This is what Ramtha has taught us since the beginning of his mission. Other great traditions in the remote past have noted these and related facts in similar terms and have called attaining the mastery of this process in its fulfilled state "ascension."

This remarkable book contains accounts of diverse ways in which a remarkable group has put into practice what they have learned in well over four decades from a Teacher without compare. Not alone were we taught how to manifest in the kind of world described by quantum physics but we were also taught knowledge and understandings that utterly date and transcend that science, which gave us perspectives that in the normal course of human events were still centuries in our future.

Ramtha taught for one hundred and twenty days at the time of his ascension. Buddha taught for a few years, and Jesus taught for two years and nine months before he had yet become an ascended Master. But we in Ramtha's school, for well over forty years now, consistently have had the incalculable privilege of the teachings and practical guidance of an ascended Master. If we look back over the entire quarter million years of the human race's history, it is glaringly obvious that the members of this school have been placed in a more advantageous position to achieve what those few great sages taught than any other individuals anywhere throughout the entire course of human history.

CHAPTER 7: HEALING OUR WORLD

"Who be friend?
All be.
Comradeship is that what we are,
we are to all peoples,
all Gods.
And in finding ourself,
truly we do not find it with the closest intimates
of our being but in all beings."

– Ramtha

HEALING WITH LIGHT – THE BLU ROOMS
Rory Sagner Photography © 2018
rory-sagner.pixels.com

"I REFUSE TO LET ANYTHING BLIND ME TO POSSIBILITY."

JZ Knight

If someone were to ask me, "What is the Blu Room?", I would first smile and then give them a big hug and say, "Have I got a great future technology for you!"

The Blu Room consists of panels of lights that are comprised of the ultraviolet (UV) light spectrum. These are long-canister, medical lights set in a room that is all stainless steel and mirrored — top, bottom, all around — in an octagon precisely according to the mathematics of Nicola Tesla. These light frequencies reach exclusively to the center of the room, the mysterious number 9. So the room is an octagon and everything in it is precisely stationed. All points come to the center of the room, which I call the "atmosphere," and it is 9.

As they first walk in, this uniquely constructed room with the panels of blue lights gives the individual a feeling like they are in a UFO. They feel out-of-worldly. They then lie down on a table that is centered in the room, which means they are lying in the center of this mind, or what I like to refer to as the "atmosphere." And it is in the atmosphere of the Blu Room where all of the divine geometry comes together with this UV reflexive light. And ultraviolet blue (UVB) is not the burning light or skin cancer light. It is the narrowest band of the ultraviolet spectrum. It is the great healer.

The longest session that I recommend is nine minutes. If you start your sessions with three minutes' exposure, you are getting about 10,000 international units of oral Vitamin D. If you go six minutes, you are getting 20,000. If you go nine minutes, you are getting 30,000 units. And after the lights are turned off, you have up to twenty minutes to just relax in this atmosphere. Vitamin D is really rather mysterious because its greatest value is not in taking a pill; it is exposure of our skin to sunlight. It is rather like a plant needing sunshine in order to create photosynthesis and needing sugars to allow it to have energy and thrive.

We could use that same explanation for the Blu Room. The Blu Room is bathing you in the vitality of UVB light. As you are lying down in an octagon, this light is now being taken into your skin and the photosynthesis effect is literally creating the mysterious vitamin that we all call Vitamin D. I like to call it the "God Hormone." And like the plant that does not have enough sunlight, does not have great vitality and is weak, a human being that does not have a great amount of sunlight does not have a great amount of vitality. All of the body's systems are weakened by this lack. In the Blu Room, the Vitamin D levels you are getting are so high that the levels create a cascading effect that alters absolutely everything about the human body to robustly begin a sensation of vitality. It really turns your body on. It turns your DNA on. It turns your cells on. And so it is from this cascade effect that clients and patients around the world have reported that the Blu Room has affected just about every malady that they came in with.

We can never say that the Blu Room cures anything, but we can say that you get Vitamin D from it and that Vitamin D in this atmosphere creates another wonderful side effect. I like to call it "stasis" — stasis. It is neither good nor bad. It is neither positive nor negative. There is a calming that happens to every individual that lies on that bed in the center of that atmosphere. It brings peace to a person's mind. And if a person's mind is brought to peace, the body is receiving the nutrient value that it needs to restore the person's whole body back to vitality. It does not matter what their pain is. People report every time a deeper relaxation, an inner healing, and a tremendous relief from pain. There is a sense of improved health and well-being. Focus deepens. There is increased creativity and greater self-awareness. And just one session will last a person two to three days. All of this is as a result of three main factors in the creation of this phenomenal room: its geometry, its stasis of mind, and its delivery of Vitamin D.

As of the first of July, 2018, our reports show we have had over 80,000 visits worldwide, and these people have reported that marvelous things have happened to them as a result of coming to a Blu Room. There are 26 operational Blu Room locations with 10 additional locations under construction. Countries with Blu Room services include Argentina, Austria, Canada, Colombia, Ecuador, Germany, Italy, Japan, Mexico, Switzerland, Taiwan, and U.S.A. Three locations are for private use or employee-only programs and the remaining locations are open to the public in either clinical or spa/wellness settings. They are going up everywhere.

It is interesting to note that doctors are putting Blu Rooms in clinics in Central and South America, and there is one doctor in Germany that has built a Blu Room as part of her medical clinic. There are also Blu Rooms in spa settings where people come in for spa treatments and now come in for their Blu Room treatments as well. So Blu Rooms have crossed over from being a valuable part of a medical clinic into a spa setting where there is also great value for those clients. In addition, there are people that own a Blu Room as a stand-alone business and end up having to build another Blu Room because the overflow is so great. Our biggest problem is not the lack of business but that people who acquire their license and build a Blu Room find themselves in need of another Blu Room. Currently, there is no Blu Room in England, but England needs it, Reykjavik needs it, Norway and Sweden need it. Especially when going into the darker winter months, the people in these countries greatly need the deliverance of a Blu Room. At this time the closest place to England where people can access a Blu Room is Germany. We have two in Germany, four in Switzerland, and two in Austria.

One of the beautiful things about the movie *What the Bleep Do We Know?* was that it showed clearly that body health is deeply tied to mental and emotional health. That is a main element of the film. I am not a doctor. I would not pretend to be a doctor. I am a scientist, although I don't have any degrees on the wall. What I am is a very intelligent woman. I have powerfully engaged my work with Ramtha for forty years and I understand that we are, first, spiritual beings — that we are mind/soul, that we are actually Spirit/soul producing mind through the brain. I came to understand that attitude was everything. I saw that people could get healed with phenomenal knowledge just because it changed their attitude.

I always wanted to be this invisible healer. I would have my costume — my little old nurse's outfit, the red curly wig and spectacles — and I would go in and heal people quietly in hospitals. That was my dream forever. No notoriety. I just wanted to go and heal people — help old people. My god, I love old people. And I especially love veterans and little children who are suffering. I just want to heal them. But in order to heal someone, they have to accept you. If they don't accept you, they won't accept anything that you have to say. So that was the reason that I wanted anonymity. They would not know who I was — they would just think I was an important person who came in.

I am a big fan of Einstein. I am a big fan of all the quantum physicists, and I am a huge, huge fan of Nikola Tesla. If you put all those minds together, I suppose that would be the neighborhood where I live in my mind, because these were individuals that had no boundaries, no political correctness, no limit to their visions and imaginations. These great minds always thought there must be something better. Their only thought was how to solve a problem. If they did not like the way something was currently being done, then they would be inspired to take that to their mind and visualize how they would solve the issue. So their minds were a natural laboratory of design and architecture and creativity. They naturally thought out of the box. Einstein was lousy at mathematics but when he deeply pondered how he could solve a problem, he learned mathematics to explain his visions. He called them his "thought experiments." Tesla did the same. All the great quantum physicists did the same. So we really found the ground of being and perhaps the first idea of Zero Point Energy through the minds of these quantum physicists. These are the minds I enjoy engaging.

When I channel Ramtha, I leave my body. Many times in these conscious journeys I would end up in this one particularly beautiful place. The moment I became aware I was there, it was like, "I have always been here." It was very odd, very strange. Everything in this realm was blue, yet I never saw the source of this blue light. There were no light bulbs. There was no blue sun. The atmosphere was blue, and there were tinctures of violet and purple and sometimes pink on the edge. The atmosphere was just beautiful. And then there were these beings — these beautiful, blue beings — and I could only assume that I was one of them. Many years later I came to realize that the light source of this beautiful blue was actually emanating from the beings, that in fact they created the atmosphere. So about three years ago, I thought seriously about this: How could I bring that knowledge, that level of consciousness, to this realm to bring stasis to an ordinary human being like myself? What could I create to allow this blue frequency to penetrate and help people? As a thought experiment in my mind, I was trying to make a machine to do this. Finally, I met the perfect doctor who became a best friend and is now my partner in the Blu Room.

Dr. Matthew Martinez is a brilliant, out-of-the-box, really beloved man. I shared this story about the blue realm atmosphere one day at lunch with him and told him what I wanted to do. This was the first time I ever spoke about it to anyone. And all he did was look at me and say, "Let's do it!" And I said, "Well, you understand it has to be built in an octagon. The table has to be laid perfectly and these lights have to be a certain way. There is an atmosphere, and I cannot tell you exactly how in divine geometry it is created but it is an octagon and it goes along with Tesla's concept of the number 9." And again he just looked at me and said, "Let's build it."

So on May 15, 2015, we opened our first Blu Room in Olympia, Washington, at his now famous clinic. At the start, we saw the Blu Room as a test. And then Dr. Matt started calling me. He would say, "Oh, my God, JZ, I mean, just the fact that my patients are relieved of pain! I had a man, a former doctor, with spinal stenosis that had been frozen for over ten years. He actually began moving around and dancing after several treatments." So that is when I went to people and said, "Come and try out this fabulous machine." I called it the Shiva machine. It is the Blue God machine. And I personally built a Blu Room on the RSE campus where I treat people with serious medical conditions for very little cost. They bring their medical records to be reviewed by our supervising physician who then follows their progress in their regular treatment plan with the addition of Blu Room sessions. I call it Mercy Blu.

The Blu Rooms started doing these marvelous things because people saw that it had no side effects except wellness. It had no side effects except "No pain." It had no side effects except "I feel better." It had no side effects but "My skin got clear." It had no side effects except "I feel joy and I have been depressed for so long," and on and on and on. When you are in the Blu Room, it is very, very hard to be negative and doubtful. When you lie in a Blu Room, you are in a unique atmosphere. As long as your mind is at stasis, your consciousness is raised, and what affects the mind affects the body. Everything changes. That is why it is a most beautiful, wonderful machine.

Eventually people started wanting to open Blu Rooms. The process is that the person buys the license and they are then given the details about how to construct it, how to advertise, and so on. Everything they need comes to them from our central office.

I had two brothers that fought in World War II, two brothers that fought in the Korean War, and one brother who fought in the Pacific. So I have a sense of what war does to people. One of the issues with veterans is that they become very ardent in pretending they are fine. They never talk about their experiences. And they would never admit that they were frightened. They would never admit that they cried. They would never admit that it was horrific, that the things that they saw and endured blew their minds. I felt that they were victims of great, grievous wars in hostile environments. And I always felt the injuries to their mind were the most underreported disease in the world.

A person can reach a stasis of the mind in a Blu Room, and if we could hold them there for a while and they could relax, it would allow time for rejuvenation and healing. So when I asked people if they were vets experiencing PTSD (posttraumatic stress disorder), nobody would tell me that they were a vet or that they ever had PTSD. Coming from the culture of the macho male military, they felt it was a terrible thing to have to admit. So what I did was reach out to all of the people in the county where I live asking who might know of veterans who had PTSD. I told these people that I wanted to provide a sixty-day free service for veterans. I wanted to study PTSD. It would not be an FDA-approved study, but I wanted to find out if the Mercy machine from that beautiful blue place could help the most injured people that I know.

As a result of reaching out, we got eleven veterans who were interested, both male and female, active and inactive. A few, when they found out it was an offer from JZ Knight, were reluctant to come — maybe because I am a famous person, maybe because they were ashamed, maybe because of whatever. But we finally got all eleven there. In my communications with them I assured them, "This is private. I won't even meet you. Just come. You don't have to spend any money. We are not going to poke you with needles. We just want you to experience this. If you choose to sign up for this, you will come see us three times a week for sixty days. We will ask you to bring your medical records. They will be kept entirely confidential. I want to know if this is going to help you, because if anybody needs to be helped, my God, it is you."

So they came. It was such a marvelous turnout that eventually some of them were bringing their family members with them to have a Blu Room session. And the really shy and frightened ones, they came, and it changed them. Little by little they got used to the environment and realized everything was going to be all right, that they were safe. We finished that study and nine out of the eleven people went through the entire process. All had a marvelous recovery. We had two particular veterans who wanted to save their last months' sessions so they could come to the Blu Room in winter when there is less sunshine here in the Pacific Northwest and Vitamin D serum levels are at the lowest. So we did that.

I want everybody to go get the veterans and get them into a Blu Room. I will pay for it. Just get them there. I wish that I could hire buses to pick up all of the vets and bring them to Blu Rooms to have their treatment done because it would bring hope to them — to their minds and to their souls — in ways that they had never experienced before.

Most people's daily lives consist of about ten percent encouragement — the rest of it is routine. And if you have emotional issues, you are as ill as anyone who has cuts or bruises or any physical disease. When you have emotional pain, when you have terrible memories, you cannot forgive those memories because they are still sitting in your frontal lobe. They are always with you. These memories then undermine the ten percent of positive reinforcement that normal people get throughout the day. So there is a huge load of unhappiness in our lives that we endeavor to cover up by acting normal and having a routine, because it feels as long as we have a routine in our life, there is some meaning in our life. But acting normal and having routines don't begin to scratch the surface of the wounds people carry or offer a way to heal them. The Blu Room is a remarkable machine that helps, and it is here for anybody and everybody.

We are 99.9 percent body/mind-consciousness consumers. We are less than one percent spiritual consumers. If only that were reversed! It is important to understand that if we were consumers of our spiritual self as much as we are for our bodies, we would be a million years advanced in our society — absolutely. We are spiritual beings, we have a Holy Spirit, we have a soul, and that is the body electric. When that blue light comes into the body, everything turns on. Every part of your DNA vibrates with very minute movements of frequency. And wherever you find frequency, you find intelligence, you find encoding, you find information. It is called consciousness and energy. So even in our tiniest, little cells, our tiniest molecules of DNA, there are little vibrations. There is a humming going on of the different coding elements of our body. And when we as Spirits and souls are reincarnated, the body is the garment we wear in order to make known the unknown on this planet. So our beautiful, beautiful bodies are sometimes hurt. If we get a brain injury we are really in trouble, because that would be like somebody injuring your computer and you are not able to do certain things because your computer is broken. If the brain is broken, we have to grow new neurons. We have to bypass the injury and go to other areas of the brain in order to make healing happen. We are not impaired as spiritual beings. But if our bodies become impaired, or if our brain is impaired, then we have difficulty making the circuitry to get all the vibrating units in the body to be healed.

The Blu Room's beautiful atmosphere is the product of the geometry of all those lights and the mirrored infinity. It all comes together in a special place in that room. And when you lie down in that place, that special light is vibrating its signature self — its ultraviolet-blue frequency — throughout the entire body and into the brain. What happens then is that we get this peace. And the moment we get this peace, the pain goes away. The moment we get this peace, depression goes away. So I am following a directive of my own experiences and building a room accessible to everyone that not only can heal us but also bring us back to what we are. If you don't believe in the spiritual — if you are an atheist — know that the Blu Room just makes you feel terrific. It makes you feel joyful and happy. Your body feels better. Your mind feels better. Everything feels better. It is not specific to religion. God is not insecure. You don't have to say you are a believer. You don't have to say anything. The Blu

Room does it in a true, magical, but very elementary way, which helps people heal themselves.

I received my U.S. patent in March of 2018, No. 9,919,162, and I have patent applications in all the other countries. I am so proud of my invention. I am so proud of all the people around the world who bought the license and built them. And I am proud of all the patients and clients — from spas to doctors' offices — who have reported such phenomenal results. Now my dream of being the curly, red-headed girl, wearing glasses and those white stockings — being the nurse who was running around anonymously trying to heal people in the hospital — I am getting there. I want to get there. I want to be that.

People can find out about the Blu Rooms around the world at the website www.Bluroom.com. And I am telling you, if there is a Blu Room where our veterans are living, go out and bring them to the room and treat them. I promise you I will pay for it if you do.

As time goes on, we will have more findings. Just know that what is happening is pretty awesome. This is a revolution in medicine. I ascribe to the concept that future medicine is frequency medicine. It is not a pill. It is not a drink. It is frequency. And we can cure everything with that.

But, again, I am not a doctor and I am not the FDA and I am not a scientist. But I am free of all the encumbrances.

---

[7]This story is based on a transcription of a phone interview with Rob Simone on the *Rob Simone Talk Show*, Los Angeles, California.

THE BLU ROOM — A PLACE OF MYSTERY

Nancy Breidenthal

In early summer of 2010, I found my dog Bushido online and I immediately fell in love with him. Bushi, as I usually called him, was of a primitive breed, a Shiba Inu. This breed is only partially domesticated and as a result it is very intuitive. At this time I was very ill and generally in bed. I was suffering from catastrophic pancreatic failure brought about by complications from my gallbladder surgery in December 2009. I thought the companionship of a dog would be a comfort and that giving love to a fellow entity would help take my mind off my health situation. However, soon after Bushi arrived, I realized he was a dog who was terrified of human contact. I was in the process of returning him when he developed parvo, a serious and often fatal viral infection for dogs. Bushi's illness caused me to miss the window to return him. So we stayed together.

From the start it was clear to me Bushi had never had nurturing, human companionship, and was traumatized because of his early treatment. Yet somehow he bonded with me on his first night, perhaps because I was the first one to offer him kindness. From that moment on, he saw himself as my dog. The Shiba Inu breed, as is true of other primitive Japanese breeds, is very loyal, and so it proved to be.

After he recovered from his parvo, I took Bushi to a gifted healer to find out how to work with such a damaged animal. She confirmed his devastating early life in a puppy mill and even questioned whether he was blind, perhaps from early trauma.

This description is to explain the great evolutionary changes both Bushi and I made over the six years we were together. I was very sick, and I like to think of the next six years as both of us walking parallel, but separate, evolutionary paths. Both of us made many breakthroughs. Just a few days before Bushi died, it seemed to me he had become a most confident, self-aware, and self-satisfied animal. He was now a kind, loving, and mischievous being. The night before he was killed, I watched him walk in front of me and remarked to a friend what an enlightened being Bushi was. Never had he seemed so whole. During this same six-year period, I had also greatly healed and had become a joyful, loving, and compassionate being myself. We had reached a peak of growth together. I had never experienced such an ongoing, intimate, and evolutionary experience with an animal before.

The Blu Room experience I would like to write about occurred on July 6, 2016. It was the culmination of a series of events which began with a breakthrough the morning of June 27, as I was engaging in the discipline of the Neighborhood Walk®, which I learned as a student of Ramtha's School of Enlightenment (RSE). As I was saying a certain phrase, I broke through a barrier within myself that opened to my awareness an attitude that was totally unrecognized by me before this moment. I immediately knew something important had changed. A significant shift had occurred within my consciousness.

On June 29, this breakthrough was acknowledged by a doctor in Rainier, Washington, that I have been working with for a number of years. During that visit, a point of grief that had caused emotional stagnation was identified and I was given instructions on how to resolve this issue.

Two days later, early in the morning of July 1, a wild animal, probably a bear, killed my beloved dog Bushido. For the next four days I was in a state of shock and grief.

On the morning of July 5, I said, "Enough! I wish to return to a state of love and joy!" By that afternoon I was able to laugh and to be filled once again with love, gratitude, and joy.

I had my culminating experience during a Blu Room session the following day.

I went into the Blu Room and lay down. I was so grateful for the love and joy I felt. I thought of Bushi and thanked him for all he had given me. I sent out a stream of love and joy as I thought of him.

All of a sudden, the love and joy I sent out came back to me and entered into my fourth seal, the heart area. I learned from Ramtha that this is the center of love and healing. The extraordinary part of the experience was that the love and joy came back not as a feeling but as a *particle*. Love and joy had become *tangible*. Love and joy were things that could be experienced in the same way as a touch, or a table. After that I became aware of a feeling of floating in the room.

My Blu Room visit lasted twenty minutes, so this was a very immediate experience. I have experienced a great amount of love and joy but never had they become "particle-ized," tangible objects. I did not know it was possible to experience such a thing until the Blu Room.

I have long thought about this experience and believe the geometry and the position of the mirrors on the walls, floor, and ceiling changed the nature of my entire being so that I was able to experience the feeling of love and joy as a tangible thing.

Bushi is always with me, as I hold him close within me. I believe my experience in the Blu Room has helped me heal the devastating loss of his death and has also given me the gift of the return of the love and joy given to another. I also believe I have found a path away from loss and grief to the wisdom of love as eternal.

THE BEAUTIFUL BLU ROOM EXPERIENCE

Captain Cynthia Williams-Patnoe

My journey to the Blu Room began with a traumatic brain injury which happened in September of 2013. I was now out of the army, living in Olympia, Washington, and working as a Youth Sports Director at Joint Base Lewis-McCord. I had just gotten back into riding my bicycle — something I always enjoyed — and planned a twenty-five-mile ride for an upcoming weekend. My husband Don had recently bought me an expensive $100 helmet and told me I needed to wear it. Well, when I grew up, you did not wear helmets on bicycles, but I did reluctantly put it on. There were several times on that ride where I wanted to take it off because it was a real nuisance. But I am utterly grateful that my husband encouraged me to wear it every time I went riding, especially on that day.

The accident occurred as I was making my last turn toward home. I was in the left lane waiting to make a left turn. The light turned green and as I made the turn, a vehicle — a large pickup truck going northbound — did not see me and ran right into me.

I have no memory of the accident actually happening. I was transported to St. Peter Hospital in Olympia. I was in and out of consciousness for twenty-four hours and barely remember being transported or being in the emergency department. When I regained consciousness, I found myself in the intensive care unit. Although my brain sustained major injury, the helmet that Don asked me to wear saved my life.

In attempting to recover, I did a lot of physical therapy and a lot of speech therapy. In addition, I had to develop systems that would help me function in my life. For example, without help I could not remember what I had to do during a day. So I started using sticky notes for everything. I would use sticky notes at work, at home, and in the car. My therapists encouraged me to use ICal, my iPhone, and iPad to stay on track with what I needed to accomplish that day. It took a lot of effort, but it did allow me to continue to work.

Eventually I began seeing a therapist regarding both my posttraumatic stress disorder (PTSD) and my traumatic brain injury. My therapist is a longtime student at Ramtha's School of Enlightenment (RSE) and is a very wise woman. She recommended that I try the Blu Room. Because I was a veteran, she told me I was being invited to use it at no cost. She made it clear that it was totally up to me to decide whether to go or not.

After thinking it over, I started going to the Blu Room in Olympia in July of 2016. The first thing I noticed was that it was very peaceful and very therapeutic. It was a time for twenty minutes of meditating and having this beautiful, blue warmth surround me. I went there twenty times very consistently — sometimes four times a week. And since those initial visits, I have continued to use the Blu Room a few times a month.

To my surprise, during the initial sessions I had several visions. I am not the kind of person that has visions. I always thought normal people do not have visions. Maybe mystical people have them but never normal people. Yet I had them in the Blu Room.

One set of visions that occurred in the Blu Room was that I was able to see into my brain. I was completely astounded at this. I was able to see where healing was most needed, which was the back, right quarter of my brain. This is not a medical term but that is where I cracked my head. So I meditated on that area. As I meditated, I got to watch my brain piece itself together. It amazed me! Another set of visions was seeing many eyes looking at me that I was able to look back at without having any fear. In another vision, doves were flying towards me. Every one of the visions I had in the Blu Room was a very, very beautiful experience.

But the thing that really excited me was that my short-term memory was coming back. For example, I began to recall that the next day I would have two appointments and I knew what time they were without having to look at my calendar. Realizing that I remembered appointments without looking at my calendar is completely remarkable for me! I am so very grateful to be able to have that kind of recall.

I believe what made my sessions in the Blu Room so amazing was that I was willing to go and that I was willing to be open to the healing that the Blu Room brings. I was raised in the Catholic Church. I do not attend the Ramtha's School of Enlightenment. I am not a person who listens to JZ Knight when she is channeling Ramtha. I am not the kind of person that ever explored spiritual experiences other than just a normal, meditative prayer. That is just not a path that I ever followed. So for me, going to the Blu Room and being open-minded and willing to be healed was a big step.

---

[8]Captain Cynthia Williams-Patnoe is a former U.S. Army Helicopter Test Pilot. This story is based on a transcription of a phone interview with Rob Simone on the *Rob Simone Talk Show*, Los Angeles, California.

A WONDERFUL DREAM COMES TRUE

Austin Hess

I graduated from high school in 2011 in Olympia, Washington. I was in the best shape of my life. But not long after graduation, my friends moved away to college and I found myself alone. Maybe it was because of the loneliness that, despite my body being in really good, physical condition, rheumatoid arthritis struck me.

At the time I did not know it was rheumatoid arthritis, and neither did the doctors. For a full year I experienced massive amounts of pain and major swelling in both knees and ankles. The only treatments doctors were able to offer were to remove the fluid in my knees and give me narcotics for the pain. For an entire year I was on bed rest. I could not get a job. I could not put my feet on the ground. And I was on heavy doses of pain medication. After undergoing multiple blood tests and multiple MRIs, the marker for rheumatoid arthritis was found. The doctors confirmed that I had juvenile chronic rheumatoid arthritis and I was prescribed Enbrel, in addition to narcotic pain medications.

This treatment helped quite a bit. But another problem arose. I realized I was heavily addicted to Percocet. I asked my doctor to prescribe a lower dose of the medication, which he did, but it was still strong enough to get me addicted — about 200 to 300 milligrams of opiates a day. I eventually realized my addiction was out of control. I was really messed up.

For a long time I did not address the problem of my addiction because I was in so much pain. But despite the pain, as time went on I decided I wanted to change my life. My girlfriend was pregnant and this was a big motivation to become sober. As my desire to change grew stronger, we decided to move to Los Angeles to make a new life. Eventually that was where our son was born. I stopped taking the heavy doses of

Percocet and got sober. Although still in pain, the California sunshine was helping my joints and I began to feel a little bit happier. Over time, I did well financially and produced enough income to take care of my family. Nevertheless, being a father with responsibilities, while being a recovering addict, was difficult. Having pain and dealing with a child — it was difficult. And there was a lot of doubt about myself which, on top of everything else, made dealing with life especially hard.

At the height of my addiction I had felt hopeless. Most people would have said about me, "That guy's not going to make it." Given the severity of my addiction, they would have been right. But I proved a lot of people wrong. That is my number one takeaway from all of this — that I am my own person and can chart my own destiny.

I had been living sober in Los Angeles for about a year when I was asked to come to Washington State and work for The Blu Room in Olympia. The number of patients using the Blu Room had increased exponentially and more staff was needed. Because I knew the founder of the Blu Room, the manager thought of me. She called and said, "Austin, we'd like you to work for the Blu Room. There are a lot of people coming in and Dr. Matt needs more help."

I thought to myself, "Well, okay, but am I going to be able to handle this? How is my pain going to be?" To reduce my nervousness, I started to do research on the Blu Room. I asked many questions of Dr. Matthew Martinez, the chiropractic physician overseeing the Blu Room, and he provided me with a huge amount of knowledge. As my knowledge grew, I grew more and more comfortable with the idea of working there.

In 2013 I decided to try it. I went to work in the Blu Room in Olympia! Almost immediately I began hearing healing stories flowing out of the people who were coming to the Blu Room. Soon I became one of those miraculous stories.

Right away I started taking regular sessions of the Blu Room light technology. I entered the Blu Room chamber — a room shaped like an octagon with mirrors — and lay down on a massage table that was placed in the middle. A staff person turned on the special ultraviolet-blue lights for three minutes. When I came out I felt like I had been brought back to life. It brought me to a spiritual awareness that I felt I was deeply lacking in my life. There was a wonderful glimmer of hope that I could start over in a life without pain. That first session was a vital moment in my journey.

I continued taking sessions every day, and slowly the time of my sessions increased from three minutes to twelve minutes and then fifteen minutes. At that point I noticed that I did not need fifteen minutes. More wasn't necessarily better. So I stayed with my sessions at nine to twelve minutes. I did about forty sessions when I noticed a lot of my pain was going away. The swelling was going down and I was able to walk up the stairs more easily. I was able to get out of bed without having to move my whole leg with my hands — a huge leap! I began to think I might be able to function without my pain medications.

At that time I made a conscious choice to take only Enbrel. When the doctor originally prescribed Enbrel, he told me to take it once a week. I injected it into my leg, yet the pain was so severe that it almost immediately came back. But after two months of being in the Blu Room, I experienced forgetting to take it. I had NEVER gone without Embrel in two years. Two months went by and I did not notice that I had forgotten to take my shot. I was amazed! I thought to myself, "Oh, my gosh, I've been doing so well without it, let's see how much further I can go." With continued use of the Blu Room, I've been going longer and longer between taking shots. Today I have gone four months without an injection.

I will soon be going to my rheumatologist, and at that time I will ask for my medical records to show the changes I have made. As time goes on, my level of pain continues to go down and my freedom of movement consistently improves. Because of the Blu Room I am hopeful and excited. I now have mental stability and my main focus is, "What's next? What other great things am I ready to experience in life?" The Blu Room is literally helping me stay nonaddicted because I don't have the pain I once had and consequently do not need the heavy narcotic drugs anymore. I know so many addicts who got sober, relapsed, went for help again, relapsed again, and then were either dead or in jail. A few recovered. I recovered and have stayed recovered — thanks to the Blu Room.

As I continue working at the Blu Room, I am becoming a person on a path to healing. I thank God every day for the Blu Room because it created a whole new reality for me. The fact that every day I wake up no longer an addict and less and less in pain is a wonderful dream come true!

RE-CREATING MY YEAR

Sharon Olson

I had an unusual December to end 2016. I was feeling unusually exhausted and decided that during this December I would spend the last two weeks, and possibly another two weeks longer, just resting, sleeping, and doing nothing. And what I further wanted was to stay with my son and his family during this rest to be even more pampered.

My family agreed for me to come and I proceeded to pamper myself. While I was there I slept an extraordinary amount of time — more than I ever had. I not only slept long nights but I also took frequent naps, something I do not even do on vacations. This was all very different for me but I really wanted to do little else, other than celebrate the beautiful Christmas high holidays.

I noticed after the first two weeks that I *still felt* exhausted and did not yet want to return to my work as a psychiatric nurse practitioner. But I did not trust that I could take another four weeks off — which is what I wanted — and still meet my financial commitments. In addition, the Create Your Year (CYY) event was coming up at Ramtha's School of Enlightenment (RSE), and this has always been the kickoff for my year.

So despite my continuing exhaustion, I readied myself to go to the event and prepared as usual: I contemplated what I wanted to create in the upcoming year and I spent time looking back at the changes I had accomplished in 2016, and was pleased by those. However, I still felt so tired that I thought about not going to the event for the first time ever as a student at RSE. I knew I could choose to view the on-demand streaming of the event at a later time when I felt more energized. Nevertheless, I made a choice and decided to go.

The morning of the event I kept getting *"Pause"* from my God, and so I did. I contemplated longer, rested, and even rejected several plans to run errands. In the late afternoon, I dragged myself to the event.

It is important that I be specific about this because that is part of what I learned from the fabulous runner I was about to experience. The term "runner" was coined by Ramtha and is a person, place, thing, time, or event that occurs in life that brings an experience, needed realization, or important understanding. In this case I realized how I, meaning my personality, *force* myself to do things and then think that was being a "hero/warrior." As is often the case, the truth is much more subtle! I eventually realized that I was not changing the state I was in, or resting long enough, when that is what I needed in moments like this. I was not willing to let go and just BE and fully trust that I could create my year at home, or fully allow myself the space or time to know what I really wanted to do.

I drove to the Create Your Year event in January 2017. It was dark by the time I set up my gear. I was just finishing with carrying my last load when I walked out the door of the RSE arena and fell over a gym bag that was in the path. After falling and skidding across the pavement, I came to rest, shocked and hurting, but thinking it was not too bad. I was promptly escorted to the on-site Shiva Blu Room for a three-minute session and then was taken to the Yelm Family Medicine clinic to get examined.

X-rays revealed that the radius bones of both arms were broken near the elbow. I was as shocked as the doctor. This was preposterous!

I went home that night with both arms in slings. I was told to see a specialist the next week to see if I needed surgery. Needless to say, I did not return to my CYY event. I contacted my friend and orthopedic surgeon, Dr. Lonnie Paulos, who had left a message to "call me as soon as you can." He was at the CYY event and knew I had fallen.

When Lonnie and I spoke, he said, "We need to get you started on stem cells right away!" I was surprised to learn that he had been using stem cells in his treatments as an orthopedic surgeon, but he stated that he had never used them on someone who had a "fresh fracture." I said, "Sure. When and where?" We set up my appointment within the week. And, of course, since the fall I had been doing frequent Blue Body® healing and focusing on myself.

So began this unknown adventure that lasted almost a full year before I felt recovered, whole, and new again.

At my first appointment Lonnie instructed me to start daily bone stimulation technology five days after the fall, which would then be followed by the injection of stem cells five days after that. I was only partially aware of how stem cells were being used and was certainly unaware that they were used to treat fractures. I had known they were becoming available locally at the Blu Room sites in both Yelm and Olympia, Washington, but had not considered them for myself, mostly because of cost and no specific health concerns. So I began researching.

Of course as a student of RSE, before receiving my stem cell injection I intently used Blue Body® healing focus on my broken bones. When the day came for the injection, in my focus I directed the stem cells to go to my fracture sites, my heart, and anyplace else my body needed healing. The nurse said it could get cold where the stem cells were injected. I did not experience the cold but was surprised when I experienced a feeling of pure joy and celebration at the injection site, as if little kids were jumping and skipping for joy at a party! I got so excited! I then went into the Blu Room for six minutes and this time, to my surprise again, I felt icy cold at both fracture sites and my heart within moments! How blessed I felt! How grateful I was to the stem cells, JZ Knight, Dr. Matt Martinez, and Dr. Lonnie Paulos!

Then from the goodness of his heart, Dr. Matt Martinez, the owner of the Absolute Health Clinic in Olympia, Washington, offered me free use of the Blu Room in his clinic "for three days a week, at least, and more if you can get in." I could not drive yet, but with the help of friends I managed to start immediately using the Blu Room three times a week. I also was doing my RSE disciplines every day, including long Twilight® sessions to focus on Blue Body® healing. In addition, I received occasional, general chiropractic adjustments and massages to make sure the rest of my body was aligned and healing.

That injury left me with little to do except my RSE disciplines, rest, and contemplate. I was humbled in a way I never had been before, needing help for even the most basic things. Initially, I was unable to dress or feed myself. A shower was now a big deal, and for months I had to get my hair washed by a beautician because I did not have the ability to get a comb through my curls.

But there was good news. After my meeting with Lonnie, he said he did not think I required surgery and could actually take one arm out of the sling occasionally and gently start to move it.

At the end of three weeks I returned for my first follow-up appointment after the stem cell injection and Blu Room sessions. Lonnie was amazed and said, "This is miraculous. I still think you don't need surgery. In fact, you could start doing some increased exercises and drive, if you feel safe. We'll do follow-up x-rays on your arms." Shannon, his wife and co-owner of the U Wellness Center in Yelm, was jazzed and said, "He *never* says that! I tell him things like this happen all the time here at the Blu Rooms, but he does not get to see them." He repeated again, "It's just a miracle." I said, "That's good. But I want to take x-rays of my right hand too because something isn't healing as quickly there."

I had x-rays the next day and was informed my right wrist had also fractured!

Now one of the decisions I made immediately after the accident was that I would not regret, blame, or feel sorry for my fall. I *know* there are no accidents or coincidences. The fall had stopped me in my tracks. I had asked my Holy Spirit for help in allowing me to rest, and this was the runner I got! I obviously needed to be STOPPED, not for a brief pause but for an elongated time to reorient myself. So this fall became my game changer. Of course one of the immediate fallouts was that I could not work. I actually did not work for the one month, even though I wanted to work but thought I couldn't afford not to. Trust just a little, as I recall Ramtha saying. This just showed me again how little the personality knows!

At times during my recovery I thought I was squandering my time because I rested and slept a lot, and I began to question if it was too late. Had I squandered my life, worn out the body, and had I really done the best I could? I knew, finally, what a true gift my body had been. Now I just wanted to rejuvenate and care for it, and I made more of a commitment to change and own what attitudes I could before this life was finished.

I have been a healer all my life, and my mom and my maternal grandmother had also been known as healers. We each have cared for and assisted others because we were able to, and we did so for decades. But now I wanted to focus that loving, attending, caring energy on Self — what *I needed,* wanted, and deserved. Is this what I had to do — to care for Self? Somehow, it was time to stop being responsible for others and be responsive to Self. Could I really just go after what I wanted? And now, what did I want?

For the second appointment with Lonnie I brought in the follow-up x-rays, and he was shocked. "It's a miracle, unbelievable. With no surgery, the arm bones are healed and in only three weeks! It's a miracle. It's awesome progress!" Shannon, Lonnie's wife and my friend, said, "Okay, is it awesome for her age or in general, compared to anyone?" Lonnie said, "It's unbelievable for anyone. And by the way, Sharon, you were right. You do have a right wrist fracture." I told him I was still having some pain in my shoulders, arms, hands, and legs. It wasn't severe enough to take pain medication, but it was unusual for me as I am usually pain free. "The pain you feel is soft tissue damage and that can take up to a year to heal. But now we have to decide what to do about your wrist. I've always done surgeries on these and then put the wrist in a cast for three months, because wrists are hard to heal. The downside to casting is that people often get contractures. However, it has now been four weeks since the fall, so it is your call." Together we decided to let it ride since the wrist pain was decreasing. I would check in again in two weeks to see if there had been more healing.

Now I was being slower, more deliberate, and kinder to my body. I was beginning to halt the usual forcefulness of my personality. I was grateful just to heal, to spend time in focus, and to see what I had not seen about myself. *Until that time I had no idea how much my past beliefs and attitudes were coloring everything I did.* I recalled Ramtha telling us students many times that we were unaware of our internal programs — that we were red in the rainbow. All these years *I thought* I was seeing my programs as they ran and that I was stopping them and self-correcting. But now I saw myself much more clearly. This process of becoming self-aware is still continuing until the present. This is the greatest, most extraordinary adventure I have ever been on — finding Self!

By six weeks post-fall I had another x-ray done on my wrist. Two weeks later I met with Lonnie again and he said, "You're healing well, way ahead of schedule. We can still turn around and do surgery if you want or we can continue as is. As your doctor I don't feel the need to do more, neither stem cells nor anything else for now. I'd like to reevaluate in two months. At that time, if you're unsure about the healing, we'll do another x-ray. You don't need physical therapy. Start gentle exercise but be easy on the wrist. You can do more with your arms. And remember the soft tissue trauma can last for months up to a year."

By the next time I saw him, Lonnie held my hands, pressed around my thumb, and manipulated my fingers. He said, "It is miraculous. In this short time and without a cast, your wrist has healed. That's amazing. There's no need for further care unless you feel you need it."

I was so grateful that my God gave me the opportunity to be in long focus to see my genetic programming and really observe, identify, and let the harmful programs go. One friend said, "You probably never thought it was that easy, given your life experience." But that is exactly what I heard my Teacher, Ramtha, and JZ, his channel, say: "YOU make it hard." Now, for the first time ever, I have deeper trust in my God Self. I ask daily, "I am a God from the future. What would a God do today?"

I am finally clear enough to have long moments of "no thoughts." I want to hear and know *my own* thoughts because they will be different from the thoughts of others. I am not critical of others' thoughts. I just want to know MINE. I want to focus on me. I do not want to live for others but want to find love for myself. I am discovering that if I do that, as I heard Ramtha say, it is changing *me!*

ORDINARY PEOPLE MANIFESTING THE EXTRAORDINARY

A MULTITUDE OF HEALINGS

Evonne LaForge

From the time I began school at Ramtha's School of Enlightenment (RSE), I have had healings. Below are accounts of some of these.

One healing involved my hearing. I had been a 4-1-1 telephone operator for Bell Telephone in Los Angeles for a number of years. The long-term use of the headset that I wore gave me what was called acoustic poisoning. There was no cure. The hearing in my left ear would come and go, but mostly go. When I learned Ramtha's discipline of Consciousness and Energy® (C&E®) in 1998, I really applied myself, and my hearing returned. It came back better than ever. I now have acute hearing.

The next healing happened in 2005, using The Neighborhood Walk®, a profound discipline for me. This is an account of that healing.

In 1978 my mother had a large tear on her uterine wall. Her uterus was saved by a wonderful woman doctor from India who was working with lasers way back then. Once treated by this doctor, my mother never had any problem with her uterus again. In 2005 I knew that the same thing that had happened to my mother was happening to me — there was a hemorrhaging of my uterus. Nevertheless, I decided to attend an RSE event, knowing it could be healed there.

I was sitting in the smoking circle on the RSE campus with a friend. I told her my problem and she said she had experienced the same thing and that she chose to have a hysterectomy. I said, "Not me." Although we students were on a meal break, I walked directly to the name-field and began focusing on The Grid®. I walked The Grid® and saw it overlaying my uterus until the bell rang and our break was over. As I walked into the arena, I felt like I had stitches on my uterus. And, miraculously, the bleeding

281

stopped. After that, my menstrual cycle returned to normal and I never thought about it again. It was done.

The next healing experience began in 1991, when my son was two and a half years old. I was a single mother on welfare. I decided to build a cordwood house. It was something I could build myself and was very affordable. The house was made of cement and firewood. I had to mix the cement by hand in a wheelbarrow. The bags of Portland cement were ninety pounds. I was willful and full of attitude and worked hard, but I did not know the consequences of my actions. My hands became severely damaged from overwork, yet I continued to ignore it for many years. Ten years later I realized my body was damaged by work, especially my hands. I applied all of Ramtha's disciplines to healing my hands: I made Fieldwork® cards, did my Consciousness and Energy® (C&E®) discipline, and danced my Blue Body® to bring about a healing of my hands. But they did not heal.

Then in 2011 the right side of my body totally broke down. This was not gradual. I just woke up one morning as an invalid. Being an invalid did not fit into how I was living my life. I had recently moved onto rural acreage, built a very small cabin, and created a great garden. I also had to support myself with a job. In one of my jobs, I had to climb up three flights of stairs. I would go up the stairs, crying and dragging myself up step by step. I could not be a cripple. There was no one to take care of me. I had to keep working.

The chiropractor had no answer. He could adjust me, but it was more than skeletal. It involved my right rotary cuff and right hip, ankle, and knee. I was wearing all kinds of support braces. I fantasized about using a cane.

I continued to attend events at RSE and applied myself in all the disciplines the best I could. Fieldwork® was my Tank® — the most physically demanding discipline — as I could barely walk. Then it struck me. I could not go into the C&E® position to participate in that discipline. So instead, I focused on my healing during the Neighborhood Walk® where I walked my

Blue Body®, and danced my Blue Body® during the Blue Body® discipline. I kept going. I did not want sympathy or to be taken care of.

In the summer I went to Assay, an RSE event where JZ had told the staff to have us walk to the back gate. I panicked. What was I going to do? I could barely go across the name-field, much less keep up with a large group. Then I made a choice: During the group walk to the back gate I was going to do the most focused Neighborhood Walk® of my life. I had to, or be defeated and stay behind with the other handicapped people.

I was so focused on my walk on what I was becoming that I went to the back gate and returned very quickly, I stayed in that focused state for every discipline. By the end of the Assay I was much improved. I never talked about it with my peers and never looked back to rate my performance or improvements.

After I went home from Assay, to my delight I could continue to do C&E®, and I continued to improve in all ways. But my hands got worse. My hands lost their strength, got spurs, and became misshapen. Eventually I started getting trigger fingers. My right hand was so bad that I had to use my left hand to pull my right-hand fingers to open them up. It was very painful. Dr. Matt Martinez, my chiropractor, would work on my hands, but it was obvious from his expression that this was beyond his ability to heal. Of course people would tell me all the supplements they were taking and that I should take this one or that group of them. I never took any. I have never believed in supplements, so they would not have worked for me.

Instead I went to the Blu Room. I had spent so much time in the discipline of Blue Body healing that when I had my first session in the Blu Room I felt I was "home." The Blu Room is a creation by JZ Knight where you enter a geometrically shaped room and lie down on a bed and rest while a special, ultraviolet-blue light shines on you for up to twelve minutes. I am so grateful for this gift of genius from JZ. I really enjoyed being in the ultraviolet-blue atmosphere. My pain levels went way down, and when I started twelve minutes in the room, something wonderful happened. I had forgotten about my hands because I had resigned myself to their disability. But suddenly I felt electrical surges in my hands — warm, wonderful currents moved through them. When the session was over I walked out of the room, and as I was gathering my things I noticed that my hands worked differently. I kept opening and closing my hands, showing them to everyone. I went to the Blu Room twice a month, and every time my hands got stronger and stronger.

Unfortunately, I have no medical records. I do know that *life is will*. If I had given in to all the maladies my body had, I would be an invalid. Pain was a great teacher. I was busy getting to the core of my attitudes so there was no room for me to indulge in foolishness and drama. I kept focused and kept going.

In summary, I reaped a lot of experience from focusing on the ultraviolet-blue frequency. And it brought me healing after healing.

THE MIRACLE

Nikki Bertone

In 1990 I was diagnosed with multiple myeloma (bone marrow cancer). My oncologist in Toronto started me on a treatment of chemotherapy involving a mustard gas and Prednisone, a steroid to control inflammation. I was on that regimen for five to six years. Eventually my skin started to turn gray, so I decided to try an alternative treatment — energy work — Chi Quong. Within six months I was told my cancer was in remission. I did the energy work twice a day.

In 2010 I started doing Chi Quong once a day, eventually decreasing the energy work. In January 2016 the cancer came back. In February 2016 I was shoveling snow and I put my back out. Because I could not get relief from the pain, I went to see my oncologist in Thunder Bay who sent me for an MRI. The MRI revealed a herniated disk and a shattered disk between T-11 and T-12.

On June 1, I conceded to start chemotherapy consisting of, once a week on the same day, Cyclophosphamide — also known as Procytox — 50 mg chemotherapy, ten pills in the morning with food. Blood work was followed by Bortezomid — also known as Velcade — a belly injection chemotherapy. Every five weeks I took Zoledronic Acid, known as Zometa, which strengthens bones but destroys the jaw bone, Dexamethasone 4 mg, a cortisone steroid, to control nausea and vomiting, amounting to ten pills for four days after chemotherapy, and Ranitidine to reduce stomach acid taken two times a day.

Prior to taking the oral chemotherapy and the other prescribed pill form medication, my sister changed the frequency of these pills so that the medications were compatible with my frequency, therefore eliminating any side effects that I would normally experience. During my doctor's appointments my oncologist alluded to the fact that I was a good stem cell infusion candidate. An appointment was arranged for me to visit the Princess Margaret Cancer Centre in Toronto.

In October 2016 I decided to go to the Univers Bleu Room in Saint-Sauveur, Quebec. Before going there I set the intention of receiving a "miracle." I had nineteen treatments in nine days. When I came back to Thunder Bay I went to see my oncologist, who was shocked to see that my myeloma count (IGA) had dropped rapidly from 19.1 in January to 1.63 in November, especially since in May the count had registered at 18.2.

In December 2016 I went to the Princess Margaret Cancer Centre in Toronto. While there, they did tests to check my heart, lungs, blood, and teeth to see what state my body was in. I then had an orientation informing me of the process involved in having the stem cell infusion. The procedure was overwhelming, so I decided not to have the procedure done.

I knew my cancer was gone because of the "miracle" I had received in the Blu Room. I feel great. My skin pigment has increased and my mobility is normal again. The pronounced curvature in my spine has decreased by 50 percent. I am elated and forever grateful to have received such a gift.

A DRAMATIC IMPROVEMENT IN DIABETES

Jaime Leal-Anaya

My name is Jaime Leal-Anaya. I am very fortunate to have experienced the extraordinary effects of the Blu Room in my life. I have been dealing with diabetes for many years with little success in holding normal blood glucose levels. My doctors mentioned in my case that it would be difficult and would take a lot of effort on my part to reach a normal level in my A1c test, which tests your blood sugars over a period of three months. To get below or around 7 would be a huge ordeal. My levels were all over the place before coming to the Blu Room. I was really not in a good place, medically speaking. And I had other related issues too with high blood pressure and cholesterol levels.

I started coming to the Blu Room from the very beginning when JZ built the first one here in Yelm at Ramtha's School of Enlightenment. I was fortunate to be able to participate here from the start. I immediately started noticing some benefits from it. After a few months of coming somewhat regularly, I noticed I did not need my blood pressure medication anymore. That was the most immediate effect that was noticeable. I stopped taking my medication for blood pressure at that time and my levels continued to be normal, as I continued to monitor it. So that was really great. That was hopeful. And I continued working on the big jump in my own acceptance for healing to reverse the diabetes and the effects it had on my body over the years. I continued coming regularly to the Blu Room and my cholesterol levels started showing normal levels. Again, I started reducing my dose of medication for controlling that and eventually did not have to take it anymore, as my test results were showing that my levels were now in the normal range again. That was really great, so I continued on.

Another aspect that I would like to share about the Blu Room is something more of a spiritual and emotional nature in my personal life. A twenty-minute session in the Blu Room made me feel somewhat disoriented, as if I had a very deep night's sleep. It was similar to waking up from deep sleep in the middle of the night and feeling disoriented, not knowing where you are for a few moments. It is interesting that the medical field explains that the body gets repaired during the deep sleep cycle and that is why we wake up in the morning feeling refreshed. I started experiencing that state in the Blu Room from the very start. After the twenty-minute sessions I would come out very relaxed, very calm, free from stress.

Stress levels actually are a very big factor in diabetes and metabolism. I started noticing very quickly that I was not reacting. I was more calm throughout the day. That was another effect from the Blu Room that was maybe not so easy to tabulate with a medical record, but it was a very real effect for me. The benefits in my health from that release of stress have also contributed, in my opinion, to my improved blood pressure, glucose metabolism, as well as cholesterol levels. So those are the effects of the Blu Room I have experienced, from the most obvious to the most extraordinary.

In December 2017 I took my next A1c test. I hadn't been able to regulate my blood glucose effectively up to that point. I was taking my medications, eating healthy, year after year, and the only thing different this time was coming to the Blu Room more often, 2 to 3 times a week, when I could. I got my blood tested and when I got the results, I almost fell backwards because I went from a result of over 10 to 7.1 in a three-month period. I was very surprised and really excited. I completely attribute it to my participating in the Blu Room because that was the only thing different I did this time. So I am delighted with that result. I have more work to do, obviously. I have to be well under 7. But having jumped from 10 to 7.1, I am filled with acceptance, which I think is another very big factor for healing and recovery.

There was something else I experienced during the flu season last winter here in Washington. It was particularly severe. Most of my coworkers and family members came down with the flu for weeks. I was completely unharmed by it and I attribute it to coming regularly to the Blu Room during that period.

Another thing that the Blu Room has helped build in me is the state of calm and a state of acceptance for healing. It is a state of detachment from the emotional reaction that often is a result of glucose swings, but maybe that is also the cause of a lot of the medical symptoms I have been experiencing. The Blu Room has helped me surrender deeply into a state of healing and restoration and inner peace. I am very grateful for that.

THE BLU ROOM AND BREAST CANCER

Maggie Barragan

I was diagnosed with cancer last year. I had my mammogram in January and by July I had a positive result of having breast cancer. That moment made a very big impact on my life. My life changed completely and my mind was spinning. "What is going to happen? What is next?" It was really scary. I had no idea what to expect. I was really anxious about everything because I did not know what was going to happen to me.

But I was blessed to know Dr. Matthew Martinez who told me about the Blu Room. So I started sessions there. At that point in my life I had to say, "I will take anything — anything. Whatever you refer me to or tell me to do, I will do it because I am scared." I took three sessions of the Blu Room and I was amazed that by the third day my anxiety was gone. I was able to sleep, which was wonderful because I had had trouble sleeping ever since I received the news.

In the meantime, I was very anxious as I waited for an appointment at the Cancer Care Alliance in Seattle to talk to the team about my surgery and all the things that I could expect for my body and my life.

I received news of having breast cancer on July 1 and eventually had my surgery in September. My surgeon asked me, "Are you doing anything else as a treatment?" and I said, "Yes. I am taking treatments at the Blu Room." She asked, "What is a Blu Room?" So I explained to her what the Blu Room was — about the lights, how I felt afterward, and how amazing it was. She asked, "What lights? Like a tanning bed?" And I said, "No, no." And I explained the process of the Blu Room to her. When I had told her that I had had anxiety and could not sleep and that after the third day of Blu Room sessions the anxiety was gone, she replied, "That is good. That is not a tanning bed. I like that. It is good. Keep doing what you're doing."

So I had my surgery. Afterward the doctors did not recommend chemotherapy, which made me happy. But they said I had to have radiation treatments. I had read all the side effects of radiation and I was really scared because I did not know how my body was going to react. I knew they would be difficult to go through.

I took thirty-five to forty sessions of radiation. Every day I went for a treatment I was asked if I felt dizzy, if I had fallen down, or if I felt unbalanced. And every day I would say, "No, I don't feel any of those. I actually feel good." They asked me if I was tired. And I said, "No. I am full of energy." Throughout all of the treatments I turned every negative into a positive.

One day after I had my radiation treatment one of the staff asked me, "How are you? How do you feel?" I said, "Oh, I feel great. I just walked out of the microwave." I thought that was funny. She said, "Oh, my gosh, I never thought anyone would say something humorous after a treatment!" And I said, "You know, it is important to be positive. You have to be positive inside yourself because that is the best way to heal yourself — doing it internally." The staff thought that was an unusual response. They said, "You are the only patient who has radiation that makes these kinds of comments." I thought, "Well, I have to be positive, you know? This is going to be over soon." My last radiation treatment was completed on December 28.

In the meantime, because of the Blu Room, my body has been healing fantastically. I feel great. And I have to say something: For me, the Blu Room has been an amazing technology. It is a tool. It is a gift that allows you to heal yourself naturally. It is an alternative way to get healed. I thought, "Why not use the Blu Room?" So I have been taking sessions and I feel great about them. I am one of those people who never takes medications. I like to use alternative, natural ways of healing. And the Blu Room has been amazing for me. You do not need to be diagnosed with cancer. You do not need to wait to be sick to use the Blu Room. The most important thing is to *heal yourself.* The tools are there, so use them!

RETURN OF OPTIMAL HEATH

Dr. Jo Linmans

In July 2015 my wife Claudia was diagnosed with a type of hyperthyroidism called Graves' disease. This is an autoimmune disease caused by an antibody called the TSH receptor antibody (TRAb).

These antibodies cause the thyroid gland to produce excess thyroid hormone T4 and T3. As a result, the thyroid gland is working too fast and causes the following symptoms: irritability, muscle weakness, sleeping problems, fast heartbeat (palpitation), trembling of hands, intolerance of heat, extreme weakness, weight loss despite ravenous appetite, changes in the menstrual cycle, and enlargement of the thyroid gland. Claudia had all of them!

The blood results in July 2015 showed very low TSH, high levels of T3 and T4, and very high TRAb levels:

TSH 0.01 (Normal = 0.3 4.5 mE/L)
Free — T3 + 15.23 (Normal = 3.23 6.47 pmol/L)
Free — T4 + 36.61 (Normal = 9.03 23.22 pmol/L)
TRAb ++ 4.1 (Normal = 0 1 U/L)

There are three main treatment options: medications, radioiodine therapy, or thyroid surgery if the first options do not work. I started to treat Claudia with the drug Strumazol at three tablets per day to block the formation of T4, which is only to treat the symptoms. A beta blocker was also added to the treatment to slow down her rapid heartbeat. With these drugs, her symptoms became partly under control but her condition was not cured. As long as the antibody TRAb is elevated, the disease is active.

This treatment is typically continued for up to two years. If during this time the TRAb goes back to normal levels, the treatment is stopped. That happens in fifty percent of patients. The other fifty percent need either radioiodine therapy or surgery to have the thyroid removed. With either choice, the patient then needs a lifelong substitution of thyroid hormone. Understandably, we did not want the last two options!

Besides the conventional treatment, Claudia started complementary treatments: homeopathy, food supplements, nutrition adjustments, frequency medicine, etc. As an RSE student, Claudia also started focusing on healing her thyroid gland.

From July 2015 to March 2016, blood tests were done every month. The TRAb stayed elevated during that period with only two short periods when the value of the TRAb dropped to normal for only a short period of time and then elevated again.

In February 2016 we got the announcement of the opening of the first Blu Room in Europe. I immediately took the opportunity and booked the Blu Room for a four-day retreat in Bad Mergentheim, Germany, in March 2016. In those four days, Claudia went five times to the Blu Room, focusing on healing.

In April 2016 — one month after her Blu Room sessions — the blood result showed normal rates of TRAb! This time the normal values of the TRAb persisted over the next several months, which gave me the opportunity to gradually wean her off the Strumazol and the beta blocker. All of her symptoms gradually diminished and she regained normal and optimal health. Since her healing, Claudia visited the Blu Room in Italy once and recently a few times to the Blu Room in Mergentheim, Germany.

From April 2016 to September 2017, blood tests were done on a regular basis. Her thyroid function stayed optimal and the TRAb values stayed normal the whole time.

We now have one and a half years of follow-up after the healing with no relapse of the disease. Claudia's symptoms are all gone and she is in good health. We are both very grateful for this wonderful healing.

A PORTAL TO ELSEWHERE

Rosa

I am from Italy and have just turned eighty. I started the Blu Room in August 2016 because of shoulder pain and general discomfort. I did two to three sessions per month and my pain level dropped from seven to three. This was the first change that occurred in my health.

The second change occurred in my Vitamin D serum level. Around my birthday each year, I get a physical and lab work.

When I was tested on November 3, 2015, my Vitamin D level was 8.2. The normal range is 16.1 to 50. So I was not just deficient — my values were scraping the bottom of the barrel. Unperturbed, I continued sessions in my local Blu Room. Then in August of 2016, a few months before my annual checkup, I did nine Blu Room sessions — two or three a month. On November 4, 2016, my blood work was taken and it was 46.7, well into the normal range. Apart from my daily focus and attention to my attitudes, the only difference was that I went regularly to the Blu Room.

JZ calls Vitamin D "The God Vitamin." She calls it that because Vitamin D helps the body in multitudes of ways. And the Blu Room — even if you are fully clothed and well into your 70s — will increase your body's ability to effectively synthesize Vitamin D "out of the blue." It is because the Blu Room is not just about ultraviolet radiation. It is a portal from elsewhere and it creates real change in the reality we inhabit.

A MAGNET FOR HAPPINESS!

Sandra

I first came into the Blu Room in July of 2015 because I heard some positive things about it. I have fought severe depression since 1997 when I was experiencing full-blown menopause. I have seen several psychologists and psychiatrists and have been on multiple medications. I went off all the medications about four years ago because I did not like the side effects.

My second visit to the Blu Room at Dr. Matt's clinic was in September. Inside the Blu Room I felt like I was in a kind of twilight. I was floating and extremely peaceful. I did not realize the effects it had until I came out into the lobby. There were four people in the waiting room and it sounded like there were a thousand. The noise was so amplified, I had to put my fingers in my ears to tell the receptionist that I needed to go outside — and not just to the outside lobby, but *outside*. I was waiting for a Dr. Matt session and told her that is where she could find me. Since that experience I have had absolutely no depression symptoms whatsoever. I haven't felt this blissful other than when I do disciplines: C&E® (Consciousness and Energy®) or Twilight®. It has been a wonderful experience and I am looking forward to my next Blu Room, which will be this coming Wednesday. It will be my fourth time. I feel blessed that the technology has been given to us.

ALLOWING MYSELF TO BELIEVE

Inge

The first time I went to the Blu Room was August 10 and the second time was yesterday, which was October 9, so there were two months between my sessions. When I was leaving the Blu Room yesterday, I realized that I had gotten an answer to a question that I had been pondering. It wasn't a question that I posed in the Blu Room intending to get an answer, but it was something that was on my mind and I did get the answer. Then I remembered that at my first visit, the same thing happened. That time I was having car trouble driving to the clinic. While I was in the Blu Room, the mystery was solved of why I was having trouble with my car. And then when I was driving home last night after my experience, I realized that I felt *so much better* with this Blu Room experience. I was just healthier, happier, stronger, and had a lot more energy than after my first experience. I was loaded with energy. I was just amazed!

HOPE

Joan

I am Joan Pulford and I've been receiving treatment from Dr. Martinez for four months for Parkinson's disease. And I also developed a tumor in my colon. Eight months ago I was given five months to live. Because of the treatment in the Blu Room, I now have the will to live, I am in less pain, and the tremors are less. You would not know it now, but they are. I have longer periods of time when I don't shake.

I started to shake intensely when I was in there, but as soon as I stepped out of the Blu Room, my tremors were gone — completely gone. Ninety percent of the time now I do not have any tremors which, as we all know, does not happen with Parkinson's disease. So this is another wonderful miracle of the Blu Room.

I know that it is my mind that is allowing my healing. It is the *allowing* — going from one point in the journey to another — that permits a fruition of healing to come through. And that is called hope.

FAMILY HEALING IN MISSOURI

Anna

I began going to the Blu Room on May 1, 2017, to increase my Vitamin D level, which at the time was 13. Normal is considered 30 and I am aiming for 50. Because of the Blu Room, it is currently 27.

The second reason is because in January 2012 I fractured my left shoulder. It has had a surgical repair with screws and metal plates affixed. After weeks of physical therapy, I still had limited range of motion (ROM). I accepted my limitations and moved on. I received a surprise on September 1, 2017, four months after going to the Blu Room two times per week. I discovered I have increased ROM in my left arm. I can now use my left hand to wash my hair, which I had not been able to do. I can now reach the second shelf of my pantry. Woohoo! I was, and am, amazed that my body healed itself even without intention or focus from me. It caused me to be aware that your body will heal itself given the right tools.

To me even more amazing things are occurring in my emotional and mental life. I can feel love and care from life, the universe, human beings, and other lifeforms. I am still at times genuinely surprised when I feel it. I find I am more clear in my thinking. I make better decisions. I am not as judgmental and can allow people and things to be who and what they are. I am more allowing about things that happen. I can say okay, not good, not bad, just as it is. I am more thoughtful. I am aware and allowing in ways I have not been in the past. To me these are even more amazing than the physical healing.

My whole family uses the Blu Room to instigate cellular healing, its immune boosting capabilities, individual needs, and to promote general feelings of peace and well-being. Our entire family enjoys Blu Room therapy. We have successfully addressed maladies ranging from Vitamin D deficiencies to anxiety.

Our bodies continue to get stronger. My teen reports less headaches. My toddler really looks forward to her Blu Room adventures. My partner reports better sleep and general health. My anxiety has been greatly reduced. My Vitamin D levels are no longer deficient. My overall well-being has been dramatically increased. In addition, my vision has become sharper and my appetite has returned.

The ladies who work at the Blu Room in Missouri, Sara and Michelle, are Earthly Angels. They are well-educated, excellent listeners, compassionate, and experts of body, mind, soul healings! Being in their presence alone promotes feelings of peace and safety. They never leave a question unanswered, nor a stone unturned. They really do go the extra mile! It is deeply comforting that my children can safely receive this therapy, from tot to teen to adult.

SEBORRHEIC DERMATITIS

Diana

I had a problem of seborrheic dermatitis which was torturing me for twenty years. It got worse last March. In addition to being ugly to see, I also had a lot of pain. My ear was burning a lot, including inside my ear. Just touching it hurt. I could not sleep on my right side because my ear hurt so much. My ear was very swollen and very hard. It often had a liquid coming out of it like pus mixed with blood.

I did not consult a physician because I did not want to take antibiotics or other chemical medicines that I was certain they would prescribe. I was eagerly awaiting the arrival of our Blu Room!

On July 3 I began my Blu Room sessions. I took two sessions close together, after which I was very tired and weak. I slept a lot and I did not eat much. After a few days, the situation changed. Everything became absolutely better. The intense pain and burning sensations were almost gone. I am still using the Blu Room three to four days per week.

My immense gratitude goes to JZ Knight, who brought us this marvelous gift. Many thanks also to Dr. Matt Martinez for his precious collaboration.

HEALING STRABISMUS

Erika

I visited the Blaue Pause Blu Room in Vienna, Austria, and healed my eye condition, strabismus, that I had lived with for nearly ten years, even after trying corrective surgery.

I have had a lot of experiences of conventional medicine with doctors. I decided to heal myself. I handed it over to God. Yesterday, August 31, 2017, in the Blu Room, I was lying in a north-south orientation. I experienced an energy flow from my feet to my head. That was everything. At the end, I sat up, opened my eyes, and let the blue light have an effect on my retina. That was the moment when I realized that I can see in a normal way. I realized that I am really able to see normally.

CHARITY, COMPASSION, AND MERCY

Dr. Ana Maria Mihalcea, of the Mercy Blu Program

The Mercy Blu Program was created by JZ Knight for individuals with debilitating health conditions who want to add Blu Room sessions to their regular medical treatment plan. Program participants provide their medical reports, lab tests, and diagnostic imaging. They must remain under the care of their regular healthcare provider or a specialist who is actively treating and monitoring their health condition.

This program is the outcrop of JZ Knight's compassion for suffering people and her unconditionally loving, healing mind who does not care about expense to help and heal people and give them the gift of reprieve from their suffering body and troubled mind in the *Mercy of Blu Atmosphere*. The idea of shining a generous light of hope on the difficult circumstance of severe chronic disease and financial limitations is a beautiful concept that is realized at Shiva Mercy Blu. People can come to the Shiva Mercy Blu Program and find healing on all levels of their being without troubles or concerns. Charity, compassion, and mercy are in themselves healing balms to the soul and body.

As the Supervising Physician of the Mercy Blu Program, I review the participants' records, interview them, and prepare reports of each participant's healing journey. The following stories are a sampling of my reports and the healing journeys to which the Blu Room has contributed.

Donna's Heart Problems

Donna is a 75-year-old woman with a longstanding history of heart problems.

She had chronic, mitral valve prolapse with myxomatous changes, causing mitral regurgitation requiring St. Jude mitral valve replacement in 1998. She has had a complex history of recurrent atrial fibrillation treated with cardioversion and antiarrhythmic drugs over several years. She did have recurrent hospitalizations with flareups, and the paroxysmal atrial fibrillation caused acute congestive heart failure, with intermittent heart pump function as low as EF 20-25%. Those numbers improved to EF 55% after further electrophysiologic intervention, intraoperative extensive Maze 2010 with bipolar radiofrequency, and removal of left atrial appendage. She then had a biventricular pacemaker placed, now with compensated ejection fraction of 55%.

Over the years Donna has had significant symptoms from her heart condition, and at times she was bedridden due to low energy. The times when she has had fast heart rates, she got dehydrated and would get short of breath with minimal activities. And she was unable to complete even the simplest tasks due to her low energy. Since Donna started Blu Room therapy, she has had less symptoms of her atrial fibrillation impacting her abilities, even though her pacemaker readings show that the problem is persistent. She has greater stamina and does not experience shortness of breath. She has experienced a more serene ability to manage stress in her life due to her Blu Room visits, which is important for healing for any heart patient. Over several months of Blu Room use, her overall condition continued to improve. Most recently she had a work-related assignment and was able to work for twelve hours in perpetual motion. All of her coworkers were amazed at her stamina and her "go-getter" attitude. Donna attributes these improvements in her condition to the Blu Room and feels they are nothing short of miraculous.

Molly's Chronic Knee Pain

Molly is an eighty-one-year-old woman who had both her knees replaced in 2003. She has had knee pain ever since. In 2013 she was unable to walk and had to have both of her knee replacements revised. After she had the second surgery to replace her right knee, she was unable to feel her leg after the procedure, and she fell. This caused her to have a complex left bimalleolar ankle fracture and dislocation of her right new knee replacement, completely opening her surgical site.

She was wheelchair-bound for three months, and her right knee continued to have severe pain, requiring opiate pain medications. She started having night sweats and fevers over a year and then developed an open draining wound on her right knee that was treated with wound care.

One year later, after several hospital visits, she was diagnosed with a failed and infected prosthesis, and the infection had eaten through her bone. Her right knee was removed and she was treated with antibiotics, having a spacer only in her leg and with the doctors concerned they would have to amputate her leg.

After three months of intensive antibiotics, she was clear of infection and was able to get a new knee. She was in chronic pain, had to use a walker, and needed ongoing opiate pain medications. She could not get up out of a chair without help. Pain in her leg was her constant companion. She tried everything from TENS (Transcutaneous Electrical Nerve Stimulation) units, topical pain relievers, opiate pain medications to rid herself of the severe, chronic pain.

Molly started going to the Blu Room in February 2017. She noticed easing of her right knee pain after each session. One day at home after her seventeenth Mercy Blu Room session, she noticed that she could walk without pain. The pain had disappeared completely and it never came back. One year later, Molly remains pain free in her knee. She is able to get up out of a chair without help and she no longer uses a walker. Molly attributes this miraculous healing to the Blu Room. Now she is working on healing her back.

Bob's Psoriasis and Diabetes

Bob is seventy-four years old with a history of atrial fibrillation and congestive heart failure, insulin dependent diabetes, and newly diagnosed marginal cell lymphoma, affecting lymph nodes in his abdomen. He has had severe psoriasis for many years.

Bob has been going to the Blu Room twice a week for two months now. Within two sessions he noted marked improvement of his psoriasis, which was severe and was covering his arms, legs, abdomen, and scalp with so much scarring that he had patches of permanent hair loss.

Bob had complete sustained remission of his psoriasis in the last two months and states that his skin looks now like he never had the disease.

During the time of his Blu Room treatments, his diabetes also improved, and he was able to lower his insulin doses from 45 units twice a day to 30 units twice a day and maintain the same diabetic control, with his last HgA1c of 6.8 indicating excellent diabetic control. He did not change his lifestyle during this time but attributes the improvement to how the Blu Room helps him heal himself.

Bob believes that his negative attitudes, emotions, and the induced stress caused his health problems. He is constantly working on improving himself and feels the Blu Room helps to "mellow him out." He feels noticeably less depressed, is able to cope better with his stress, and maintains a positive outlook on life which helps his overall health status. He does not have significant heart-related symptoms.

Bob chose not to undergo chemotherapy or radiation for his lymphoma. He is feeling healthier and is able to cope with the stressor of having been diagnosed with cancer. He feels the Blu Room helps him to look deeper at his attitudes, and he experiences a personal sense of forgiveness in the Blu Room. He says, "Everything is gone" when he is in the Blu Room. When he goes back to his life, reality sets in — but slowly he is seeing life is changing for the better. Bob notes that the Blu Room changes he is experiencing are subtle but represent powerful and profound levels of personal transformation.

Doris's Healing Pain From A Life-Altering Collision

Doris is a seventy-eight-year-old woman. In November 2015 she sustained life-threatening injuries in a car collision. Doris remembers driving down the road, preparing to make a turn, and hearing a loud voice in her head say, "You are going to die!"

Doris found herself yelling, "Nooo!!!" At the same moment she wondered why she was yelling out loud, since she was alone in the car. The next thing she remembers is waking up in the hospital. She had been in a coma for more than six days.

Doris sustained traumatic, displaced fractures of three ribs, two cervical vertebral fractures, along with a fracture and dislocation of the left clavicle. She also had severe traumatic brain injury and intracranial bleeding from severe head trauma. Her daughter reported that while she was in the hospital, Doris would mention that her deceased mother would come to visit her. The daughter asked Doris what Grandmother wanted and Doris said, "She wants me to go with her." Doris had replied to her mother "I'm not ready to go."

After one month in the hospital, Doris was discharged to a nursing facility where she remained for three and a half months. She required assistance with all daily activities of living, like bathing and dressing, help with transfers, and help to go to the restroom. She required the use of a wheelchair and later a walker. Doris did not want to use narcotic pain medication. While convalescing in the nursing home, she weaned herself off all opiates.

Seven years prior to the car collision, Doris had a two-vessels coronary artery bypass graft with aortic valve replacement. She has not had any chest pain or shortness of breath since her bypass graft. Due to the multiple rib fractures, however, breathing had become quite painful and the pain in her chest at times almost unbearable.

After being discharged from the nursing facility, Doris started going to the Blu Room once a week in 2015. Her progress was gradual. She was unable to drive. She still needed considerable assistance. All her movements were very slow, her balance was impaired, and her memory poor.

In 2016 she was able to use the Blu Room for two weeks every day. When she began these two weeks of daily Blu Room visits, she needed help to be able to lie down on the table and to transfer and move around, and could not get up by herself. After two weeks of daily treatment, she had substantially decreased pain and was able to get up by herself. "I almost jumped off the table by myself!" she proudly says.

Doris experienced an enormous difference with decreased pain through regular Blu Room use, which was a relief beyond the descriptive power of words.

Chronic pain can be a devastating experience for patients who live with it, often leading to severe depression, hopelessness, substantially impaired functionality in life. Pain can become an all life-consuming experience of suffering. The gift of relief from this through the Blu Room without the need for debilitating use of mind-altering pain relief drugs has been of unspeakable value for Doris.

Since the rib fractures were displaced, they were unable to heal appropriately, and she still was experiencing substantial pain with movement, walking, lying down, and any position change. Doris was determined not to take any chronic pain medications at any time because she did not want the side effects of clouding her mind and her ability to think.

After the motor vehicle accident, it had been recommended to Doris to undergo neurosurgical treatment for the two vertebral fractures in her neck. Doris declined and was able to progress with her healing without surgery. She was in a hard-collar neck brace for several months. Unfortunately, since her rib fractures were unable to completely heal — as the bones were dislocated and the shattered, left clavicle fracture was causing pain when she was lying down — she felt compression to the soft tissue in her neck occasionally giving her even a choking sensation. Most recently in early 2018, during a reevaluation by a surgeon regarding the option to repair the dislocated, nonhealed, left clavicle fracture, Doris opted against surgical intervention at her age. She prefers to heal herself.

In fact, her right shoulder had substantially decreased mobility due to previous injury from the accident. Since starting the Mercy Blu Room Program, she developed increased range of motion in her right shoulder. Now she can lift her arm and shoulders, reach for things, and comb her own hair.

Her overall mobility in her arms and upper torso have improved so much since April 2018 that Doris can drive again. She hadn't been physically able to do so since the accident. Doris also no longer uses a walker. She's careful not to fall and moves slowly. She is well enough to not have to utilize an assistive device. She fights for her independence of living alone and says, "I clean corners," meaning she cleans her house a little at a time and then sits down and rests, but she does it all herself. She can even use her own vacuum cleaner. Only someone with her experience understands what a miracle that is.

For many months Doris had difficulty sleeping due to ongoing pain. Her sleep has significantly improved with her Blu Room use. She proudly says, "Now I sleep like a log!"

Doris feels that her mood is uplifted, and she is much improved. To maintain a willful, optimistic, and enthusiastic outlook when physical suffering is ongoing for so long is an extraordinary feat.

Throughout her journey, the Blu Room has been healing Doris significantly and on many levels of her being. Doris felt that the Blu Room was helping her to recover an enthusiasm about life and support her determination to be able to master this challenge mindfully, emotionally, and physically.

Doris has been using her focus to continually heal herself. Due to the severe brain injury, she had developed significant memory loss and problems with her balance. Gradually, with ongoing use of the Blu Room, her memory started improving. Doris has been going into the Blu Room with specific intents like healing her brain from memory loss. She would diligently work with her healing focus in the Blu Room and noticed that her ability to concentrate was improved and deepened.

Doris notes that she also underwent a profound personality transformation. She has been able to be more allowing of others and letting go of control in her life. Doris feels that the extraordinary challenge of surviving from this motor vehicle accident and continually fighting to improve her physical and mental function have brought a wisdom and peace to her, and the Blu Room has been supporting her to hold that tranquil, peaceful place in her daily life.

At seventy-eight years old, Doris marvels at her own recovery, her determination to heal, and prides herself that she's living independently, taking care of herself.

Throughout the years since the accident, her goal was to master her own suffering, and the mischievous twinkle in her eyes shows her knowing that she's doing it! Doris feels the Blu Room has been a tremendous gift in supporting her healing and rehabilitation to a functional life.

Pat's Chronic Open Wound Healed Through Blu Room

Pat is a seventy-seven-year-old woman with chronic arthritis of the knees, severe degenerative arthritis of the lumbar spine, morbid obesity, and gait abnormality. She fell in September 2017 with her walker and ripped open the skin of her right lower leg, causing an approximately 5 cm open laceration. Pat was seen by her healthcare practitioner and the wound was treated with standard wound care. She then developed a nonhealing, open wound that got infected, and she required oral antibiotic treatment twice. For months the wound would not heal with bandages and topical treatment.

In March 2017 Pat started coming to the Mercy Blu Room Program. Her wound was still open and had not changed much in appearance over the last six months. She exposed the wound to UV light in the Blu Room and it took two sessions for the wound to completely close. She still had surrounding erythema but that also quickly resolved.

The effectiveness of UV-light therapy use for chronic wound healing has been long established in clinical research studies. Prominent wound healing centers like the Advanced Wound Care Clinic at the University of Southern California utilizes UV light for advanced wound healing with remarkable success. UV activates genes that influence cell division and immune responses, acts as a bactericidal, and thereby promotes wound healing by diminishing the toxic effect of bacterial overgrowth on fibroblasts in the wound bed.

Pat has a well-healed scar without any pain and is now working on healing her arthritic pain.

David's Healing Posttraumatic Stress Disorder

David is a seventy-one-year-old Vietnam veteran with a history of posttraumatic stress disorder (PTSD) who had a severe heart attack in April 2014 and, subsequently, a stroke in August of the same year.

His heart attack was so severe that on the way to the hospital he went into cardiac arrest. He was successfully resuscitated and required stents in two of his heart arteries. The sustained heart damage caused him to have congestive heart failure from severe ischemic cardiomyopathy with a heart pump fraction of 30%, normal being about 65%.

Only four months after this heart attack, he had a severe stroke that left him with right-sided weakness and expressive aphasia, the inability to speak. He had a vocabulary of two words: yes and no. After his stroke he was in a rehabilitation center for a month. He has been doing speech therapy for the last four years.

David started using the Blu Room in February of 2017 and has been coming twice a week for more than fourteen months, sometimes more often. He still has speech difficulties and his memory is affected, but he is doing a lot better. He must pause and find his words but is able now to speak in full sentences. Sometimes he has to try several times to say what he means before it comes out with the meaning he intended. His speech therapists are amazed at his remarkable progress. He gets teary-eyed when he talks about his journey with the Blu Room. He says it is not because of his PTSD — he only killed one person in the war and was able to cope with the horrible things he saw — it took him about eight years after the war to come to terms with his life. There was something else that happened.

David explains that he experienced the Blu Room as both negative and positive for 150 sessions. Then something happened to him in January of this year and since then all his sessions were positive. He says that it was not the Blu Room that was negative; it was that something in his being was out of sync. David did not realize that his body and mind were not in harmony. Then in January he felt in the Blu Room like his body, his age, and everything about him caught up with himself. After that, everything was all right.

His neighbor Helena notes that she was the one he came to when he had his heart attack in 2014 and she called 9-1-1. Having known him for many years, she describes David's transformation over the past year nothing short of miraculous. She says David used to be a grouchy, grumpy man, easy to get angry and have a temper. In the last few months she notes that he is so sweet, completely transformed, moved to tears in his emotions, and able to express them with the people around him. Helena notes that this is not the old David. He is completely new, completely transformed, and unrecognizable from his former self.

David explains that the Blu Room can help you heal at your own pace. If you add to it by intentionally working on healing yourself and your attitudes, it can help you speed up your healing. He says he added to his healing by looking at this "negative" in his life, his "shadow," this being out of sync with himself. He explains that if you are adding more to your healing, then it will take even less time in the Blu Room, until there is a time where the negative "issue" is diminished to "nothing." The negative disappears; it just is gone one day. David says it depends on what you are doing and how you are in your own healing. That is what happened to David in January in the Blu Room. His negative disappeared to nothing and what was left was Love.

He cries, exhausted, after he explained this, and the look in his eyes speaks to a much greater understanding than he has words for.

David describes that after January the Blu Room helped him heal something that now is peaceful and calm, like a shadow that got lifted. He cries because he has no words for what happened to him. How do you express with words something in the depth of your being that you felt throughout your life but could not give words to, something you could feel sitting there with every breath like a nagging shadow? That is what got healed in David through the Blu Room. He can best express it in his eyes with his tears, and this thing that happened is bigger than words. And yet because it happened, he is now able to speak better and his brain is continuing to heal.

David continues to improve, and he surrenders to his journey. He is scheduled to get an implantable defibrillator put into his heart soon, due to his low pump function. A few months ago he had some chest pains but now, despite his poor heart function, he does not have any symptoms of heart failure. He is accepting his journey and is doing what he needs to support his improvement, including following up with his doctors and continuing the Blu Room treatments.

In Closing: Final Thoughts

"I want you to work on the architecture of your new self.
I want you,
to whatever degree you wish to do that,
to participate in your own redemption,
indeed your own spiritual growth
that enables you to be inwardly responsible
and then use it."

– Ramtha

Designing Your Extraordinary Self

Designing an extraordinary life, free of disease, suffering, and pain is clearly within our grasp. Thanks to JZ Knight and the Blu Room and Ramtha's teachings, we have the ability to be radiantly healthy and to live a long and prosperous life. We have perhaps a new view of how the people in this book have gone about designing their reality, where they have harnessed the power within them to heal themselves, their animals, their families, their community, their attitudes. Today we are living in a time where ancient wisdom has married new technology, where the future of medicine is frequency medicine.

As a result of these new developments and breakthroughs, it is not hard to see that the following words by Jaime Leal-Anaya are an extraordinary reality within our reach:

> *"The greatest legendary masters who have survived and are still remembered in history offer us their life's example as a testament of truth that immortality and a life worthy of being remembered throughout time is not mere fantasy but something reachable and real for those who understand what those legendary beings knew and learned and still know. It is true, nevertheless, that such a conquest is the crown of glory of a splendid, radical few!"[9]*

We — the ordinary, common people of all races and walks of life — are transforming our minds in an age where our natural evolution is imminently possible to realize a great future. What better time for all of us than now!

---

[9]*Ramtha, The Mind Gladiators of the Future* (Hun Nal Ye Publishing, 2016).

RAMTHA, JZ KNIGHT, AND
RAMTHA'S SCHOOL OF ENLIGHTENMENT

Ramtha communicates his wisdom by channeling through the body of JZ Knight. JZ Knight began publicly channeling Ramtha in 1979. RSE was established in 1988 in Yelm, Washington, and more than 100,000 people from around the world have attended Ramtha's events.

JZ Knight is the unique channel of Ramtha and author of the best-selling autobiography, *A State of Mind, My Story*. Historians and religious experts who have studied her life's work call JZ Knight the Great American Channel and recognize her as one of the most charismatic and compelling spiritual leaders of the modern age. JZ Knight is the only channel through whom Ramtha has chosen to deliver his message. She and Ramtha have inspired audiences worldwide for the last three decades, bridging ancient wisdom and the power of consciousness together with the latest discoveries in science.

The home campus sits on 80 acres of pastoral, lush grounds and towering evergreens in Yelm, Washington. Great cedar and fir trees grace the grounds, and a sense of timelessness prevails. Events are conducted in the Great Hall, which can accommodate up to 1,000 students. RSE facilitates live events in many languages at the Yelm campus, at venues around the world, and via Internet streaming.

For more information on Ramtha's teachings, his disciplines and techniques for personal transformation and focus, please visit or write to:

Ramtha's School of Enlightenment,
P.O. Box 1210, Yelm, WA 98597, U.S.A.,
www.ramtha.com.

RAMTHA'S SELECTED GLOSSARY:
ADDITIONAL TERMS AND DISCIPLINES

Analogical Mind: Being analogical means living in the Now. It is the creative moment and is outside of time, the past, and the emotions.

Bands, the: The bands are the two sets of seven frequencies that surround the human body and hold it together. Each of the seven frequency layers of each band corresponds to the seven seals of seven levels of consciousness in the human body. The bands are the auric field that allow the processes of binary and analogical mind.

Binary Mind: This term means two minds. It is the mind produced by accessing the knowledge of the human personality and the physical body without accessing our deep subconscious mind. Binary mind relies solely on the knowledge, perception, and thought processes of the neocortex and the first three seals. The fourth, fifth, sixth, and seventh seals remain closed in this state of mind.

Body/mind consciousness: Body/mind consciousness is the consciousness that belongs to the physical plane and the human body.

Mother/Father Principle: It is the source of all life, the Father, the eternal Mother, the Void. God the creator is seen as Point Zero and primary consciousness, which came out of the Void. The Source is the Void itself.

Sending-And-Receiving: Discipline created by Ramtha to develop the brain's innate ability for telepathy and remote-viewing, both with a specific target or a partner, anywhere, anything, or any time, past, present, or future.

Seven Levels of Consciousness and Energy: The seven levels of consciousness and energy is Ramtha's model of reality and it explains our origins and destiny. It is expressed graphically as a triad, with the seventh level at the top and Point Zero at the apex. Consciousness and energy are inextricably combined and the seven levels of consciousness correspond to the seven levels of the electromagnetic spectrum. They also represent levels of energy, frequency, density of mass, space, and time. The levels or planes of consciousness and its energy from the first to the seventh are: 1. Subconsciousness and Hertzian; 2. Social consciousness and infrared; 3. Awareness and visible light; 4. Bridge consciousness and ultraviolet blue; 5. Superconsciousness and x-ray; 6. Hyperconsciousness and gamma; and 7. Ultraconsciousness and Infinite Unknown.

Seven Seals of Consciousness and Energy: The seven seals are powerful energy centers that constitute seven levels of consciousness in the human body. The bands are the way in which the physical body is held together according to these seals. In every human being there is energy spiraling out of the first three seals or centers. The energy pulsating out of the first three seals manifests itself respectively as sexuality, pain, and/or power. When the upper four seals are unlocked, a higher level of awareness is activated.

Void, the: The Source. The Void is defined as one vast nothing materially, yet all things potentially.

Rosette Publishing, LLC

P.O. Box 1068
Rainier, Washington 98576
USA
Email: sophie17sykes@gmail.com

Made in the USA
Columbia, SC
05 April 2019